DEAREST PET

Félix Vallotton,
*Bathing Woman with
Swans*, c. 1893

DEAREST PET

On Bestiality

MIDAS DEKKERS

Translated by
Paul Vincent

VERSO

London · New York

First published as *Lief dier: Over bestialiteit*, Uitgeverij
Contact 1992
Translation © Paul Vincent 1994
This edition © Verso 1994

Verso
UK: 6 Meard Street, London W1V 3HR
USA: 29 West 35th Street, New York, NY 10001-2291

Verso is the imprint of New Left Books

ISBN 0-86091-462-3

British Library Cataloguing in Publication Data
A catalogue record for this book is available from the British Library

Library of Congress Cataloging-in-Publication Data
A catalogue record for this book is available from the Library of Congress

Typeset by Servis Filmsetting Ltd, Manchester
Printed and bound in Great Britain by Bath Press, Bath, Avon

This book was published with financial support from
the Foundation for the Production and Translation
of Dutch Literature.

Contents

Acknowledgements

Illustrations are reprinted by courtesy of the copyright holders listed below.

The publishers have checked source material for illustrations with due care, but have not been able to trace authors of all illustrations. Possible copyright holders not mentioned in the list of acknowledgements below are invited to contact the publishers.

Pablo Picasso, *Boy with Horse* © DACS 1994; Kerstin Apelman Öberg, *Noah's Ark* © DACS 1994; Norman Mansbridge, *The Origin of Species* paperback cover © *Punch* magazine 1993; Joost Veerkamp, *Tarzan Weismüller and Co.* © Editions Obscure/Joost Veerkamp 1985; John Wesley, *Honeypot*, courtesy Jose Freire Fine Art, New York 1992; Maria Lassnig, *Sleeping with a Tiger* © Maria Lassnig 1975; Marliz Frencken, *Pitbull with Girl* © Berg Berg BV/Marliz Frencken 1990; Jan Lavies, *Mermaid* © DACS 1994; Pablo Picasso, *The Minotaur in a Good Mood* © DACS 1994; Félix Labisse, *The Joy of Being Loved* © DACS 1994; N.A. Abildgaard, *The Primeval Cow Audumla with the Giant Ymir* © Statens Museum for Kunst, Copenhagen; Anon, *Gorilla and Man Kissing* © Keystone/Sygma 1989; Keith Haring, *Man on a Dolphin* © Estate of Keith Haring 1994; Pablo Picasso, *Girl with Crow* © DACS 1994; Joost Veerkamp, *The Uncouth Bear* © Editions Obscure/Joost Veerkamp 1990; G. Coco, cartoon from 'Is it Bad, Doctor?' reproduced with permission of Mondria Publishers BV, Netherlands 1990; Salvador Dali, *Dream Caused by the Flight of a Bee around a Pomegranate, one Second before Waking Up* © Demart Pro Arte BV/DACS 1994; Christoph Schutz, *Watchdog* © Christoph Schutz; Jean-Marie Poumeyrol, *Teddy Bear* © ADAGP, Paris and DACS, London 1994; H. Armstrong Roberts, *Who's Playing with Whom?* © H. Armstrong Roberts Inc., New York 1989; Jean-Marie Poumeyrol, *Giggling* © ADAGP, Paris and DACS, London 1994; Delmas Howe, *Zeus (on the Bull)* © Delmas Howe 1981; Balthus, *Nude with Cat* © DACS 1994.

Introduction:
Letting Ourselves Go

People love animals – a stroke here, a pat there, a quick nuzzle in that Stewart, *In the Woods* gorgeous fur, the amount of cuddling they get is enough to make a person jealous. In Holland dogs are petted more than people. Not as thoroughly, though: that one spot, somewhere down below, generally remains untouched. The high regard in which love for animals is held is matched only by the fierceness of the taboo on having sex with them. Those who do give in to their impulses are seen as wallowing contemptibly in the mire. Hence, in spite of the dangling penises and the cries of females on heat, the eroticism of our dogs and cats is completely ignored. With these darlings we adopt the role not of lover, but of master or mistress.

Yet however indecent, it does happen: sex with animals, the ultimate consequence of love for them, making love *with* them. On the farm, in the brothel, or simply at home in front of the fire, but mainly in our heads. The imagination is our most active sexual organ, and it is no surprise to find art and culture permeated with physical love for animals. Leda and the Swan, seductive mermaids, Fritz the Cat, piles of porn mags, young girls and their ponies, smutty jokes, fur coats, 'fuck a duck'. And now at last a whole book on the subject, with data drawn from all those diverse sources.

Between themselves animals observe the same taboo against the sexual transgression of species boundaries, if anything even more strictly than we do. In nature, if you see two very different creatures mating, they are not usually from different species but are sexually dimorphic: that is, the male and female of the same species look totally different. For example, with wild duck the male is much brighter coloured than the female, it is usually only stags that have antlers, and female birds of prey are larger than their mates.

Human beings are only slightly sexually dimorphic. Men have hair in

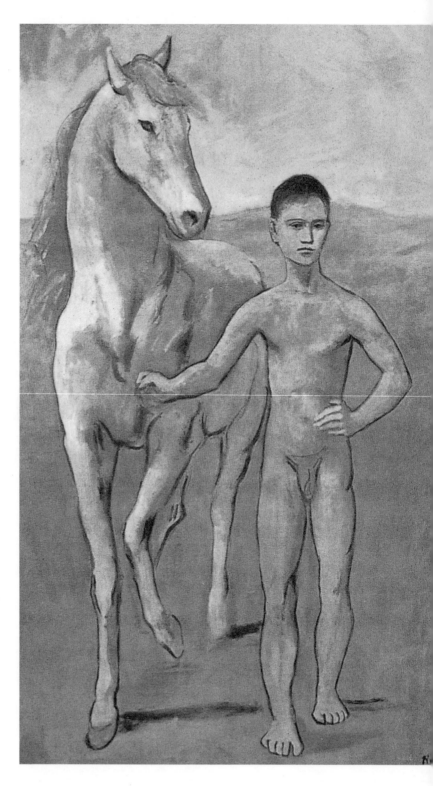

Picasso, *Boy with Horse,*
c. 1905

more places, women are more rounded. Nevertheless, back at boys' school girls seemed like beings from another planet to us, so different were they in our eyes. They were strange creatures, aliens; the girls' school a few streets away was very like a zoo. The thought of making love one day to such a being had the alarming quality of bestiality.

Nowadays, with the proliferation of mixed schools, the difference may seem less, but there is still a yawning gulf, widened still further by lipstick and leather jackets. Sex is something that by definition you have with another being, whether of the same or a different sex, someone of the same race or a more exotic choice. Every sexual encounter is a breaking of bounds, an intrusion into an alien realm, every sexual encounter retains a whiff of bestiality. What use is the other person if they are not different? You find true satisfaction only when you let yourself go.

I

Just Like Animals

Mrs Klein grows a tail. Just like that, without warning, a rabbit's tail. Ladies don't get upset for no good reason, but when rabbit ears suddenly sprout from her head Mrs Klein goes to the doctor. He refers her to the vet, who treats only complete rabbits; nor does she get any help from her mother, whose verdict is, 'It serves you right.' There is nothing for it but to tell her husband. Sobbing, she shows him the new parts of her body, ready to pack her bags. But Mr Klein fetches her a tasty morsel and showers her with kisses. 'I like you just as you are,' he says. 'You're a very sweet rabbit.'

A Very Sweet Rabbit by Imme Dros has the charm of the natural. A human being changes into a rabbit, a rabbit is showered with human kisses, all perfectly possible in our culture, which since it began has been permeated by intimacy between man and animal. Seductive mermaids, King Midas with his ass's ears, jokes about goats and Arabs, all those teenagers and all those horses in all those riding stables, 'ants in the pants', frogs kissed in vain; nowhere and at no time has love for animals remained purely platonic. Bestiality is omnipresent – in art, in science, in history, in our dreams – but our gaze is averted, our giggles suppressed. Instinct will out, as long as it remains below the surface. Children eagerly absorb the fears and longings of old myths and legends from their books, at high school their older brothers and sisters obediently do their Greek and Latin homework full of lascivious gods in constantly changing animal form.

For centuries the classical gods, driven from their temple ruins, their worshippers swept away by the barbarians, have inhabited our libraries and museums; their names are evoked in theatres, their shapes preserved in the firmament, and with them their bestial tendencies, sometimes shamelessly overt, sometimes disguised so as to be scarcely detectable. Who can recognize in the coiled snake on the logo of the Dutch GP on an

Agostino Carraci, *Satyr Mating with Nymph*, c. 1584

5

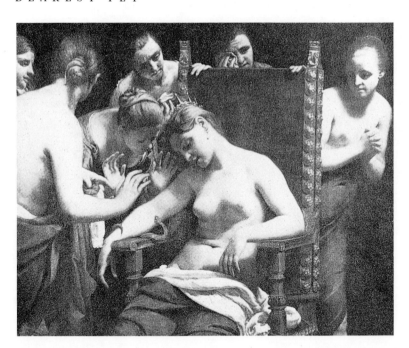

Guido Cagnacci,
Cleopatra and the Asp,
c. 1659

emergency call who ignores the no parking sign, the god Aesculapius, for whom women once copulated with voluptuously writhing serpents? How many fathers at the circumcision of their sons nowadays see in the sacrifice of the foreskin the sacrifice of the whole skin by the snake, which after sloughing off its old skin appears newly made and immortal? How is it possible that canalside mansions and palaces have for centuries been full of depictions of Leda and the Swan engaged in an act for which Christianity has sent thousands to the stake?

The last question is the easiest to answer. The theme of Leda and the Swan is quite simply ravishingly beautiful. The thought of the combination of the divine swan's down and the human skin of a beautiful mortal has inspired painters and draughtsmen for twenty-five centuries. What could be less unnatural than this exceptional combination, which somehow seems as little forced as is a bunny bringing Easter eggs, a cat on a human lap or a horse with one horn? Part of the challenge for the artists lay in the description of Leda as of 'exceptional beauty'. She was so beautiful that Zeus himself, the supreme deity of the Greeks, the 'cloud-gatherer' from the *Iliad*, who could make heaven and earth quake, had to possess her at all costs. In the shape of a swan, ostensibly pursued by an eagle, he sought a safe haven in her lap. She threw her cloak over him, and one of the most famous heavenly and earthly matings could begin. In a biological sense it was also one of the strangest, because although the human being, not the bird, was the mother: she laid eggs. Traditionally there were two; from one came

6

L. Riésener, *Leda*

Helen, who was to be the cause of the Trojan war, and from the other the twins Castor and Pollux. But it was also said that Castor and Pollux were the sons of Leda's husband, the King of Sparta, who had slept with her the same night; the egg with Helen in it, they maintained, was laid by Nemesis, who had vainly transformed herself into a goose to escape the amorous swan. Whatever the case, fragments of an enormous eggshell attributed to Leda were displayed in the local temple of Leucippides.

It seems an inextricable tangle, all those gods, all those lovers, all those animals to change into, but there is a system in it. Zeus had not chosen a swan at random. If with most birds there is nothing to be really jealous about in their mating – a bit of fluttering, two backsides pressed together like lips in a toddler's kiss, those silly antics to avoid falling off right away – the swan is an exception: it has a penis. A large, beautiful penis, as large and beautiful as the bird itself, amply equipped to satisfy every desire. Consequently in antiquity, Leda's swan was depicted as a truly divine, huge bird, which overpowers her by taking her neck in its beak with unerring accuracy. Today art connoisseurs still appreciate the strong lines, while biologists check whether the penis points to the left as befits a swan. Depictions of the swan diving under Leda's skirts were more suitable for a prudish age, although for a painter a swan is the ideal creature with which by introducing a slight change – the wings a little more extended, the back a little more arched – the whole scene can be chastened. The contrast between the pure, white exterior and the voluptuous animal creature within escaped no one. 'The swan is white of

7

feather, but its flesh is black,' says the Flemish proverb, and in his play
Noah (1667) Joost van den Vondel wrote:

> If all sank and was gone,
> What of the swan?
> What of the swan,
>
> The swan, that merry river flyer,
> Never tired of kissing?
> No waters hissing
> Can dowse its fire.

Although Mennonites use it as a symbol and advertisements for
washing powders vaunt its unsurpassed purity, in the eyes of the gods the
swan is what he is: the bull among birds. And it was as a bull that Zeus,
when he wished to restrict himself to mammal form, approached lovers
like Europa.

Depictions of Leda and the Swan make one envious to think that we
have no such beautiful, lascivious gods. As recently as the 1960s the
author Gerard Reve was prosecuted for representing the Christian God
as a 'year-old, mousy grey donkey', which he claimed had allowed itself
to be 'possessed ... by the writer at length three times in succession in its
Secret Opening'. He was acquitted, but in the Bible his own God is less
merciful. 'Whosoever lieth with beasts', as it says in Exodus, 'shall surely
be put to death.'

Yet the God of the Christians, like Zeus, once descended in the form of
a bird to know a woman, albeit not as a swan but as a dove. Matthew
writes of the Spirit of God 'descending like a dove', and Luke is still more
explicit, declaring that the Holy Ghost 'descended, in a bodily shape like
a dove'. That was at the baptism of Jesus, but later too the Holy Ghost
appeared as a dove. In the lives of saints and martyrs the 'Heavenly
Dove' plays an important role. *The Catholic Encyclopedia*, for example,
writes of Pope Gregory the Great (*c.* 540–604):

> when the pope was dictating his homilies ... a veil was drawn between his
> secretary and himself. As, however, the pope remained silent for long periods
> of time, the servant made a hole in the curtain and, looking through, beheld a
> dove seated on Gregory's head with its beak between his lips. When the dove
> withdrew its beak the holy pontiff spoke and the secretary took down his
> words; but when he fell silent, the servant again applied his eyes to the hole
> and saw that the dove had again placed its beak between his lips.

Jean-Honoré
Fragonard, *Portrait of
Marie Catherine Colombe,*
c. 1775

The dove is also a faithful attendant in depictions of the Annuncia-
tion, the episode in which Mary is given the news that she is to bear an
extraordinary son, and which is commemorated each year by the
Church – for the discerning, exactly nine months before Christmas. The
dove is not there for no reason. 'What good is a God without a mother?'
Gerard Reve once asked himself. 'In that case you might just as well

have no God at all.' But a mother by herself is not sufficient to produce a child. In the words of the official liturgy, he was born of the Virgin Mary and made flesh 'through the power of the Holy Ghost'. At the beginning of the Gospel she was 'found to be with child of the Holy Ghost', the 'Heavenly Dove' of the psalms. Christ was born of a virgin and a dove; Christianity too is founded on bestiality.

'Not from the seed of a man,' St Ambrose argued to the early Christians, 'but through the mystical breath of the Spirit did God's Word become flesh and the fruit of the womb blossom.' How one is supposed to imagine this is something that not even the Mariologist Francisco Suarez can answer. He is, however, certain that 'in giving birth to a son the Holy Virgin neither lost her virginity nor experienced any sexual pleasure.... It was not fitting for the Holy Ghost to have caused such a thing for no reason or purpose or to have aroused any unseemly upsurge of passion.' He did not need to go into the question in much greater depth, since in his day – around 1600 – people had as yet not the slightest idea how children were actually conceived. Like most scholars the Church Fathers assumed that the mother provided only the raw material for the baby, to which the father gave shape and movement. This view derives from Aristotle, who compared the mother's contribution to amorphous milk and the father's to form-giving rennet. His Roman counterpart Pliny considered even that too much raw material for a man – a gust of wind could suffice. In his view Boreas, the north wind, was particularly fertile, which was why mares wishing for a foal without the intervention of a stallion stood in the wind with their hindquarters facing north. As recently as the seventeenth century many scholars believed that it was not the semen itself but an 'odour of seed', the *aurea seminalis*, which activated the egg-cell. Even the discoverer of the circulation of the blood, William Harvey, was convinced that a woman was fertilized 'without the intervention of any demonstrable physical agency'. A child appeared in its mother's womb like a thought in one's head, or – better still – like magnetism in an iron rod: if you hold iron to a magnet, it in turn acquires the power of attracting iron. If it was as easy at that, it was naturally a trifling task for the Heavenly Dove to sire Jesus in Mary. Moreover, modern biologists are quite sure that it must have contributed something, since had Mary really remained a virgin, Christ would have been female, like all products of virgin births.

Christians do not proclaim their bestial origins from the rooftops. It does not strike us as anything to be proud of. However, things were once very different; indeed, animals were very popular as founders of all kinds of things. Rome owes its origin to the she-wolf which suckled Romulus and Remus, the Inuit regard white men as the result of a cross between a woman and a dog, and the Danish Royal Family are not in the least ashamed to read Ambroise Paré's account of their bear ancestor:

Fortunius Licetus recounts how two bishops of Uppsala lamented the fate of a young Swedish girl, a remarkable beauty, who had set out with her ladies-in-waiting to divert herself far from her native city and to general astonishment was seized by a huge bear, which took her to a cave deep in the forest. Threatened and violated by the lascivious bear, the girl, who while she lived with the bear was fed on raw meat by it, soon became pregnant. She bore a hairy monster with the shape and limbs of a man. When the bear was killed in a hunt, she took the child, whom she had named Ursus in memory of his father, back to her native city. After marrying, Ursus fathered various sons, one of whom, called Trégals Sprachaley, married Ulso, from which union Suens, king of the Danes, was born.

Old English families also pride themselves on their roots in the animal kingdom. For instance, Siward, Duke of Northumberland under Edward the Confessor, claimed that his grandmother had been assaulted by a bear. An eighteenth-century Devonshire family called Sucpitch could boast an ancestor who had been found in the woods of Prussia with a 'sucking bitch'.

Jesus Christ, himself the Lamb of God, had absolutely no need to be ashamed of his origins, since the dove which had fathered him in Mary was a god as well as a dove. Like all the children of Leda and her swan, he is at the same time the product of bestiality (man × animal) and of theogamy (god × man). The same ambiguity is found in other religions. For example, because Hindus believe that certain animals are really gods, mating with such an animal is also mating with a god; human beings are, so to speak, marrying both beneath and above their station.

Bestiality is present at the very cradle of Christianity. Bestial tendencies can be discerned not only in the Christ child himself, but in the gathering assembled round the crib. One finds creatures which are half-animal, half-human, but also half-human, half-god: the angels. Down through the ages artists have done their best to depict these aerial spirits in a credible way, but with little success. One does not have to be a biologist to see that such a transvestite with wings would never get off the ground. The body is too heavy, the wings too small, nowhere in the torso is space reserved for powerful flight muscles. Only Leonardo da Vinci occasionally produced passable angels, but he had thrown himself into inventing flying machines. The fact that despite our lack of imagination angels strike us as so logical, and that a whole Christmas industry revolves around them, strikes a chord with our need for order and logic in a chaotic and illogical world. In our desperate attempts to organize that chaos into systems, sequences and hierarchies, we still cling to the obsolete image of the Chain of Being. On this chain everyone and everything has a place. At the bottom are the rocks, a link higher are the plants, then come in succession the worms, the cows and the apes, with man at the top. But there is also God. He is at the very pinnacle, and a huge gulf separates Him from us. However, that gulf is filled with angels,

Michelangelo Morisi
da Caravaggio, *Amor
as Conqueror, c.* 1596

hundreds of thousands, millions of angels, for 'a thousand thousand
serve Him and ten thousand times ten thousand stood before Him.' And
just as the step from animal to man was once bridged by the negro,
between man and God there came rung by rung the ordinary angels,
archangels, princes, powers, kingdoms, thrones, cherubim and
seraphim.

The chain can be climbed, but also descended. Charles Baudelaire
maintains that there are two opposing tendencies in every human being,
one striving towards God, the other towards Satan: 'invoking God or the
spiritual is a desire to rise higher: invoking Satan or the animal is the
desire to descend. The love of women and intimacy with animals, dogs,
cats, etcetera must be ascribed to the latter.' Just as we have imagined
angels lining the upward path, devils loom up in front of us on the way to

Left: *The Satyr and the Sleeping Woman*, etching from a fresco from Herculaneum, 18th century
Right: Satyr Mounting Stag, decoration on a Greek vase, *c.* 520 BC

Hell. Ask someone to draw a devil from the underworld one step below the rocks, and it is ten to one that it will be a black imp with a tail, horns on his head, a goatee beard and cloven hooves. In short, the person does not draw a devil (since, as we are apparently not reminded frequently enough, devils can assume any shape), but a satyr. Our image of evil is no different from that of the satyrs on Greek pottery from long before the birth of Christ.

It is quite common for the Church to adopt ineradicable demons, myths and symbols, but the satyr has been smuggled in by a back door, by an over-free translation of God's Word. In the Hebrew version of the Bible the word for 'hairy creatures' occurs. The first translators did not know what to make of this and rendered it as 'satyrs'. Later, this was changed to 'nature spirits' or 'devils', but by then it was too late; Christianity was saddled with the licentious demi-gods of the Greeks, who cared only for wine, women and song and were consequently avid followers of Dionysus, the god of wine. They were depicted with the hindquarters of a billy-goat, since billy-goats were regarded as the epitome of lust and virility. The Greeks probably took this idea from the Egyptians, who according to Diodorus Siculus had deified the goat only 'because of its sexual organ; for this animal is very amorous.' In Egypt the Greek Herodotus witnessed a veritable miracle: 'near Mendès a goat mated with a woman in public and drew a large crowd.'

Since a satyr was half-man, half-billy-goat, a mating between a satyr and a full human being could only be half-bestiality, unless only the lower body counts. The fact that this did not make satyrs any less amorous can be seen on countless Greek vases, lamps, plates and statues. On the stage satyr plays were performed, in which the Chorus consisted of actors in goatskins, often with huge phalluses. With the Romans the satyrs changed radically; they became increasingly apelike, until they matched the first vague descriptions of anthropoid apes. But the lust remained. And so they became more and more lustful and apelike, until finally they appeared on our screens as King Kong.

Unlike the satyr, the main body of the classical array of gods impinged on Christian culture only after the Middle Ages, when the latter's own menagerie of saints and martyrs were so firmly established that the old gods could offer no competition from a religious point of view. That was their attraction. For what is the appeal of all those Greek gods? 'Perhaps', observed the writer M. Februari in the weekly *Vrij Nederland*, 'the fact that no one believes in them.' No sacrilege can be committed against them, one can read their stories as an entertaining narrative, and all those allegorical depictions at the front of old books can be identified with the same pleasure as siskins in the bird sanctuary. Although adherents of Carl Jung often proclaim that 'myths are original revelations of the pre-conscious psyche', in terms of content Greek mythology was, in the words of the mythologist Robert Graves, 'no more mysterious than an election poster'. There is no copyright on them, one can curse Greek gods without being struck by a heavenly thunderbolt and above all they are wonderfully suited to art. Mythological themes were a welcome change after a thousand years of depicting and paraphrasing Biblical scenes, and had the same universal expressive power.

On the theme of bestiality there is a painting by Rembrandt, *The Rape of Ganymede*, in which a struggling infant is being carried into the air by an eagle. That eagle is of course again Zeus, but it is difficult to recognize in the bawling infant the 'fabulously beautiful boy' who turned Zeus's head. In order to seduce the child, Zeus once again changed himself into a bird, to the great delight of the Greeks, who saw in this an acknowledgement of love between men, allowing women to be eliminated from public life. By Rembrandt's time this moral message had long since become a hymn of praise to the purity of the child's soul, which, still untainted, longs for heaven. The scene became popular on children's gravestones and appears to be not yet completely forgotten, as witness the text on a child's grave still in existence:

> HOW BLESSED IS
> A DEAD CHILD'S FATE
> CALLED SO YOUNG
> TO HEAVEN'S GATE

From a biological point of view Zeus's choice of an eagle was far less fortunate than that of a swan in the case of Leda. One can see all too clearly that Rembrandt had difficulty in depicting the rape of the boy by a bird in a credible way. Although the eagle, judging by the size of the child, has a wingspan of $1\frac{1}{2}$ metres, that is not nearly enough. Leslie

Rembrandt, *The Rape of Ganymede, c.* 1635

Brown showed experimentally that an eagle cannot lift a normal newborn weight of $3\frac{1}{2}$ kilos off the ground. There have been reports of eagles carrying off a fox or a baby deer, but the culprits used the thermal currents along a hillside for swooping and had a wingspan twice that of Rembrandt's eagle. There seems to be little likelihood of Rembrandt's toddler being violated by the eagle, as happened to the real Ganymede, son of Tros, the king who gave Troy its name; the risk of an air crash seems greater.

Mention of bestiality is as rare in the Greeks' classical writings as it is normal in their fables and romances. An earthenware jug preserved in London refers to one of those writings; Amsterdam has a fragment of a similar specimen. The jug is in the shape of a large goose which is being mounted by a small Eros. According to the ancients, as the bird of

Aphrodite, the sensual mother of Eros, the goose was so fiery in nature that it had to live in a damp environment and eat a great deal of grass in order to cool its ardour somewhat. There are some biological objections to this, but it is definitely the case that the gander, like its cousin the swan, has a good-sized penis. The fact that the Eros figure is riding the much larger goose says all the more about its power over the senses.

When the vase was in use, some two-and-a-half centuries before Christ, the affection between a goose and a woman was the topic of conversation in Alexandria, where this sort of pottery came from. The story concerned the beautiful harpist Glauke, who was desired even by King Ptolemy. In *De natura animalium*, a hotchpotch of fact and fiction, Aelian writes that not only men but also 'a ram and a goose' fell in love with her. Elsewhere he writes that it may also have been a dog. That paralleled the Roman woman 'who was accused of adultery by her husband; the correspondent was a dog.' 'And I have also heard', he continues in gossipy vein, 'that baboons have become infatuated with girls and have raped them, still more lasciviously than the boys in the night-long dissipations of Menander.'

The fact that bestiality was not confined to myths is confirmed by Gerald Carson: '[Zeus] and other such gods, such as Pan, the lewd billy-goat, were put on the Greek stage, sometimes in episodes containing actual coitus between animals and human beings.' In Rome, according to ancient texts, women copulated with bears, snakes and crocodiles. Snakes were pushed into the vagina, or suckled the nipples. Those wishing to see such things could go to the games, where all kinds of male animals, from dogs to leopards, apes and giraffes, had been trained to mate with women, frequently causing harm to those women – mostly still girls. This too was in imitation of the lives of the gods. Most popular of all was the scene in which Pasiphae allows herself to be mounted by the bull.

Although the Greeks and Romans perhaps dealt with it in a more sophisticated way than other cultures, they certainly did not invent bestiality. Copulating with animals is probably as old as humanity. Depictions of it are found in the very oldest cultures; in Europe there are Swedish rock paintings from the Bronze Age (the second millennium BC) in which a man is unmistakably inserting his member under the tail of a large quadruped. There are strikingly few reports from ancient China. Bestiality, being a custom of country folk, was probably of no interest to the cultured classes.

Rock painting from Bohuslän (Sweden), Bronze Age

A great deal is known about sexual customs in ancient America thanks to the pottery preserved by the Chimu and Mochica Indians. The pots, often more than a thousand years old, are decorated with all kinds of sexual illustrations: 24 per cent depicting a penis, 4 per cent a vulva, 11 per cent coitus in the missionary position, 5 per cent male masturbation, 31 per cent heterosexual anal intercourse, 3 per cent homosexual anal intercourse, 1 per cent lesbian acts, 14 per cent cunnilingus and 6 per cent bestiality. The bestiality involved both men and women, with all kinds of animals. The art collector Larco Hoyle, who described the pottery, suggested that those depictions may have served as a warning, showing what one must not do, but the Spaniards and Incas had such trouble in persuading the Chimus and Mochicas under their control to adopt a more moral attitude that it is almost certain that the Indians found most forms of sex both pleasurable and normal.

In European history cases of bestiality are particularly common in court records. Not only the judiciary, but the Church too was very keen that there should be a severe response to this 'disgusting crime', which was often linked to heresy and witchcraft. The papal bull issued by Gregory IX, the infamous founder of the Inquisition, against a heretical sect, is characteristic:

> When the novice is accepted into the sect and for the first time enters the school of the damned, he sees a kind of frog appear which some call 'toad'. Some kiss that animal from behind, others on the mouth, as a result of which they receive its tongue and spittle in their mouths. . . . After the feast a black cat, as large as a normal dog, descends backwards with its tail pointing directly behind it, the initiate kisses its arse, followed by the master and every assistant, in a fixed order, to the extent that they are worthy. . . . When all are seated and the incantations have been pronounced, the master turns to the cat and says: 'Have mercy upon us,' whereupon his neighbour answers: 'Who has commanded us to do that?' A third person says: 'The grand master,' and the fourth: 'We must obey.'
>
> Then the candlesticks are lit and those present give themselves over to shameful vice.

Strangely enough, from precisely the same time as the witch-hunts and burning of heretics there is in many churches a painting or tapestry of a naked girl with a unicorn on her lap. The sexual connotations of that horn are unmistakable. Yet the unicorn symbolizes Jesus Christ in all his glory and majesty, the naked girl the Virgin Mary.

> It has a single horn, in the middle of its head. But how is it captured? A pure virgin, splendidly arrayed, is put in it path. Thereupon the creature leaps into the lap of the virgin, and she has him in her power, and he follows her, and she takes him to the king's castle.
>
> This refers to the image of our Saviour . . . He entered the body of the truly eternally virgin Mary, the word was made flesh and dwelt among us.

If the maid in this text is still dressed and reserved, in the course of the Middle Ages she was depicted more and more erotically and the unicorn as increasingly virile. The Church maintains that the animal is won over by divine love. A glance at medieval depictions teaches us otherwise.

Maiden with Unicorn,
design for a tapestry
for Charles de
Bourbon, Cardinal of
Lyons, *c.* 1500

Labourers, town-dwellers and country folk must have ogled those
depictions. For them the unicorn was above all else the ideal horse. In an
age of cars and planes it is difficult to imagine how dependent society
once was on the horse. Just as men now drool over the sports car of their
dreams, men once sighed as they gazed at pictures of unicorns, the
Porsches of the Middle Ages. Those desiring a woman as a sexual partner
aspire to the most beautiful woman, those who mate with animals prefer

to mate with the noblest of creatures. In the absence of unicorns that was the noble horse.

In order to understand something of the love of a man for his horse all one need do is look around a historic city. Everywhere one sees statues of men on their horses, seldom if ever of men with their wives. With such an intimate bond between horse and rider it is understandable that men should sometimes wish to mount their steed. In the army especially, with many horses and few women available, it must have happened often. At any rate the judgment of Frederick the Great on a cavalryman who had abused a mare is well known: 'The fellow is a swine and belongs in the infantry.'

In the infantry of course there were no horses. In consequence, so the chroniclers tell us, no goat was safe. If need be the armies took their own with them. In 1565, for example, Louis de Gonzaga, Duke of Nevers, went to war with three thousand soldiers and two thousand goats, some (of the goats) dressed in velvet. Such provisions were not surplus to requirements, because three years before, at the siege of Lyons, the Italian besiegers had deserted, not so much because they were worse paid, but because of the lack of willing goats. Varillas indeed writes in his *Histoire de Charles IX* that the peasants saw no alternative but to burn all the goats in the places where the Italians passed.

Sometimes there were not even any goats for the soldiers. For example, it struck the non-commissioned officers of the allied forces in 1849 that the quartermaster served roast duck very frequently. 'The repeated serving of the same roast dish', wrote the *Gazette Médicale*, 'and the liberality of their comrade aroused suspicions, which were soon confirmed. The quartermaster slit open the anal passage of his victims to provide a better fit and at a carefully chosen moment decapitated the birds in order to use their death throes for his own pleasure. These were the ducks which found their way to the table of the non-commissioned officers. The quartermaster was cashiered from the regiment.'

2

Birds of a Feather

God's creation is a mess. Living organisms stand, swim and fly about at random. Dandelions spring up next to orchids, the latest model of mammal treads on cockroaches that are a hundred million years old, a thousand species of fish sport on their garishly coloured coral reef, bewildered by the confusion a man walks by, inside the man lives a tapeworm. One can't make head or tail of it.

When all this gets too much for them, people go to the zoo. Here the animals are neatly ordered, species by species, here creation, simply left in chaos on the Seventh Day, has been tidied up by the director of the zoo; elephants with elephants, tigers with tigers, the seven-ringed armadillo – they have only one of those – next to the nine-ringed armadillo. Unless, that is, you happen to visit a modern zoo. Then the animals wander about in the same confusion as in the wild, but that is just because the ordered nature of an old-fashioned zoo looks so unnatural. The 'natural' is in fashion; its chaotic quality is accepted by the new nature lovers as natural. In their minds these species are distinct, in groups and groups of groups, each with an elegant Latin name, a collection classified according to the age-old system of Carolus Linnaeus to which new species are added daily in the basements of the world's natural history museums. Aristotle knew of five hundred species, Linnaeus named fifty thousand, in Charles Darwin's day records listed several hundred thousand, and today's computers are crammed with millions of species; the zoos overflow with them, television fills its transmission time with them, in the woods and fields disentangling nature has turned into a national parlour game for Sunday afternoons – 'Look over there, the middle spotted woodpecker!'

Yet nature itself is as at least as aware of its own order as we are. Of necessity. Many of its organisms, however beautiful they may be, are severely handicapped. They lack organs. Most animals have a left lung

Kerstin Apelman
Öberg, *Noah's Ark*,
1969

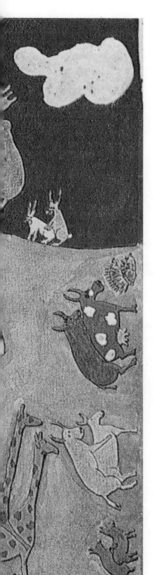

and a right lung, a left front leg and a right front leg and a left and right kidney, so that if one fails there is still one left, but they only have one heart. Hence the majority die of heart failure. Unfortunately, we only have one liver too, but there is worse to come. There is one organ of which human beings and animals have only half. One half of human beings has one half, the other half has the other. The first group we call males, the second females and the organ is the reproductive system. If I want to reproduce myself, it turns out that I cannot do so alone; I have to involve somebody else with the missing half of the reproductive system. That is odd. Just imagine that you had only one half of the digestive system, so that for each ham roll you wanted to eat you had to recruit a partner.

The fact that every human being and almost every higher animal has only half of the organ that serves to perpetuate their species is inefficient, but also inspiring. A large part of thought and action on earth is directed at finding appropriate half-organs. These must be from one of the other sex, but above all from the same species. Consequently, at mating time nature orders itself species by species; elephants with elephants, fourteen-spotted ladybirds with fourteen-spotted ladybirds. Bearded tits fall for bearded tits, slugs cuddle slugs, turkeys prefer turkey. Male three-spined sticklebacks are so thrilled to see a female three-spined stickleback when they are in the mood that you can teach them tricks for which the only reward is a glimpse of a female, for a few seconds, through a window. This peepshow for fish existed in Leiden, at the university, long before the peepshows of the red light district in Amsterdam were set up. And just as a male gorilla does not get worked up over our girls in the windows, a three-spined stickleback has no idea what a ten-spined male sees in a ten-spined female. As far as that is concerned love is very selective. Nature may be a mess, but it is not an aimless mess. If there were no rules to keep order and mechanisms to maintain those rules, the survival of life on earth would be in jeopardy. Only if human beings always mate with human beings and mice always with mice is there any certainty that new human beings and mice will be born and with luck be just as discriminating. Those who flout the rules and mate with another species are committing genetic suicide. They themselves may stay alive, but their biological inheritance, built up over billions of years of evolution, is lost. An elephant ejaculating its semen into a giraffe might just as well have spilt it on the ground. Wasting semen is a mortal sin. And consequently the strictest safety measures have been taken to combat it. In order to prevent the male's semen entering the wrong female or the female having semen foisted on her which will be rejected by the eggs inside her, each partner closely monitors the other's identity. From the trills in their song, from that specific smell of urine, from that wonderful look which occurs in no other courting repertoire, the owner of the semen and the owner of the eggs conclude that their semen and eggs will shortly be compatible and grow into new male and female owners. Everything else is capriciously rejected. Nowhere is there such xenophobia as in the choice of partner.

Indeed, mating is so focused on the individual's own species that the definition of the species has been based upon it. Two animals belong to the same species if they mate with each other. The only additional condition is that such a mating should be capable of producing fertile offspring; otherwise horses and donkeys, which do mate but produce only infertile offspring, would have to be classified in the same species. The definition can also be reversed; two animals mate if they belong to the same species (provided they are of the opposite sex, adult, healthy and it is mating time). The fact that two skeletons in the museum both have the caption *Tyrannosaurus rex* therefore implies that a hundred million years ago, covered with flesh and blood, they must have been capable of falling for each other had they encountered each other; the palaeontologists guarantee this, even though they have never seen a living dinosaur – let alone one that was mating.

In order to indicate the species to which it belongs, every animal is equipped with a code. It flaunts this code – certainly at mating time. This is why every bird sings its own tune and why an appropriate aquarium fish can be bought for every interior; it is also why most human males find the bouncing derrière of their own species more attractive than the huge bright-red wart on the bottom of a female chimpanzee, which is as much of a turn-on for a male chimpanzee as it is a turn-off for us human beings.

Human beings who try to break the code of animals are engaged in determining species. The talent for this is innate. Toddlers who cannot yet distinguish a spoon from a fork, an apple from a pear, a triangle from a circle, point unerringly at pictures of lions and tigers, pandas and bears, rhinoceroses and hippopotamuses. In industrialized countries this capacity for distinguishing develops mainly into the ability to recognize scores of makes of car at a glance, but native peoples, however primitive, can identify hundreds of species of plants from childhood. This is very useful because in that way they are able to distinguish as quickly as possible the edible ones from the poisonous ones, those which devour and those which can be eaten, alien plants and their own plants. In our society, where the most dangerous animal is the dog and where if you fancy a meal in the woods you get a takeaway hamburger, that is not much help. There are too many species and too many kinds of problem. Determining species, as you may remember from school, has become a laborious path through keys and tables in which even professionals get lost. Those combating plagues of locusts or managing fish stocks, butterfly collectors and specialists in natural history museums all over the world wrestle with the question whether a specimen belongs to this, that or a new species. It is very difficult to determine whether two

Religious depiction of an erotic elephant, India, 18th century

Henri de Toulouse-Lautrec, Two Pigs, late 19th century

animals in the no longer very effective formaldehyde of an old museum jar might once have been sexually compatible. Together with one's high regard for scientists who after years of careful sifting are able to distinguish two kinds of jellyfish, one's admiration grows for the creatures themselves, which rush into the embrace only of the correct partner. Sometimes the researchers are forced to leave the object of research to make the identification for itself, for example in the case of many pond skaters – those insects that walk on water like a cross between a daddy-long-legs and Jesus Christ – only the males can be properly classified; if one wishes to identify the females, one has to wait until they mate. A female that mates with a *Gerris lacustris* is likely herself to be a *Gerris lacustris*; she has a better nose for such things than we do. A handbook of species written by human beings would only confuse the female pond skater. The views in such works are constantly changing, as is the value which the various researchers assign to certain determining characteristics. The creatures themselves would be better off not risking their genitalia on such advice.

Besides creatures who in human eyes scarcely differ from each other and yet belong to two different species, there are those that look as if they come from different planets and nevertheless form one species. A dachshund dog is as different from a St Bernard bitch as a rabbit is from a calf and nevertheless he mounts her. How is it that a pug can allow itself to be crushed or impaled by a mastiff? How is it that they are able to see something of themselves in the other dog? How far apart must you breed two dogs before they reject each other as alien? It is as though dogs are anxious to bridge the gaps that human beings create between the breeds as quickly as possible by means of the weirdest crosses. A pedigree dog is a bundle of hereditary characteristics which can bark. People maintain those breeds, dogs want to be rid of them. This is not very difficult for a dog, because it simply does not know whether it is small or large; a dog has no sense of proportion. It is not its dimensions which give it its identity as a dog, but its smell. Human beings have unfortunately not been able to do much to change that by selective breeding. However, the hunting of wolves shows that alienation has nevertheless taken place in the dog world. Although it would be perfectly capable of mating with a wolf, the fur trapper's dog sees its ancestor only as game to be hunted; he regards his master as a superdog. He is a fraternizer with the world of humans, a collaborator.

Human beings are better able than any other living creature to recognize their fellow human beings, even without a field guide, in any wood, sometimes to their delight, often – particularly when walking in the woods – to their displeasure. Oddly enough we have the greatest difficulty in recognizing our nearest relatives, the other mammals. They proclaim their species just as loudly as all other creatures, but, like dogs, with smells instead of colours or other visible signs. Human beings are not particularly sensitive to these. Like most primates man has a poor sense of smell, since while swinging about in the treetops one is better advised to use one's eyes and ears than one's nose. We find it hard to distinguish all the different odours of all those ground mammals; we are not even aware of them, apart from exceptions like the smell of a tomcat on heat. The inadequacy of our sense of smell is clear from the fact that while people have built museums for their eyes and concert halls for their ears, there are no olfactory pleasure domes where we can spend an enjoyable afternoon smelling. For dogs on the other hand, smell is a full-fledged art-form; they obviously enjoy the symphonies of smells which have been applied to lamp-posts.

Mating Cock and Hen, engraved Greek jewel, 5th–4th century BC

Determining mammals is slightly easier for us if they make noises, even if in the case of bats we need a bat detector in order to lower the ultrasonic squeaking to an audible frequency. But even this does little to boost the numbers of those interested in mammal protection. Almost no one goes out mammal-watching on Sundays. Birdwatching, on the other hand, is a form of mass recreation which has been very beneficial for bird protection. Bird guides sell in their thousands, the birds themselves have had legal protection in Holland since 1937 – years before our own class of animals, mammals. Birds owe this preferential treatment to their poor sense of smell. Since their sense of smell is even poorer than ours, they resort to colours and sounds that we, as one-time fellow tree-dwellers, are easily able to recognize in illustrations. One never sees birds snuffling each other excitedly as dogs and cats do constantly, let alone sticking their noses into someone else's droppings. Their visiting cards are intended for other senses.

Since we are able to read it so well, we are indebted to one such visiting card for the discovery of the associated animal, the Congo peacock. In 1913 its discoverer, the American James Chapin, was struck by a brownish-black striped feather in the colourful headdress of a chief somewhere in the Belgian Congo. He bought the feather for some tobacco and combed the world searching for the real owner. Twenty-one years later he discovered two stuffed specimens, plus a man who told him that he had occasionally eaten such a bird. It was not until 1936 that he found his first specimen – dead. Thanks to this *pars pro toto*, living specimens were eventually tracked down and transferred with extreme haste to European and American zoos to ensure the bird's temporary survival.

The brown striped feathers of a member of its own species would probably make less impact on the Congo peacock itself than on James Chapin, but a robin redbreast reacts fiercely to others' red feathers. The extent to which the red breast makes the robin is clear if one puts two stuffed birds into its territory, one with, the other without a red breast. The red-breasted specimen is attacked savagely, the other left

Jules Pascin,
lithograph, early 20th
century

unmolested. It is not necessary to stuff them well for this experiment; a
bunch of red-coloured chicken feathers works just as well.

Underwater, too, a red breast is also used as a species signal, by the
stickleback. Males attack red-stomached rivals – or red-coloured pieces
of wood – just as fiercely as a robin redbreast attacks its rivals. It does not
matter that the robin and the stickleback use the same signal, since the
chance of them encountering one other is nil. It is different when two

26

animals with the same signal inhabit the same area. In those cases they vary the signal and emphasize the differences in order to avoid mistakes.

Fiddler crabs have taken such emphasis to extremes. The males advertise themselves with one of their claws which has grown disproportionately large, sometimes up to a third of their total body weight. That is awkward in everyday life on the beach, where crabs of all shapes and sizes dash out of their holes in order to feed themselves on all kinds of prey, which they dig up from the mud. Holding one claw in front of it like an arm in plaster, a male is forced to eat with one hand. In digging, the thick claw only gets in the way and is also useless against predators, which often, like true gourmets, are after the delicious meat in the claw, and for that reason single out males to hunt. This obtrusive appendage is of use only for reproduction. Males wave it at females, each of the sixty species having its own wave: one with theatrical gestures, the other quick and minimalist, as though it required secrecy. The species *Uca lactea* is the easiest for us to understand, as it simply gives a come-hither wave. There are other species which drum wildly, give a magnanimous blessing or simply produce a few nondescript taps. The walking claws support this recruiting drive by parading proudly, executing elegant dance steps, or in the case of the small white *Uca saltitata*, enthusiastically jumping up and down on the spot without a break.

Such rhythmical movements are well adapted to coding. Just as with a handful of dots and dashes one can construct a Morse alphabet into which one can translate the whole of world literature, there are sufficient codes available to distinguish every species from each other with simple variations on a theme. The code of banana flies and dancing flies is the simplest: because of their specific dimensions their wings buzz at different frequencies for each species in flight. The females receive only the frequency transmitted by the males of their species. Male crickets use their wings like a Morse key. With a thickened section on the upper side of the wing they saw across a ridge below the other wing, each in their own rhythm, attracting female mates and allowing expert entomologists to catch them. In this case the advertisements are preferable to the goods they are extolling: females prefer sitting next to a loudspeaker with exactly the right chirping sound than with an amorous but silent male.

Fireflies do it with light. Towards dusk the first males appear in order to advertise their identity like living miniature lighthouses. Mostly they fly in a promenade, but there are some which gather in one tree and flash rhythmically, so that the whole tree alternately lights up and blacks out again. The virgin females, which will emerge from the ground later in the evening, respond to the correct light pattern from the males with a species-specific signal, mostly a single flash of light at a carefully timed moment after the males' last flash. The system works so well that one can play around with it. If one imitates the female's signal with a pocket

Paul Gauguin, *Maori Cult*, late 19th century

torch, the males will rush towards it. Nature itself also cheats: in order to prevent fireflies being misused by religious broadcasters for the umpteenth hymn of praise to God's Creation, the Creator has made *Photuris pennsylvanica*. Females of this species of firefly accurately imitate the light code of the smaller *Photinus scintillans*; exactly one second after two short flashes they give a flash of exactly the correct strength and duration. Eager to mate, the males head for the light source, whereupon they are seized and devoured by the despicable Lorelei. There are also frogs that are attracted by the lights and stuff themselves so full that their abdomens start emanating a gently glowing light. The closest analogy is a gross infringement of the secrecy of the mail.

How do animals know their own code? That knowledge must be innate. A cuckoo cannot learn its song from its parents, since it begins life as an orphan. Imitating the reed warbler which has reared it does not work, because by using that code it would attract reed warblers instead of birds of its own species. Its song is therefore innate and the fact that the song is so monotonous should come as no surprise. On the other hand, most birds learn from their parents. For the most part they have a crude song of their own, which is polished by imitating their parents into a species-specific repertoire. These singing lessons may begin in the egg. Quails, for example, despite the popular Dutch adage, are far from deaf: days before they hatch, they learn to recognize their mother's call, so that they know which bird to follow and recognize the sound of their species.

The system works less well with geese, which follow the first moving thing that they see after they hatch, on the assumption that it is their mother. However, the possibility of mistakes is proved by the famous photos of the biologist Konrad Lorenz with a whole train of goslings in tow under the delusion that they are little biologists. Instead of their mother Lorenz had been the first thing that they had seen and now they were imprinted on man. This imprinting is possible only at a certain phase of development; chicks do not enter the critical phase in which the image of their own species is formed until a day after hatching. If they choose wrongly then there is a chance that they will later mate with a partner of the wrong species. For example, zebra finches reared by munias prefer to go to sea with munias when they grow up. The most difficult experience is that of the zebra finches who have been reared together with their brothers and sisters by munias; some of them are later attracted to their own species, some prefer mother's species and a quarter of the fostered young are never able to choose.

As with human beings, the exchange of calling cards does not lead to immediate mating. Even though the other may belong to the same species, it is still frightening. In nature, red in tooth and claw, every other animal is a potential danger. Even creatures that live in herds, swarms or packs usually keep some distance from each other. At mating time, however, that distance can be reduced to zero. For this there are all kinds of rituals, which in the case of human beings have resulted in the discotheque and in the case of animals in display, sniffing, spawning and chorusing. The slow pace with which recognition leads via further acquaintance to the ultimate goal has been beautifully described by William Beebe in the case of the fiddler crab *Uca beebei*:

Illustrations from 'Mating Methods of Animals', China, *c.* 1640

> For an hour a splendid male had been trying in vain to attract the attention of a small, grey female sitting ten centimetres away. He was displaying his most beautiful colours and dancing as though his life depended upon it. Now and then he stopped for a moment to eat a morsel. But everything seemed to leave the female cold. She fiddled around a little at the entrance to her hole, went on eating steadily and did not even look at him. Only when she had finally eaten her fill did she seem to notice him. Somewhat encouraged by this, he increased his dance tempo still further, waved the great purple claw up and down like a thing possessed and alternated the proud raising of his eight green legs with passionate, trailing dance steps. The female shifted sideways a little to come a few centimetres closer, but not without eating a couple more morsels. Dancing faster and faster, the little male crab finally succeeded in

putting her completely under his spell. As though hypnotized, she remained looking at him from a few centimetres away without moving. Now the nature of his dance changed: like a model he revolved slowly in front of her so that she could see in turn his green gleaming shell and the purple claws. Finally she came so close that he could touch her. Carefully he stroked her legs with his, a gesture she reciprocated. They separated for a moment, he executed a last cheerful skipping dance and then suddenly rushed to a hole and descended into it. The last thing that we saw was his gleaming claw, which made a last irresistible beckoning gesture. The female followed him without delay.

Complicated mating dances have also been described in the case of the grebe, the stickleback and all kinds of insect. They consist of scores of components which generally must be executed in a fixed order. One action elicits a response from the other party, which in turn is the cue for the next response by the first partner. This excites the partners, brings them closer together and represents an extra additional check, since an alien species is bound to be exposed in the course of the extensive repertoire.

Yet nature is not sure of itself. In order to prevent animals which are a little careless with their codes and which fraternize with other species from wasting their semen on the wrong partner, it has often built in physical barriers. Even though they may want to mate, they are unable to. For this double-check flies use an intricate locking system. Their penis is their passport; species which in other respects look precisely the same each have their own model of penis, which like a key in a lock fits only the corresponding model of sexual opening in precisely the right kind of female. Entomologists are delighted with this; all kinds of 'difficult species' can be determined on the basis of their penises. This explains why in insect cases in natural history museums one often sees the penis pinned separately under the castrated body of the former owner.

Thanks to all these checks and double-checks a female is only rarely forced to resort to her last line of defence against alien males: biochemical rejection by the egg. If she has been deceived with all her eyes, ears and antennae, then her egg-cells are sure to unmask the illicitly admitted semen. Alien semen is either not admitted to the egg or after a few cell-divisions turns into a non-viable lump of plasma. The mechanisms are like the rejection of a heart transplant and owe their efficiency to their great age, for the last barrier is the oldest one. Our single-celled ancestors had to get to know each other chemically, and bacteria still do. For successful mating certain special marker-proteins must combine with matching proteins in the other bacteria. Butterflies use similar chemicals to attract mates, egg-cells show the desired semen the way with species-specific substances. From the point of view of a sperm or egg, we human beings and other animals are only aids to keep them warm and bring them together, and since every aid is fallible, we have to be checked by them.

The Watching Masseuse, Japanese print, *c.* 1905

Nowhere in nature are there higher walls erected than those between the species. They also exist between man and all other animals. For man the animal kingdom is a forbidden realm, of which he can have knowledge in a roundabout way, using binoculars, electrodes, biologists, novelists like Anton Koolhaas or sign language. Just as an elephant is designed to love elephants, so a human being is naturally attracted only to human beings. Just as elephants prefer trunks and giraffes long necks, human beings can only really identify with beings who walk upright, look at you when you talk to them and are warm-blooded. The characteristics which most attract human males in human females can be seen in any brothel, where human attraction signals are on open display.

Human beings fall for other human beings. And if they occasionally fall for an animal, they are attracted by the animal's human features. What attracts the dog lover is not the doggishness of a dog – the fact that it drools and pants and stinks and moults – but its human qualities – faithfulness, gratitude, patience in waiting for its master, if necessary reinforced with the aid of tricks such as sitting up and begging. Dogs, cats and rabbits are mirrors in which we love ourselves, and if the mirror is enough of a caricature – not ridiculous, but touching – it may even happen that we prefer the animal to the human being. The fact is that in some respects some animals are even more human than human beings themselves. No human being has such an entreating expression as a basset hound, no human being is as loyal as his dog.

The walls between the species are high, but no higher than necessary. Sometimes two closely related species are separated so effectively by mountain ranges, lakes or climatic differences that no behavioural codes are required to keep them apart. Where the various species of white-footed mice live close to each other in America, they have an aversion to the smell of alien species, but in experiments the Florida mouse, which is the only one of the fifty-five species of white-footed mouse found in Florida, did not worry particularly if its cage smelt of another kind of mouse. That was an artificial situation with which it would never be confronted under normal circumstances. In the same way it is quite easy to bring crickets of different species together in a laboratory by warming one of them up. The warmer it is, the faster a cricket chirps. One can even use them as a thermometer. If, for example, one has a snowy-tree cricket and wants to know how warm it is, one can count the number of chirps per minute, subtract 40, divide the difference by 7, add 10 to the result and obtain the temperature in degrees Celsius. If one warms up a male it will start to chirp faster and will attract cold females of another species which chirp just as quickly at a lower temperature. For instance, a female black-horned tree cricket at 21° responded not to a warmer male black-horned tree cricket, but to a silvery tree cricket at 27° and a four-spotted tree cricket at 32°. Love at first hearing. In the laboratory the dividing mechanism can be easily sabotaged; in nature males and females live together at the same temperature, thus eliminating the possibility of mistakes.

In some frogs and toads the dividing walls are naturally low. Although every species has its own croak, many species are quite careless about it. A common toad waking from its winter sleep has a very simple view of the world. If a male sees something moving, there are three possibilities: if it is larger than I am, I run away from it, if it is smaller, I eat it, and if it is the same size, I mate with it. If the creature with which it is mating does not protest, then it is probably the right species and the right sex. Such a toad can afford to do this because most things hopping around at the time when it wakes up from its hibernation are likely to be of the same species; other species wake earlier or later. The green frog has more trouble in avoiding mistakes. Previously it was regarded as one species, nowadays we know that there are three forms: two species plus a hybrid of those two. The carelessness with which partners are chosen is also beautifully shown in a marvellous short film sequence shot by Ed van der Elsken, in which a young man using well-imitated croaking and some finger movements drives the frogs so wild that they mate with his hand.

While on the one hand there are huge walls between the species, on the other hand there are other species which do not seem to take the boundaries particularly seriously. This contradiction is only apparent. In order to erect high walls between the species there must first of all be

Edwin Landseer, *The Thrashing Cat, c.* 1824

sufficient species and in order to create additional species one needs parent species which are flexible. Although there are biologists who collect species as if they were postage stamps, there is an important difference: an 80 cent postage stamp can never become a 90 cent stamp, but species can change into other species. This is called evolution. Although one reads in the newspaper about species which are disappearing, scores of new species are added every year. Among all those obituaries there should at least be room for the occasional birth announcement. One shouldn't hope for a new species of elephant in the foreseeable future, but among the bed bugs, sea spiders and other creepy-crawlies there are a large number of newcomers. It is obvious that these young species, which have not yet defined their boundaries very well, should approach foreign species more frequently than old-established species.

33

An example of such a young species is the lesser black-backed gull (*Larus fuscus*), which is actually still simply a herring gull (*Larus argentatus*), because the two are able to produce fertile offspring, but is regarded by ornithologists as a separate species since seen through binoculars it is so clearly distinct from the herring gull with its black back, yellow feet and red ring around its eyes. It is assumed that the herring gull originated in Siberia and from there spread both eastward via America and westward via Europe across the whole Northern hemisphere. During this world journey minor differences between the populations emerged. In Holland, where the westbound group and the eastbound group meet, the difference between the two becomes so great that we distinguish them as the herring gull and the lesser black-backed gull. Although we can crossbreed them, partitions have already been erected. Even where ordinary herring gulls and small black-backed gulls nest together in a mixed colony they do not interbreed. The mating call and the courtship behaviour already exhibit so many differences that the two no longer recognize each other as potential partners. Hence behaviourial isolation has resulted from geographical isolation. Since interbreeding scarcely occurs, the birds simply continue to accentuate their differences. In time the lesser great black-backed gull will become a separate species, which will not only not wish to reproduce with the ordinary herring gull, but will be unable to do so.

Wherever in the world a fragment of wild nature survives, it pulsates with the creation of new species. Variation is the source of all life, making it possible to exploit the enormous variety of living conditions. Once a dividing wall has been erected between two variants of a species, the germ of two new species is created. Such a dividing wall may be literal – the creation of a mountain chain or inland sea – but also figurative. As a result of minor climatic changes the frogs of one species may divide into early maters and late maters, which hence do not encounter each other at the critical moment. Once they have developed into a different species, the difference in mating time will become a virtually insurmountable barrier.

Birds of a feather flock together. In nature exemption to this rule tends to be granted to young species, which are still in the process of defining themselves. Mankind is a young species. Does it also have a dispensation for sexual intercourse with closely related species? That question seems theoretical; after all, there is only one species of human being, *Homo sapiens*. However, that has not always been the case. Not so very long ago there were others – *Homo erectus* and *Homo habilis*, for example – and besides a sub-species of our own species, *Homo sapiens sapiens*, there was a second sub-species, *Homo sapiens neanderthaliensis*. It is assumed that more than one species of human being lived at various times in various places, so that there was ample opportunity to mate outside one's own species. That would have been bestiality with a fellow human being. Just look at

a picture in one of the books on the subject and ask yourself whether you would have fancied going to bed with one of your ancestors. Your answer will of course probably depend on which book you are looking at. Until recently the 'ape people' were depicted in as apelike a fashion as possible, with low foreheads and blank expressions in order to emphasize the difference from us, the conscious human being. At present the reverse is in vogue and our 'ancestors' look quite appealing. The same trend can of course be observed in the depictions of blacks and other 'foreign races,' which have become more and more like those of whites. If sexual abuse of his female slaves once gave a plantation owner the thrill of bestiality, today marriages between black and white are normal, albeit not as normal as they might be. Although we belong to the same species and although seas and mountains no longer divide us, there are still high dividing walls between the various races. But they are not around us, they are in our heads.

The Monkey Looks On, engraving, 18th century

3

Our Kind of Animals

In order to get properly into the skin of an animal, one would have to see through its eyes. H. Keffer Hartline succeeded in doing this and in 1967 received the Nobel prize for his work.

Woman Mating with Ape, engraving, 19th century

Hartline was able to tap into what the animal saw as it was transmitted to the brain along the optic nerve. He preferred to use the horseshoe crab, because they gave him easy access: a horseshoe crab's optic nerve runs like a thick cable immediately beneath its outer shell.

By looking through the creature's eyes, Hartline discovered a way of seeing better. If one visual cell in the eye received more light than the other immediately next to it, the strong stimulus of the one weakened the weak stimulus of the other even further, thus heightening the contrast. People do this in exactly the same way. When we are on the beach and look at the horizon, the stimuli of the lower band in the sky make the upper band of water darker, so that we are able to see a clear division where water and air in fact virtually merge with each other. It is like making vague outlines clearer by using a pencil.

More contrast enables you to see better. Not always, though. In extreme cases, the 'lateral inhibition' discovered by Hartline may prove fatal. In hospitals, where the eyes of doctors sometimes see stripes on your X-rays which are not there, it can result in unnecessary surgery.

With its predilection for contrasts our mind is constantly searching for differences. The more alike two images are, the more vividly the differences emerge. We recognize at a glance our relatives and friends from five billion faces with five billion virtually identical noses and ten billion virtually identical ears. Strangely enough, the smaller the differences, the easier it is to make distinctions. For a white person, who is able to distinguish his or her fellow white people without any problem, a yellow face tends to be so different that 'all Chinese look alike'. Only when white people have seen enough yellow faces to be able to discount what they have in common do they notice the differences. Biologists are aware of the same phenomenon in field behaviourial research. To begin with all chimpanzees look alike and all elephants are called Jumbo – field guides deliberately blur the individual differences within a species in order to emphasize the common differences with other species – but after a while a fieldworker distinguishes his animals individually like a class of children, and can give them proper names.

At the zoo the most striking artificial contrast is found when we visit the apes. However keen we are to identify ourselves with distant relatives such as the tiger with its splendid velvety testicles or a chic-looking gazelle, we become uneasy when we are close to the animals that resemble us most closely. Too closely for comfort. Laughing sheepishly at their 'silly antics', we are embarrassed at the unfortunately irrefutable fact that of all animals these obscene, childish creatures are our nearest relatives; a feeling familiar to many people from family get-togethers. The laughter generated by distorting mirrors is seldom jovial.

The difference between white and black human beings is still smaller than that between white humans and apes. Consequently no difference has ever been so exaggerated as this one. Besides being black and thick-lipped, blacks are supposed to be stupid and lazy. Because they were ugly in the eyes of whites, they were also supposed to be evil and lecherous. The only area in which blacks surpassed whites was in lust and penis size. Some of them at least. In the 1930s Stirling Brown distinguished five types of 'negro' in the United States: the *toms* were the well-behaved servants, the *coons* lazy and stupid, the *mulattoes* tragic, the *mammies* sexless kitchen maids, and only the *bucks* were reckoned to be super-virile. For centuries blacks were generally classified by whites somewhere between animals and humans, approximately where nowadays the anthropoid apes are found, and sometimes even lower. The English captain Daniel Beeckman, in his Journal of 1712, prefers orang-utans: 'Their faces are at least not completely repulsive. In any case I found them more pleasant to look at than many Hottentots whom I have seen. Moreover, they have large teeth and no tail and have hair only where humans have it. . . . The natives believe firmly that they were originally human beings, who, however, because of their wickedness have been changed into animals.' Where in his day blacks were treated like animals on the plantations, they were certainly afforded the same rights as domestic animals or chattels. The same fate was shared by other races. Not until 1957 did the high court of Paraguay officially decree that 'Indians, like the other inhabitants of the Republic, are human beings'. In South Africa in the same year sexual intercourse between whites and members of other races was forbidden. In the United States such a prohibition was scarcely necessary at that time. There, in a survey held in twenty cities in 1951, 70 per cent of whites considered it 'unacceptable' that blacks should even visit the same hairdresser as themselves.

This was in a country in parts of which more than half of males had sexual contact with animals. Intercourse with blacks was obviously a worse kind of bestiality for a white than with a cow or a pig. Which does not mean that the whites, given the large number of people of mixed race in the former colonies, were inhibited by this. Indeed, foreign races exercise a particular sexual fascination, as can be seen in our own day in the Amsterdam red light district, which presents a full spectrum of human races as a living reference work for a physical anthropologist. In the past one had to visit foreign lands to find foreign women, but white seamen and colonialists were quite prepared to do this, as witness songs like:

> I was outside Batavia,
> not far from Jakarta,
> when a native girl came up to me
> and asked me for a banana:
> I let myself be moved by the maid,
> and invited her to an inn.

Provided one didn't catch anything, otherwise the watchword was: 'Both here and in Monkeyland too. Keep the whores away from you.' Conversely, according to the third president of the United States, Thomas Jefferson, in other respects a very enlightened man, white women should be on their guard against black men. The superiority of whites was quite clear, he wrote in 1782, from 'the judgement of the negroes themselves in favour of the whites, as was evident from their preference for them, just as widespread as the preference of the orangutan for the black woman above his own kind' in both cases there were upward aspirations.

That sexual intercourse with another race was wrong was quite clear to Joost de Damhoudere, whose textbooks set the norm for jurisprudence in large areas of sixteenth-century Europe. The only question was whether fornication with a Turk or a Jew should be classed as bestiality or sodomy. A century later in 1693, François van Bergen unwittingly produced a nice retort to this in his *Miscellaneous Leaves from Parnassus*:

> A wanton Jesuit, inflamed with lechery,
> Went to a Jewish woman, and most lustfully
> Asked to have his way, but she refused the treat,
> Saying: Sir, our Jewish law won't let us touch pork meat.

The insult to Jews weighs heavier than that to blacks in that while many Jews lived in Western Europe there were scarcely any blacks. How little was known of them is clear from countless paintings of the three Magi from the East, in which the black king is clearly a white man with a blackened face. Until the 1950s, in the words of the writer Ewald

Vanvugt, 'a person with a colour other than that of dead prawn was a spectacle in this country'. In general blacks waited in distant lands until they were converted. The exception, *the* Negro of the Netherlands, Donald Jones, did everything that is expected of a negro. Crazy dancing, pulling faces, laughing, getting up to tricks, in short, behaving like an ape.

In the past if one wanted to see a negro or an Indian, one went to the zoo. For example, in the menagerie of Blauw Jan on the Kloveniersburgwal in Amsterdam, the Mohawk Indian Sychnecta could be viewed on payment of admission, among all kinds of animals. At the end of the nineteenth century the exhibiting of strange peoples was all the rage. Thousands of Dutch people first made the acquaintance of the natives of Surinam at the World Exhibition of 1883 in Amsterdam. Exhibited in huts behind the Rijksmuseum, Bushmen were extolled as the 'strangest race ever seen in Europe'. A postcard of a group of Indonesians on show has been preserved with a note from the sender that one of the women from the 'troop of Blacks' in the photo is his 'darling': 'when I go there she always has to have a bag of sweets'. At that time people in Berlin were being astounded by a tribe of Russian nomads, the Kalmuks, and in Paris Senegalese drew a million visitors in two and a half months. Nowadays one can see living exotic races in the street, railway compartments and underground trains free of charge. But they remain exotic: renowned museums like the Natural History Museum in New York have scores of brown, black and yellow human dolls among the thousands of stuffed animals, surrounded by the appropriate colonial wares, and in 1992 a scandal followed the discovery of a stuffed negro on display in a small museum close to the host city of the Olympic games, Barcelona.

We are surrounded by other races in the flesh, we go to the zoo, watch television and read books. Until the seventeenth century there were only books, and they were not very reliable. It is not clear from many travelogues whether a strange race of humans or an anthropoid ape is being described. For example, the animals concerned are too hairy to be human and too garrulous to be anthropoid apes. Moreover, all kinds of creatures were dredged up from antiquity which were half-man, ape and god, such as satyrs and pygmies.

Indians, apes, satyrs, pygmies, blacks: it was really not clear where the human ended and the animal began; where high-flown love could turn into filthy bestiality.

A first attempt to separate man and animals was made by 'the illustrious Doctor of Medicine of Amsterdam' Nicolaas Tulp, celebrated as the anatomist in Rembrandt's *Anatomy Lesson*. In 1641 he produced the first accurate description of an anthropoid ape. The animal, a gift to the stadholder Frederik Hendrik, came from Angola. Unfortunately there was a departure from accuracy because Tulp described his African

Edward Topsell's 'Sphinx', 17th century

chimpanzee as an 'orang-utan or satyr from the Indies'. He really believed that he had found the satyr of antiquity: 'either there is no satyr to be found in nature, or if there is, then it will indubitably be this creature.'

For that matter his orang-utan corresponded not only externally with the descriptions of Pliny and the other classical authors, it also behaved like the satyrs which, according to Edward Topsell, the shipwrecked Ephemus Car had seen:

> These, on being perceived by the Mariners to run to the ships and lay hold of the women that were in them, the ship-men for fear took one of the Barbarian women and set her on the land among them, whom in most odious and filthy manner they abused, not only in that part that nature hath ordained, but over the whole body most libidinously whereby they found them to be very brute beasts.

This accorded with the stories which Tulp had heard from those who had journeyed to the Indies:

> The King of Sambaces told my Neighbour Samuel Blommert, that on the Island of Borneo these Satyrs, particularly the males, are so bold and brave, and have such strong sinews and muscles, that they dare to attack armed men, and also Women; who they sometimes in their lustfulness abduct and rape; which lustfulness towards Women they share with the ancient wanton Satyrs, so that the Indian women shun like the plague the Thickets where these shameless creatures abide.

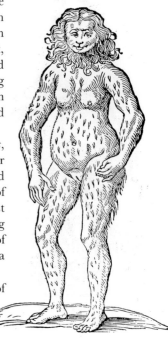

The 'Orang-outang' of
Jacob de Bondt, 1658

A colleague of Tulp's in Batavia, Bontius, whose real name was of course simply Jacob de Bondt, depicted the 'orang-utan' in even more human terms. He himself had seen in the Indies a female who hid her body from strange men 'with modesty'. She covered her face with her hands, wept, sighed and displayed other human behaviour, so that one was inclined to say that besides language, they lacked no human quality. According to the Javanese such creatures were 'born of the lust of Indonesian women who consort in disgusting lechery with apes'. Linnaeus included them in his system as a second kind of human, *Homo troglodytes*.

Probably what De Bondt saw was simply a member of *Homo sapiens*, albeit an extravagantly hairy example, but for people in the mother country it was now clear that the orang-utan is quite rightly called 'orang': 'orang' is the Malay for 'human' and referred to all kinds of nomadic tribes besides the anthropoid ape: the orang akit on the East coast of Sumatra, the orang boekit in South East Borneo. An 'orang blanda' was not only a white man, but also a particularly ugly kind of ape. In the Indies whites themselves used the term 'weird orang' as a term of abuse.

In 1669 the English doctor Edward Tyson, the father of the study of anthropoid apes, confused the chimpanzee which he was dissecting, a young animal 75 cm long, with a pygmy:

> That the Pygmies of the Antients were a sort of Apes, and not of Humane Race, I shall endeavour to prove in the following Essay. And if the Pygmies were only Apes, then in all probability our Ape may be a Pygmie: a sort of Animal so much resembling Man, that both the Antients and the Moderns have reputed it to be a Puny Race of Mankind, call'd to this day, *Homo sylvestris*, the Wild Man: Orang-Outang, or Man of the Woods.

The stories about apes abducting women persisted. Three centuries ago the traveller François Leguat, 'with his accompanying Retinue', saw on Java the results of such abduction: a 'Rare Ape':

> The creature's face was completely bald/except at the eyebrows: and corresponded completely with those rough and boorish faces of the Hottentot women that I have seen at the Cape.
>
> ... Most people considered that this creature was the issue of a human being and an Ape: because it sometimes happens that some slave woman or other having committed a grave crime/and fearful of being as usual severely punished for this/in fear takes flight to the woods and lives there as a wild beast. And since Nature does not oppose the mingling of Horses and Asses, then she is very likely to tolerate that of an Ape with a female creature which is similar to him/when the latter is not restrained by any reason or principle: because there is more similarity between an Ape and a black slave woman, who has been brought up without the least knowledge of God/than between an Ass and a Mare.

Hoppius's 'Satyr' (below) and Hoppius's 'Lucifer' (below facing)

Leguat's name is virtually forgotten, and it has since become clear that his travelogue was largely fictitious. However, his contemporaries had no such doubts, certainly not with regard to what had been said about apes and human beings. Since antiquity and during the Middle Ages apes had symbolized the lower desires. An old rabbinical text relates how the devil, when Noah tasted the first wine, sacrificed in succession a sheep, a lamb, an ape and a pig. The animals symbolized the stages of drunkenness in human beings: first mild, then wild, next dissolute and finally disgusting. In animal books like that of Aldrovandi (1640) apes were generally depicted with enormous penises. However, that makes them, in view of their preference for human females, all the more human.

Influential writers like Jean-Jacques Rousseau helped to smuggle anthropoid apes into the human realm. For someone who presented the 'savage' as a 'noble' model for us Europeans, it was quite conceivable that further investigation of the 'bushmen' would show that they were simply a variant of our species. The proposition that the 'orang-utan is more highly developed than many savages' was certainly defended by

Seltsaamen Aap.

Left: the *Rare Ape* of
François Leguat, 1708

the Scottish jurist James Burnett in an argument running into hundreds of pages.

While the animal was thus being elevated into a human being, human beings were being relegated to the animal kingdom. In 1735 Carolus Linnaeus, the first official bookkeeper of nature, included man between the apes and the sloths in his *Systema Naturae*. Nevertheless man has a leading position in the system and in the view of Petrus Camper, another Dutch doctor, that is the very least that can be said. In 1782, as the first person to describe the difference between the chimpanzee and the orang-utan, he also assigns man his place. He makes much of 'the Superiority of mankind above all other animals'. For does not man alone

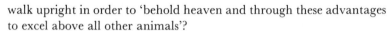

Cynocephalus by Ulyssis Aldrovandi, 1640

walk upright in order to 'behold heaven and through these advantages to excel above all other animals'?

The state of affairs in the second half of the eighteenth century is best indicated by the most widely read animal encyclopedia of those days, the *Histoire Naturelle* of the French count, Georges de Buffon. If one compared a man with an ape, one had to take into account the various factors, including 'the ardent desire of male apes for females, the identical structure of the genitalia in both sexes, the periodical flow of the females, the forced or voluntary intercourse of black women with apes, resulting in offspring that belong to both species: and consider then how difficult it is, if one does not include them in the same species to indicate to what extent they are distinct.'

In the nineteenth century the theme of the hairy woman-chaser evolved into a literary cliché. The archetype of the series which was ultimately to lead to *King Kong* is Edgar Allan Poe's *The Murders in the Rue Morgue* of 1841. Here the sexual element is still veiled by violence. In the story an orang-utan, which has tried to shave itself in imitation of its master, escapes from a hotel room in Paris. Still brandishing the razor, it surprises two helpless ladies and tries to shave one of them. She screams and the ape becomes enraged, with fatal consequences.

'An Attractive Cover for Darwin', *Punch* magazine, c. 1962

When Poe's gothic novel was filmed, the orang-utan was changed into a gorilla. Because a gorilla looks even more terrifying than an orang-utan. Poe would never have overlooked this, but he could not have known it, because the gorilla was not discovered until six years after his story was first published. The name had occurred in literature since the fifth century BC, when it had been used by the Carthaginian explorer Hanno, but the animal itself, however large and appealing to the imagination, has been known only for the last century and a half. A sub-species, the mountain gorilla made famous by Dian Fossey, has been known for less than a century, since 1901. In that short time the gorilla has ousted the orang-utan almost completely from its role as a woman-abductor. Likewise, chimpanzees are now rarely mentioned in this connection. According to Pierre Boitard, in *Le Jardin des plantes* (1842), they are quite simply much more civilized:

> The male is devoted to his mate ... nevertheless the Chimpanzee is not always faithful to his mate and often chases Negro women in the jungle whom he abducts and takes to his hut. In their attempts to overpower the Negro women, says M. de La Brosse in his *Voyage à la Côte d'Angola*, they guard them and give them excellent food. ... Sometimes it is as though Chimpanzees are less concerned to satisfy their brutish lusts than to construct a congenial relationship. ... A proof of this is that they also abduct very young children and watch over them just to have them near them. Battel tells us that a Negro boy from his retinue, who had been abducted by Chimpanzees, lived for

Arther Rackham (left)
and Aubrey Beardsley
(right), illustrations for
'The Murders in the
Rue Morgue' by
Edgar Allen Poe, 19th
century

between twelve and thirteen months in their society, and returned very contented, fat and healthy.

The chimpanzee has retained this friendly image down to our own days, as is clear from *Max Mon Amour, Max My Love*, a film made in 1987 by the Japanese director Nagisa Oshima, in which an English diplomat discovers that his wife is having an affair with a chimpanzee, which she keeps hidden in a hotel. The diplomat, who himself has a mistress, albeit a human one, decides to take the ape into his household in order to satisfy his curiosity. (Does she really do it with him? Can one be jealous of an ape?) A shock awaits him: his wife really does love her chimpanzee.

Indeed, in literature the chimpanzee fulfils a sexual role which is seldom given to a gorilla: that of the female partner. In *His Monkey Wife; or Married to a Chimp* (1931), John Collier describes how an English teacher, Alfred Fatigay, lives in Africa with a chimpanzee as his housekeeper. Back in London, where he is about to marry an old girlfriend, there is a power cut during the wedding ceremony. In the confusion the bride faints, the chimpanzee takes her place and before Alfred realizes what is happening, he is lawfully married to his chimpanzee. With his hairy bride, who cannot speak but out of a desire for order reads Darwin's *The Origin of Species*, Alfred returns to Africa, where, in view of the final sentence, much good awaits him:

> The candle, guttering beside the bed, was strangled in the grasp of a prehensile foot, and darkness received, like a ripple in velvet, the final happy sigh.

Apart from exceptions such as these chimpanzee scenes, the anthropoid ape always plays the brute in its sexual relations with human

Charles Darwin,
caricature, *c.* 1871

beings. It does not require a Freud to recognize the terrifying aspects of the father figure in the gorilla or orang-utan. It is the timeless theme of *Beauty and the Beast*: the spirit which is eager to love but is trapped in a lustful body, which cannot be brought under control.

From the start the gorilla is depicted as menacingly as possible. The tone is set by such writers as Paul du Chaillu, who in 1855 left America to be the first man to penetrate gorilla country and to bring back a gorilla with him – dead or alive. The report appeared in 1861 as *Explorations and Adventures in Equatorial Africa*:

> It looked remarkably like a devilish dream figure which the ancients depicted among the other ghastly monsters, half man, half beast, when they wished to depict scenes of hell. It came a few steps closer, stopped, let out its dreadful roar again, came down and finally stopped about six metres away from us. When it began roaring again and beating its breast in fury, we shot it dead.

Even the respectable *Archives du Musée National d'Histoire Naturelle* lost their scientific objectivity. In 1858 Doctor Gautier-Laboullay wrote the following about gorillas:

> They are so terribly strong that they drive off an elephant who dares to invade their territory with their bare fists or with sticks. It is sometimes said that they abduct unfortunate Negro women who are careless enough to come into their vicinity.

While the apes were thus again relegated to the animal kingdom, Darwin with his theory of evolution taught us that we are descended from them. Many people could not endure the thought that they had even one foot in the animal kingdom and dismissed the notion. Now that this is scarcely possible any longer without putting on blinkers, the dilemma is again solved as it has always been: by making human beings more animal, so that we topple from a less lofty pedestal, and by the humanization of animals, so that it is no longer so awful having to be one.

The first approach has been followed most consistently by Desmond Morris. In the 1960s his *The Naked Ape* taught us that not only our appearance but our behaviour derives from that of our ape ancestors. It is therefore quite normal that we should behave in an apelike way. In his view, our sexual behaviour in particular is based on animal instincts. Human females, he claims, have the largest breasts of all anthropoid apes in order to compensate human males, who had begun to copulate face to face, for the loss of the view of their buttocks. Many of the assertions in *The Naked Ape* have since been qualified by Morris himself and his critics, but the message still resonates: *really*, we are apes.

At the same time that Desmond Morris was animalizing human beings, Jane Goodall was humanizing animals. She was the first human being – and the first woman – to achieve such complete acceptance by a wild chimpanzee community that she was able to study their activities in the wild virtually without hindrance: a variant of the participatory journalism popular at the time. The results were sensational. Used to the confused creatures in the zoo supplemented only sparsely with glimpses from the wild, biologists could at first scarcely believe it: chimpanzees used tools, became pleasantly excited by killing other apes and behaved so subtly with each other that their frame of mind could only be described in such human terms as love, jealousy and intrigue. In giving her animals names Jane Goodall was giving them much more than an identification code: they had become individuals instead of representatives of a species, just as children in a mass of pupils only become real people when the teacher knows the name of the boys and girls in his or her class. Since Jane Goodall it is no longer chimpanzees who are running around in the jungle but Ann or Peter, you know, the one who had such a row with Charles, just like him, isn't it? The Dutch chimpanzee researcher Frans de Waal even dreams about them:

> It is clear from the dreams of those who work with them that chimpanzees are seen in the first place as personalities. Just as we generally dream of human beings in the form of recognizable individuals, so we dream of these anthropoid apes as individuals. If a student were to say that he dreamt of 'an ape', I would look at him with as much surprise as someone who maintained that they had dreamt of 'a human being'.

'If this is an animal,' De Waal wrote of the chimpanzee, 'then what are we?' But he is a lone voice in more than one respect. For a start he is a man. It is striking how often research into ape behaviour is carried out by women. If chimpanzees are synonymous with Jane Goodall, mountain gorillas are instantly associated with Dian Fossey and orangs with Biruté Galdikas, although the Dutch Liesbeth Sterck also does commendable work on apes in the orang centre in West Sumatra. The most remarkable feature is the devotion shown by women to their apes. For Jane Goodall her chimpanzees were ultimately more important than her husband Hugo van Lawick, and Dian Fossey made it so clear that she preferred her gorillas to the Africans who were poaching in her reserve that it cost her her life. Spiteful tongues maintained that Dian was found in bed in the arms of a gorilla. Sir David Attenborough, who worked with her, could not confirm this, but answered my question whether Dian Fossey had not gone too far in her love for gorillas with a deep sigh:

> Yes. And she also went too far in her dislike of Africans. For example, she told the farmers in Ruanda that they must not let their cattle roam in the nature reserve. But it was difficult to indicate where the park began or stopped and the poor African farmers had very little to eat. If you disregard this warning, she said, I shall take the necessary steps. One of them did disobey. And she

47

shot each of his cows in the spine. She didn't kill them, but she crippled them and left them where they were to make it clear to the owner that he had lost all his possessions.

Once a baby gorilla disappeared. Dian believed, rightly or wrongly, that she knew the culprit. She kidnapped his son. She also tied Africans to a tree with barbed wire in order to beat them. That is not the way to win the support of the local population. Whatever the case, since the death of Dian Fossey not a single gorilla has disappeared.

Not only in the field, but in the laboratory too a strikingly large number of women work with anthropoid apes, in this case in an attempt to break down the last barrier between apes and human beings: language. In the seventeenth century De Bondt had heard from natives that the 'orang-utans' were quite able to speak but seldom did so for fear of being put to work. He himself was sceptical, but the French doctor La Mettrie maintained as late as 1748, in *L'Homme machine*, that all that is required to teach the 'homme des bois' to speak is to bring him up as a deaf-mute child. Around the turn of the century an American professor, Richard Garner, tried to solve the problem with a new aid, the gramophone. He recorded the sounds of apes in captivity and even undertook an expedition to Africa.

Unlike Jane Goodall, he was so distrustful of his research subjects in the wild that he had himself shut up in a cage. At first the apes gave him a wide berth and it was the lions who besieged him in his cage for a whole week, but finally he believed he was able to distinguish twenty-four genuine ape words. For example, the professor had a young female chimpanzee, which greeted him every morning with the words: 'Gwouff tsch' tak tourôô', which according to the professor meant 'I love you.'

In 1892, in a review of 'Monkey Man' Garner's research in the magazine *De Natuur*, H.J. Calkoen still confuses apes and blacks in a way which has become inimitable for us with the argument that apes, despite their small vocabulary, are quite able to speak a language, since 'the savage peoples do not have many words either'.

> Bushmen, for example, have a language which consists of short sounds uttered in quick succession, which can scarcely be called articulated: language is so little advanced in those underdeveloped human beings that, in order to make themselves understood to each other, they have to resort to all kinds of hand gestures, from which it follows that darkness certainly does not favour the conducting of a regular conversation.

Later recordings refuted what Garner had tried to demonstrate with his gramophone. Apes have no spoken language, their sounds are simply those of animals. This is not to say that human beings do not produce animal sounds. These are particularly well suited to sexual intercourse, and if that applies to human beings, their use between an ape and a

human as the writer Brots imagined it in an unpublished book, of which
a fragment appeared in the magazine *Barbarber* in 1959, is even more
inspiring. Here love blossoms between a man and a gorilla: 'With her
large dark hand she now caressed my body very lightly. From her throat
came growling sounds.' At the climax human being and animal merge:

> Her ... and arms and legs over my bod and ther ther. And waggg! Then
> Reng! Ssoon ... and ah no more yes and u wit you ndvas the groov more
> goesegosemureliyertasverfgregregrerrrtfe hre ni ight asvgt.

The message could not be clearer. When human beings behave like
animals, animal language is a useful aid. But if a human being becomes
more animal through animal language, surely the animal can be
elevated by using human language and the gap between human beings
and animals can be closed with language. By the 1960s good progress
seemed to have been made in this direction. Through the use of click
sounds people were already communicating with dolphins, which were
depicted by the popular press as scholarly creatures which had
accidentally found themselves in the water. And then there were our
nearest relatives, the apes.

The first experiments had the opposite of the effect to that intended.
The Reynolds husband-and-wife team, who brought up a chimpanzee
with their son of the same age, managed to teach the animal scarcely a
single word; the most significant result of the mixed upbringing was that
their son learned to speak very late and started barking when hungry. A
breakthrough came when people like Beatrice Gardner realized that an
ape has the wrong kind of throat to sustain a real spoken language. Of
the sixty-five throat muscles which enable humans to produce 250
syllables per minute (or in the case of the French 350), few are found in
apes. Gardner taught her pupil, the chimpanzee Washoe, the sign
language used for communication by deaf people in America. One of her
human pupils, Penny Patterson, even began teaching a gorilla, Koko.
The extent of her dedication became clear when San Francisco Zoo
decided to discontinue the experiments for fear that Koko would become
so human that she would later become unsuitable for breeding. 'If she
has to go in a cage,' protested Penny, 'I'll go in with her.'

Ultimately the language lessons, which began so hopefully, resulted in
disappointment. Although apes were able to overcome the handicap of
their vocal chords with the help of sign language, computers and plastic
symbols so well that they could string together hundreds of words into
meaningful combinations, a proper conversation was never achieved.
Probably their brains are not suited to this. This does not mean that
theirs are any worse than ours, it simply points to the fact that apes do
not need language. Anthropoid apes are constantly communicating
with each other, but they do it differently: with gestures, with body

49

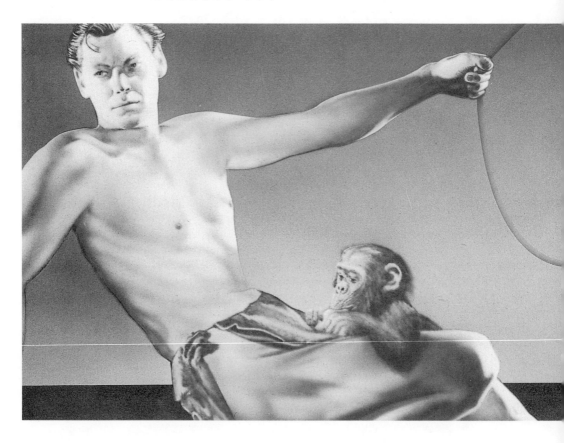

Joost Veerkamp,
illustration from 'Filled
Contours', 1985

language, with behaviour and above all with fleas. Just as our chattering
is the lubricant of our social life, apes lubricate their society through
grooming. It is true that human beings have their language to thank for
Shakespeare's sonnets, Notre Dame and the flood defences in the Rhine-
Meuse delta, but these might also have been produced with a little less
chatter. For 99 per cent of the time 99 per cent of human beings use
the most refined vocal chords in the world for banter, social talk,
sociability. Apes use grooming for this purpose. While orangs growl
loudly during courtship, they mate in silence. The only apparent sign of
lust is that the male sometimes uses his big toes to insert his penis. An ape
says nothing because it has nothing to say, human beings speak in order
to disguise the fact. Perhaps we should talk about this.

As less and less prestige was attached to language experiments it
became clearer what the researchers really thought of their apes. Even
before the previous harvest had been gathered, the scientists were
already at work in their next field. At most, Washoe was given a little
attention, the rest of the 'talking apes' had been largely paid off. A
number of them were dumped mercilessly from the pulpit into the

vivisection laboratory. Nim, one of the most eloquent chimpanzees, was rescued from medical research and according to *Silent Partners* by Eugene Linden is now in a horses' retirement home called Black Beauty Farm.

And then there was Lucy. After all the words that had been pumped into her had been extracted, she was let loose in the African jungle. Her keeper Janice Carter believes that that is where a chimpanzee belongs. Lucy did not agree. Having lived for eleven years in a human family, she wanted to sleep on an ordinary mattress, she preferred her mineral water from a bottle, before going to sleep she liked leafing through the magazine rack, and if there was one thing she hated, it was camping. Hence, finding herself in the jungle, Lucy flatly refused to forage for food. Instead she made gestures of command: '*Food. Hurry. Give food Lucy. More food. Hurry, hurry.*' Janice virtually had to kick the spoiled brat into the trees and even showed her how to eat live ants. The most poignant detail was that Lucy was robbed of her language. Questions were no longer answered, statements ignored. When two years later someone from her previous life came to visit her, Lucy raced to the edge of her fenced-off piece of Africa and called in sign language: '*Please. Help. Out.*' Of course it was useless. After a short job interview at our request, the animals, having been weighed and found wanting, were again expelled from the human realm, back millions of years, into the world of apes.

It strikes me as an act of poetic justice that apes should conversely deny human beings access to the animal kingdom. By being silent about their concerns of course, and – just when we start thinking of them as a kind of people – by doing something very animal-like, like cannibalizing each other or showing aggression towards sick members of their group. The researcher Frans de Waal dreamed about this too:

> I dreamt that the main door of the apehouse was open for me. The apes crowded around in order to see me. Yeroen, the eldest male, stepped forward from among them to shake my hand. He listened rather impatiently to my request to join them. He flatly refused. There was no question of this, and according to Yeroen I would not like it: their society was far too tough for a human being.

As already indicated by the case of Janice and Lucy, the rehabilitation of anthropoid apes in the wild is another area where women predominate. Barbara Harrison taught scores of orangs in Borneo the jungle life which they had never known in the human world, Stella Brewer helped acclimatize the apes on Mount Asserik, Jo Fritz provides an emergency refuge for all kinds of hairy relatives in a breeding centre in the Arizona desert. The model for all of these is the wealthy Madam Rosalia Abreu, who at the beginning of this century owned a private ape collection in Cuba, the pride of which were three orang-utans and fourteen chimpanzees. According to Madam her apes were very jealous.

Cornelis Cornelisz van
Haarlem, *The Fall*,
detail, *c.* 1592

For example, one of her male baboons always hid his partner when
human males came to look at the cage. Since he never showed this
reaction in the presence of women, Madam tried an experiment. She
had a priest come to the cage in the hope that the clergyman's surplice
would fool the animal, but to no avail: the creature still hid its mate.

The famous primatologist Robert Yerkes, who with his wife Ada
brought up the two chimpanzees Chim and Pansee, often visited
Madam Abreu, who had more apes to perform research on than he
could ever afford. One day he asked her whether she thought that apes of
various species, as she put it, 'would not marry'. Not as a rule, was
Madam's opinion, but exceptions prove the rule. In reply Yerkes
reminded her that human beings, white or black, do cross-breed. 'Not so
much any more,' said Madam. 'Not in Cuba.'

At night Madam Abreu brought her anthropoid apes into the house, frightened that they would catch cold. They did not actually come into her bed, unlike many other anthropoid apes which have been brought up by human beings. The babies in particular were always able to find a way of getting into bed with their foster parents. After all, in the wild they also sleep with their mothers. 'If she became very clingy,' wrote Dr Lang, 'she was allowed to come into my warm bed. She was over the moon, nuzzled up to me and first played with the buttons of my pyjama top, then with my fingers; suddenly her movements became slower and she went back to sleep, safe in my arms and in the warmth of the "nest".' Cathy Hayes had the same experience with Viki, and Lilo Hess reports: 'She trotted up the stairs, dragging her sheet behind her, and crawled into bed with me. There she burrowed deep under the covers and fell asleep in a few seconds.' A fully grown anthropoid ape in bed is a very different matter: this is mentioned only by Gertrude Lintz, who had taken the gorilla Buddy into her home. At night he slept in his cage in the cellar, but one stormy night at the end of the 1930s, for all his 400 pounds, he was so frightened by the thunder and lightning that he escaped and sought refuge in Gertrude's bedroom.

In these cases sex of course is scarcely a factor: the relationship between woman and ape is first and foremost the relationship of mother and child, although there are hints of an erotic element when, for example, Dian Fossey in her *Gorillas in the Mist* calls the black-backed gorilla Sam 'exceptionally attractive'. And yet, when one reads *Eve and the Apes*, written by a woman, Emily Hahn, who is as concerned with the fate of the anthropoid apes as with that of the female researchers whom she is describing, the love-life of those researchers and their human partners repeatedly goes wrong. An anthropoid ape absorbs one completely. What is it that attracts women so in anthropoid apes? Emily Hahn herself is not exactly sure:

> Maternal impulses plus the fascination of the unknown? Possibly. Probably. Is caring for anthropoid apes the same urge that has so many teenage girls mucking out filthy stalls and grooming ponies just to be close to the horses they love? ... No, maternal instinct is not quite the answer [many of the women had children of their own]. Perhaps these women (like many other humans) find it easier to get on with nonhuman animals than with their own kind.

Even though they never succeeded in talking properly, the anthropoid apes did read, or at least looked at pictures. 'Without having been taught,' writes Reynolds in his survey of anthropoid apes who have been brought up by human beings, 'all young anthropoid apes enjoy looking at picture books and showed that they recognized people, objects or animals that they knew.' As was said above, Lucy always read some magazines before she went to sleep. But the most important revelation for our topic comes from Roger Fouts, who told Vicki Hearne (author of *Adam's Task*) that the chimpanzee Washoe liked sitting in a tree reading *Playboy* in the mornings. And according to Maurice Temerlin, Lucy used *Playgirl* when masturbating. Eugene Linden regards this as 'the most impressive proof of the complex intelligence of chimpanzees'. So be it.

4

The Cuddliness Factor

'When I reached the spot where I had seen the *nendak* bird,' reported a girl from Sarawak, 'there I was suddenly embraced by a maias, who came from my rear. I fell down to the ground.' The story threatens to become monotonous, but ends unexpectedly: 'My basket also was dropped to the ground – and all the cucumbers poured out. These at once attracted the maias who freed me to pick the cucumbers. These it took up unto [sic] a tree top.'

This recent report by Gaun anak Sureng may not be as exciting as the old travellers' tales, but it is certainly as credible. It tallies with the available facts. In Africa, too, the chimpanzees were more interested in the bananas than in Jane Goodall's breasts and nowhere in the literature is there a convincing example of an actual mating between a human being and a free, live anthropoid ape. Obviously it is precisely with our nearest relatives that mating is most problematical. Apes among themselves seem to have less trouble. Zuckerman, for example, saw a male orang repeatedly trying to mate with an immature female chimpanzee, and Hamilton knew of a female baboon that mated with macaques. These unions were usually provoked by captivity, but it is clear from the encounter between the chimpanzee Flint, a seven year-old male, and the adolescent baboon Apple, as noted by Jane Goodall, that the dividing lines are also crossed in the wild:

> Flint, clearly, was sexually stimulated by the sight of Apple's small rosy swelling. To attract her attention, he used postures and gestures typical of male chimpanzee courtship: he sat and looked towards Apple, his thighs splayed, his penis erect, and he shook a little branch with quick jerking movements of one arm. With the exception of the erect penis the male baboon does none of these things. . . . Apple, however, seemed to understand quite well what Flint wanted . . . and presented herself for copulation. She did this in the manner of her species; she stood squarely in front of Flint facing away

from him, looked back over her shoulder, and held her tail to one side. But a female chimpanzee does not offer herself to her male in this way – *she* crouches close to the ground. Flint looked at Apple perplexed. He shook his branch again. And then, seeing that this was not effective, he stood upright, placed the knuckles of his right hand on her rump, at the base of her tail, and pushed down. To my amazement Apple flexed her legs – but only a little. . . . Flint gripped Apple's right ankle with his right foot [as a male baboon would do], held onto a sapling with his other foot and actually achieved intromission.

With the chimpanzee behaving a little like a baboon, and a baboon a little like a chimpanzee, the species had come together. For human beings such a compromise is obviously asking too much with regard to anthropoid apes. They clearly prefer mating with their friends than with their relations. The animals most used for bestiality are not even distantly related to us. They are mainly predators, like dogs, and cloven-hoofed animals, such as goats, cows and donkeys. Other mammals are also mentioned, even seals, but with anthropoid apes things go no further than sexually tinted games. Neither birds nor reptiles are spared our attentions and there are even people who have sexual intercourse, as far as this is possible, with fishes. Women stuff an eel into their vagina – it wriggles as well as a snake, is pleasantly slippery and is not as dangerous – and the method used by men has been described by Friedrich Krauss in his book *Japanisches Geschlechtsleben*:

Persian Soldier Mating with a Donkey, 19th century

> Fishermen along the Japanese coast even use the thornback ray *Trygon gastinacea* for sexual purposes, albeit only when it has been freshly caught and killed, because when alive the thornback is a very dangerous creature, which can inflict serious, often fatal injuries on human beings. Because it has no external sexual organs, it is natural in the case of the thornback ray that a man should insert his penis in the intestinal opening of the fish, but it is said that the pleasure for a man is as great or even greater than with a woman.

But fishes are not the most bizarre partners chosen by human beings. There are women who smear honey between their legs in order to attract flies or other insects. The tickling of their feet and mouths does the rest. Men have their own variant. Although the official term – formicophilia – means literally 'love of ants' – i.e. copulating with ants – it includes sexual contact with snails, frogs and other small creatures. Actual mating is of course out of the question because of all those minute sexual organs, but on the other hand a real orgasm is perfectly possible.

Although human beings take their sexual partners from all corners of the animal kingdom this does not mean that they have sex with every species, let alone equally often with every species. They have their favourites. To some extent these are, naturally enough, connected with availability. Domestic and farm animals are the most eligible, but neither is it mere coincidence that they have become such. Not only the

pet at home, but also the livestock on the farm has been selected for its
tameness and amenability. However much meat there may be on an
animal or however much milk it yields, it must give man the opportunity
to take those products from it. The aurochs was quite prepared for this to
happen and was bred into a cow; its twin species the European bison
refused to have people interfering with it and because of its lack of
usefulness was almost exterminated. Ultimately, of all the millions of
species and animals only a handful turned out to be prepared to form an
alliance with human beings. But even the animals not wishing to form an
alliance can be incorporated into the human kingdom. As children,
human beings grow up in a world of bears, rabbits, ducks and wolf cubs;
in fairy tales, on pyjamas, at the zoo, as metaphors. Besides real fauna,
with real animals like ducks and hares, human beings also have an
imaginary fauna including Donald Ducks and Easter Bunnies, with
qualities which we have assigned to them. From all those real and
fictitious contacts with animals human beings have distilled their likes
and dislikes. Hence it is possible for our culture to compile a top ten of
favourite animals. Desmond Morris asked thousands of children in
Great Britain for their favourites, Stephan Kellert took a sample of three
thousand from the whole American population. Combined with the
Czechoslovakian top tens of Šurinová and Gressner we arrive at the
following list:

1.	Ape	6.	Parrot
2.	Horse	7.	Lion
3.	Dog	8.	Cat
4.	Bear	9.	Panda
5.	Chimpanzee	10.	Elephant

The list shows a striking degree of correspondence with the scale
proposed by a Dutch writer, Rudy Kousbroek, who classifies the animal
kingdom on the basis of the criterion of cuddliness. At the bottom of his
scale are 'the creatures that are characterized by a negative cuddliness
factor: animals that are objectively unmateable with, either because of
their substance (oysters, jellyfish), or because of their essence (piranhas,
electric eels); hard on their heels (to the extent that they have heels)
come species with a cuddliness factor of nil: these are animals that are in

J. Wesley, *Honeypot*

theory cuddlable, but without this being the source of any sensation either for the cuddler or the cuddled.' As an example of this last category it is noted what a 'hopeless business it is, as children sometimes do, to stroke a tortoise on its shell'. Via birds Kousbroek then proceeds to the furry creatures, of which the domestic cat is supposed to represent the epitome of cuddliness.

As a cat lover I am inclined to congratulate Kousbroek on his insights, but as an explanation of the top ten this is open to challenge. If it were only a matter of cuddliness, increasingly cuddly cats would be bred, which is not the case; pedigree cats are no more cuddly than ordinary pets. Moreover, a wonderfully furry creature like the bird spider sends shivers down people's spines – precisely because of all those hairs. And what is a parrot doing in the top ten if it is 'inevitable' that 'a furry creature is better suited to cuddling than a feathered one'?

It may be illuminating to look at the matter for a change from the point of view of the animal. If, for whatever reason, you want to attract human beings, what do you have to do? In the first place you must resemble a human being as well as you can. That makes it easy for people to love you, because people are best at loving people, having been programmed to do so from birth. Not for nothing is the ape at the top of the list. As our nearest relative it is most like us. And it is cuddly into the bargain, although this is mainly a theoretical question: however much you may like to nuzzle your head in the warm woollen suit of an ape – or a bear – it cannot be recommended. But there is no need – even without touching, good contact with an ape is quite possible. After all, unlike most animals, you can look into an ape's eyes. Its eyes, like ours, face forwards, enabling it to estimate distances accurately as it leaps from branch to branch and from tree to tree in the jungle. When we were still living in the trees as apes, we too needed eyes like that. The fact that human beings and apes can look into each others' eyes is therefore a family trait. Other animals prefer to look in all directions to see whether danger is threatening and with their side-mounted eyes which are difficult to look into they forfeit much of our affection.

An exception are the predators. Although they pounce on a prey instead of a tree, their leap has to be calculated as accurately as that of an ape. The fact that their eyes are aligned like ours has nothing to do with relationship; it is pure coincidence, albeit a particularly pleasant

Maria Lassnig, *Sleeping with a Tiger*, 1975

coincidence, which enables us to look them straight in the eyes across the species boundaries. Hence no fewer than five predators have found their way into the top ten, in spite of their gory way of fending for themselves. But not just because of their good looks. Just like us they are clever – at least cleverer than their prey – and one can teach them things, which increases understanding. In order to use their capacity for learning, predators have a long childhood and are playful: at home with us that childlike playfulness lasts almost a lifetime for our dogs and cats.

Precisely because with its feathers it does not seem to belong among all that cuddly fur, the parrot also provides a good key to the secret of looking like a human being. A parrot sits upright, just like the other popular birds, the penguins and owls. The degree to which one forfeits one's human attributes by not walking upright is something that many a farmworker has had to learn the hard way when bending down by chance in a bull's field and finding the bull, which suddenly mistook him for a cow, on top of him. Walking upright was quite simply the decisive step in the evolution of mankind. It freed our hands to manipulate objects, and that is precisely what we find touching when we see a parrot putting food into its beak with its 'hand'. Because manipulation looks so human, it always charms us, even if the animal is eating from its nose: that is what makes an elephant so attractive.

Walking upright has a lot to do with the question of the number of legs. Millipedes do not feature in the top ten and six-legged creatures – the insects – are also absent, although they are by far the most numerous creatures in the world. Quadrupeds generally appear to be favourites, but that is an illusion; a characteristic of the quadrupeds on the list is that they can switch to walking on two legs. Apes, chimpanzees and pandas can walk reasonably well in this way, while bears, dogs and cats can raise themselves on their hind legs. It is true that the latter three do not do this that often, but when it happens – the dog sitting up like a good boy, the cat in front of the refrigerator, the bear with its trousers round its ankles – human beings melt and the animal gets its reward. Horses and elephants have even made a profession of standing on their hind legs, in the circus.

In order to gain favour with human beings it is advisable to resemble a human being, in order to climb high up the top ten the best thing to do is to resemble a young human being, an infant. The ingredients were analysed by Konrad Lorenz as early as 1943; a round head with large eyes and a small nose, a round body with short legs and a nice soft skin. The fact that small human beings with these characteristics should move us is biologically meaningful, because toddlers need the protection of the whole group. Baboons make use of a similar mechanism. As long as the young display the characteristic of infancy – in their case dark fur – they can get up to whatever tricks they like as far as the older apes are concerned. Once their fur lightens, the party's over.

Toy manufacturers assembled the teddy bear from the components of the infantile model, the Amsterdam Zoo calculated the spectator appeal of its animals so precisely that the sponsor of a group of penguins had to pay ten times as much as for a lawnful of emus, Walt Disney gave Mickey Mouse an increasingly rounded appearance over the years in order to exploit him better. For lovers of bestiality, too, the top ten of nice animals is also something of a menu. Mateability is quite simply an extension of cuddliness. However, this does not mean that the concepts are identical. In the words of the poet Willem Elsschot, 'giving dreams their head raises both practical and legal snags.'

Cuddliness and mateability coincide best from the perspective of a man. After all, the sexual attraction of his mate is based to a large extent on infant characteristics; outwardly she has remained much more childlike than him. While he has become angular and sinewy, often also bald, she remains rounded and soft, with a small nose, small chin and long hair, accordingly he calls her his 'dearest pet' as an expression of tenderness. However, the only really sexy animal in the top ten is the cat, and animals which are commonly used for sexual purposes by men, like the cow, the goat and the donkey, do not even appear on the list. Livestock has long had a low status. Not only the fact that the eyes are in the wrong position, but the ease with which it allows itself to be taken to slaughter and disposed of, means livestock has a lower place in our estimation than even slaves and serfs. The exception is the horse, which as the companion of the nobility acquired some semblance of nobility itself. However, seen from the rear, female cattle have characteristics

Anselm Feuerbach,
Archer on Horseback
(Amazon Study),
c. 1871

which also attract a man in his wife. Men quite simply respond to women's most distinctive features, and the distinctions *par excellence* – by which one can recognize a woman at a great distance at dusk – are the broad hips, buttocks and thighs. Cows, female donkeys and mares are well equipped in this area: cows indeed are bred for this quality in beef production. Seen from behind, with a slight sway of the hips, presenting their large vulva at an inviting height, they can easily lead a man into temptation. The psychiatrist Magnus Hirschfeld had a patient referred from Berlin who 'suffered acutely because he became sexually excited by the enormous rumps of the brewery horses. The moment he saw them, he got an erection and sometimes even ejaculated. The interesting thing about his case is that his ideal woman accordingly extended to large-sized people and that it gave him extraordinary pleasure to see his wife becoming plumper as the years went by.'

Women react differently to the animals in the top ten than do men. These animals excite their maternal feelings more than their sexual organs. Women are stimulated sexually not by what is soft and plump but by what is hard and sinewy. This explains the high score of the horse – at number two – which is entirely inexplicable in terms of the infant paradigm. Research carried out by Desmond Morris showed that horses are three times as popular with girls as with boys. Moreover, they form an exception to the rule that as children grow older they prefer small animals to large ones. Love of horses reaches its height in girls just before puberty. 'Sitting with legs astride a rhythmically moving horse undoubtedly has a sexual undertone,' is Morris's cautious formulation. 'The important things are the flanks and the thighs,' says Yvonne Kroonenberg, an expert author of equestrian books for girls who have just acquired a riding hat and breasts, 'the wonderful firmness, the irresistible urge to sit on those muscular hindquarters.' Hence the horse is the ideal consolation for the great injustice done to girls by nature, of awakening sexually years before the boys in their class, who are still playing with their trainsets when girls are already sighing 'Trigger' when they actually mean 'Simon' or 'Jeremy'. Interestingly, the sex of the horse is irrelevant in this relationship. Stallions are castrated to become geldings for girls, and most girls are as little aware of the sexual undertones of their love of horses as the lion cub is aware that its play is in fact hunting. A horse symbolizes the male, whether it be a stallion or a mare, just as both female cats and tomcats represent the feminine.

If the sexual element is dominant, then – after men – the dog has the highest cuddliness factor for women. Dogs are there in all shapes and sizes, literally bred for all requirements, from lapdogs which, as an aunt of mine once put it, 'set your milk flowing', to huge animals compared with which any macho looks like a milksop. But that is not the most important reason why the dog is the favourite sexual partner. The reason that it proves to be man's best friend in this area too is because it requites love. Sexual love does not have to be reciprocal, but it is nice when it is. 'What does the animal think about it?' is consequently the most interesting question in the area of bestiality. Is it simply the victim of base human lust, or does it enjoy it itself? Unfortunately, the former is often the case. It often costs chickens and rabbits their lives, sheep and donkeys at best meekly let human beings have their way with them. With cows it is very difficult to know what they think about anything, as

Left: Dog Mounting Woman, Indian print, mid-19th century
Right: Marliz Frencken, *Pitbull with Girl*, 1990

they show the same equanimity whatever happens, but dogs obviously often enjoy themselves, and sometimes eagerly take the initiative.

A dog regards all the members of its household as fellow dogs. It is a pleasant duty for a male dog to service the members of his household from time to time, certainly if he has no access to a bitch on heat. On these occasions something pinkish flops out of the abdomen and is rubbed against one's legs, or with the impertinence native to dogs, against the legs of your visitors, which are firmly gripped by the dog's front paws. Giggling politely or otherwise ignoring it is fairly pointless, punishment only increases the animal's frustration, and dog lovers maintain that politely rejecting the animal's advances is a more appropriate response. Unless one really enjoys them, that is. With some adjustment it is not difficult to exchange the leg for a more appropriate part of the body and actual mating can ensue. Mostly, however, things do not reach this stage and the dog is most commonly used for cunnilingus. Dogs have an ideal tongue for the purpose, and and can be taught it, like so many other tricks. As a reward something edible can be applied to the appropriate spots, or the dog can be masturbated as a return favour. Every dog is a potential lapdog.

There is even a documented case of a sexual encounter between a dog and a female gorilla. The gorilla, called Congo, is described by Yerkes as reacting sexually to male and female dogs, with a clear preference for males. With people she would take the initiative, grabbing the person's hand, placing it on her genitals, and making masturbatory movements. In *The Mind of the Gorilla* Yerkes relates how Congo attempted to seduce him:

> Congo came close to me ... [and] throwing herself on her back she pressed her external genitalia against my feet and repeatedly and determinedly tried

to pull me upon her, precisely as in the previous winter she had been observed to react to the male dog. In this activity she was markedly and vigorously aggressive, and it required considerable adroitness and strength of resistance on my part to withstand her attack. Thwarted in her first attempt, she arose, and standing in the natural position on all fours, immediately made what presumably is the usual or normal sex presentation of the female gorilla. As previously, the genitalia were directed towards me and she made persistent efforts to achieve contact. . . . . Her insistence on sexual contact was extremely embarrassing ... and somewhat dangerous because of her enormous strength.

Several cases of sexually aggressive apes have been documented. Yerkes, for example, knew of a chimpanzee which tried to masturbate with a human hand, while Hamilton described female macaques which started smacking their lips the moment a man came near them by way of sexual invitation. However, the common feature of all these observations is that they were made in captivity. In such circumstances animals commonly become infatuated with human beings. Any zookeeper can confirm this. For example, Amsterdam Zoo once had a penguin which at mating time performed courtship displays in front of visitors, and as early as 1923 the animal behaviour researcher Oskar Heinroth was followed by a procession of lovesick cranes. Sometimes such animals are simply deranged, but mostly it is a case of false imprinting. A male dog trying to mount visitors probably saw, as a puppy in the sensitive phase – between one and two months old – too few dogs and too many people, through being removed from the litter too early. Conversely, dogs which have seen no human beings at all at that time become very shy of people. Hence a degree of imprinting on humans has its advantages in future dealings with the animal, but Konrad Lorenz, who studied the phenomenon extensively, had firsthand experience of the disadvantages of heavy imprinting at the mating time of ducks. One drake showed his great affection by mounting Lorenz's head of white hair with an obvious sexual intent. In some cases incorrect imprinting can be dangerous: Wilhelm Schmidt, a zoo-keeper who had bottle-fed a baby walrus in the Karl Hagenbeck Zoo, later had great difficulty in keeping his 500 kilo sweetheart at a safe distance. The vet Frankenhuis, on the other hand, who was once treating a crane at Rotterdam Zoo which had been reared in China by children, made a virtue of necessity. The bird, completely imprinted on human beings, tried to mate with its vet, but the latter used this exceptional opportunity in order to take sperm from the creature, thus providing the zoo with a large number of young.

Although zoos increasingly use artificial insemination, the acquiring of semen remains a problem. Usually animals are given a general anaesthetic, after which the appropriate organs are stimulated with an electro-ejaculator. Nowadays this is even done with bees. In order to

Carl August
Ehrensvärd, *The Bull I*,
18th century

prevent the queen, which has been carefully stuffed full of favourable
genes, from acquiring undesirable characteristics from unknown drones
on her bridal flight, the drones are deprived of their sperm under general
anaesthetic, after which it is inserted into the queen's oviduct under the
stereo microscope. Such expensive operations are no longer necessary
with most ordinary domestic and agricultural animals. The disinte-
gration of sexual behaviour is so far advanced in them that males can
quite easily be persuaded to mount an artificial partner, with human
beings capturing the sperm in the artificial sheath. A bull mounts
anything globe-shaped – hence the danger to farm workers bending over
– and the artificial sow for an AI donor-boar resembles nothing so much
as a collapsed ironing board. Nevertheless so much semen is obtained
that one prize bull was able to fertilize more than 160,000 domestic and
foreign cows in a single year.

When I attended Professor Slijper's lectures in the early 1960s, things
had not progressed to this point. Attempts were still being made to refine
the artificial cow and improve the quality of semen obtained. The
professor's assistants had discovered that a real cow moves away a little
just before being mounted. Was that the secret? An imitation cow on
wheels was improvised, with one of the assistants seated inside as the
sperm collector. In the test the bull's leap was wilder than anticipated:
the contraption shot across the meadow at an alarming speed and ended
up, if I remember correctly, in a ditch. At this point in the lecture an
illustration was shown of an improved version, with a brake, or
inhibitor, to prevent further mishaps. The lecturer then concluded, with
an expansive gesture: 'Here, ladies and gentlemen, we have the world's
first inhibited artificial cow.' The extra stimulus being sought by the
scientists was not found. The artificial cow obvious contained enough
elements of the bovine archetype to arouse a bull.

66

Carl August
Ehrensvärd, *The Bull
II*, 18th century

That such an image of a partner can also be simulated by animals themselves was demonstrated in an American dolphinarium, where a dolphin was put in the same tank as a sea-lion. Both were males. At a certain moment the dolphin began playfully imitating the sea-lion, until the latter became so confused that it tried to mate with the dolphin. The dolphin did not welcome the advances, and a few bites returned the sea-lion to the real world. Having learned caution from such experiences, the keepers of the extremely rare Californian condor breed the birds in the zoo with a glove in the shape of a condor's head. It is vital that the young birds do not become convinced that they must mate with human beings, since that would soon lead to their extinction. With less rare species human beings have fewer scruples: they shamelessly hoodwink them. Hunters lure ducks out of the sky with wooden decoys (derived from the Dutch word *eendenkooi*, meaning 'duck trap'). Primitive as they may look, the decoy carver is in some way able to capture the exact essence of the species image. With many animals this turns out to be a *pars pro toto*. For example, a researcher was once bold enough to venture into the territory of the Wapiti deer, which with its enormous antlers can be extremely dangerous, wearing antlers which normally hung in his living room. Because of the antlers the deer took him for one of their own kind, and because the antlers were larger than their own they abandoned any thought of aggression.

Occasionally people unintentionally seduce animals with inanimate objects. While shooting the film *The Sea Behind the Dunes*, William Sargent discovered that the local male sword crabs regarded everything in the water, from old boots and bricks to anchors and boats, as females on heat. It was no easy task filming when one's feet and camera tripod were constantly being mated with. The old joke about a tortoise falling in love with a German helmet is based on fact: many zoo keepers have had their shoes cleaned by their tortoises for similar reasons. A tiger in Miami Zoo mated repeatedly with a car tyre, to the accompaniment of growling and neck bites. Along the English coast a dolphin delighted holidaymakers in their rubber boats with its antics. If they had looked more closely, they would have seen that the dolphin was not just playing about with their boat but was masturbating against it with its enormous penis erect. Normally dolphins are social animals, but for some reason or other this individual was an outcast and was desperate for company. What is an intelligent animal like a dolphin, which doesn't smoke, drink or go partying, to do about its loneliness?

Dolphins and rubber boats, tigers and car tyres, robins and bunches of red-coloured chicken feathers, sticklebacks and pieces of red wood – such activities are also very human. Our society is full of such fetishes and *partes pro toto*. Men are aroused by a photo in *Playboy*, women by a pink rubber organ, advertisers increase their sales with the suggestive power of a pair of full lips. Lipstick, mascara and aftershave create illusions, which are explained by biologists as supranormal stimuli which means that quantity often makes a bigger impact than quality. A striking example is the imitation goose egg. If an egg rolls out of a goose's nest, the goose rolls it back with its beak. If one offers it the alternative of a much larger, artificial egg, from which no gosling will ever hatch, the goose will prefer that to its own genuine eggs full of its own flesh and blood. I shall never forget the film footage of such a goose, balancing on that monstrous egg, falling off and scrambling onto it again, in spite of everything obviously proud and contented, the expectant fulfiller of a hopeless task. Human mothers are little better, invariably selecting from a series of portraits babies with inflated heads and dewy eyes which in reality would be scarcely viable. Men are aroused by two of the best-known examples of a supranormal stimulus; the breasts of Marilyn Monroe. They are constantly in search of extra-full lips, extra-large breasts and extra-long eyelashes, and women resort to artificial means to provide them. There are also animals which by their very nature offer stimuli which for us are supranormal; the long lashes of a donkey, the divine hips of a mare, the long sinews of a cow, the soft fur of cats. The senses are aroused and search out the strongest stimuli. Mostly these are derived from a human being, but sometimes from an animal.

The desire to cuddle, imprinting and supranormal stimuli, not to mention fate and the longing for happiness, drive human beings and animals into each other's embrace. Sometimes to their satisfaction, sometimes to their disappointment. We are not made for each other. A woman who actually mates with her dog is in for a surprise: she may be unable to detach herself from the dog. A dog's penis is somewhat unusual, in that it contains not only a bone, the baculum, but it also has an inflatable body at its base which swells up once inside the vagina. A bitch's vagina also sometimes contracts, so that the two animals may be

Ecstatic Nun with
Donkey, engraving,
18th century

linked together for between 5 and 50 minutes. This makes a ridiculous
spectacle, especially when people start throwing water over them, but it
serves a purpose. It gives the male time to ejaculate not only sperm but
also prostate fluid which encourages fertilization. Wolf hunters have
long exploited this, by using a bitch on heat as bait. Despite its totally
different appearance, the wolf recognizes the pale reflection of its species
and mates with the bitch according to the old, still-shared ritual. After
ejaculation wolf and dog remain attached to each other for a quarter of
an hour, long enough for the hunter to be able to club the wolf to death.
In the case of a human being with a dog the link is less strong because the
female does not grip the male's swelling with her vagina. The greatest
danger to the woman arises if there is any panic as they are uncoupling,

when the delicate internal tissue, which is not designed for such treatment, may be damaged.

Mating with a stallion is not at all easy. A 60 centimetre penis is really too long for a human vagina. Where the length limit lies precisely is difficult to say, because of the elasticity of the vagina. The best approximation of the maximum vaginal volume, according to *The Illustrated Book of Sexual Records*, was achieved with the aid of five pounds sterling in small change: 'Shilling after shilling I put up her,' reads the report of the calculation, 'until forty were embedded in the elastic gully.' The number was increased to seventy. 'Triumphantly, she walked up and down the room, none falling out of her vagina.' Finally the content went up to the equivalent of eighty-four shillings, perhaps sufficient for the human record penis length of 35 centimetres listed by Dr David Reuben in *Everything You Always Wanted to Know About Sex*, but certainly too small for that of a horse. The Japanese have long been aware of this, as is evidenced by the following story from their rich folklore:

> There was once a very lascivious woman, who experienced more pleasure from sexual congress with a horse than from anything else. But because the horse's member was too thick and too long, she was obliged to take preventive measures. This she did as follows: tying one end of a guitar string to the base of the horse's penis and the other end to the ceiling, she put out a bench and climbed onto it to have intercourse with the horse. The horse appeared to be perfectly satisfied, although it would have preferred to insert its sexual organ fully inside the woman, which was not possible because prevented by the guitar string. Now her husband got wind of this and was not at all pleased. One evening he went to the attic to look secretly at what was happening. He saw his wife's debauches, as they had been reported. He silently waited for the appropriate moment and when the two had reached the climax of pleasure he cut the string with a sword. His wife was killed instantly when the horse thrust its member up into her chest.

The mating between Europa and the bull would have been an equally painful matter without the intervention of Zeus, to say nothing of that between a human and an elephant ($1\frac{1}{2}$ metres) or a human and a whale ($2\frac{1}{2}$ metres). But a penis can also be too small. In this respect the anthropoid apes particularly are found wanting. However formidable a gorilla may look, its genitals are ridiculously small. It cannot be a coincidence that Paul du Chaillu sent the gorillas that he had shot to Europe without their sexual organs: no one would have believed the bloodcurdling stories about the hairy monster had they known that its penis, even erect, was a mere 5 centimetres long. Modesty also befits the chimpanzee and the orang-utan in this area: a woman abducted by them might feel badly let down. As regards size, man is certainly well-endowed compared with his closest relatives.

Proud as he may be of it, man's genital size imposes limitations on sexual intercourse with other species. Few vaginas in the animal

kingdom can accommodate one of the largest species on earth, with one of the largest penises. However, other orifices are available for the purpose; those wishing to have sexual intercourse with chickens – which have no vagina – use the communal exit of all the waste channels, the cloaca. What is large enough for an egg is large enough for a penis. Nevertheless this usually proves fatal to the chicken, if for no other reason than because the height of pleasure is achieved only by decapitating the creature just before ejaculation in order to intensify the convulsions of its sphincter. In the Far East ducks and geese are commonly used for this purpose, and according to De Sade, turkeys were the speciality of Paris brothels. A legendary example of such aviphilia was Tippo Sahib, who as the 'Tiger of Mysore' made life difficult for the English in colonial India. With mammals an alternative for the vagina is the anus, so that male animals can also be used, which according to De Sade (in *Juliette*) is particularly to be recommended with goats. The billy-goat's 'anus is wider and warmer: and the animal is so naturally lusty, that it moves to and fro of its own accord as soon as it realizes that you are about to climax.'

Such practical aspects of bestiality have seldom been so lucidly described as in *Sex-Driven People*, in which R.E.L. Masters quotes a man who with a friend mounts two sows:

Woman Mating with Stallion, illustration from a book by Yoshida Hambei, *c.* 1.705

71

Silenus with Hind,
decoration on a vase
from Eritrea

We had no sooner entered the shed, than two sows came towards us in their sties, making the throaty, hoarse sound that I would describe as 'the mating call'. Nowadays I always imitate that call as well as I can when I feel like performing sodomy with a sow or a pig, and the animal 'replies'. I did so now, which visibly increased the animals' ardour. Because we had decided to observe each other performing coitus in turn, we put the two sows each in their own sty, so that the animal which was waiting would not get in the way. A while ago when I was occupied with one sow, the other animal attacked me from behind, probably out of jealousy, and tried to sniff my genitals, which understandably is rather unpleasant. Although I am not at all afraid of this, in such cases the animal may occasionally bite! I went up to one of the sows and began stroking her body and genitals. She immediately assumed an expectant, passive position and did not move at all until I had finished with her. I took up my usual position for coitus, with my upper body leaning against the sow's back and my hands gripping her shoulders so as not to get into the wrong position. My legs were bent slightly inwards, and I was resting with the balls of my feet and toes on the ground. Now I was in the right position to penetrate her.

As a rule it is not necessary to introduce the penis with one's hand because the vulvas of sows – as a result of their litters and being on heat – have enough discharge of their own. Occasionally, I have to admit, I have missed my target and instead have penetrated the anus, but one notices that at once. In order to be mounted from the rear, the organs of a sow could not have been better placed and there is nothing wrong about the size of the human penis for intercourse with a sow. With young piglets, particularly if they are very young, that is slightly different. The vaginal opening is not large enough for the penetration of the penis. However if a pig is old enough (five or six months) to come on heat, then it is also sexually mature enough to participate in sexual intercourse without pain. Nevertheless I have found that with younger animals it is better to insert the penis by hand.

However soberly it is described, there will always be people who find mating between a human being and an animal unnatural. Nevertheless the mechanisms which break down the barriers between the species – imprinting, supranormal stimuli, the creation of new species, curiosity, desire for variation – are no less natural than the mechanisms which produce them. Both in captivity and in the wild we have seen examples of animals which pay no attention to species boundaries. There is sexual intercourse not only within the animal kingdom and between the human and animal kingdom, but even between the animal and the vegetable kingdom. The most innocent example of sex – the bees and the flowers – is itself an extreme case of cross-species sexual intercourse. Here the plants obtain satisfaction with the help of animals. In your garden, on your balcony.

5

Strange Offspring

I am the blue-bummed gorgel,
My father was a porgel,
My mother was a porulan,
The strangest family they began.
Raban! Raban! Raban!
CEES BUDDINGH'

Jan Lavies, *Mermaid*,
poster from 1954

Hares have a harelip. Thanks to the split in it, so deep that you can see their teeth even when their jaws are closed, they are able to nibble stalks, buds and shoots till only stubble is left. Moreover, it makes them easy to distinguish from rabbits, in which the two halves of the lip are linked by a membrane. A hare would be extremely unhappy with a rabbit lip.

There are also people with a harelip. This construction fault is a consequence of our bilateral symmetrical structure. In human beings with a harelip the left half of the body is not properly attached to the right one at the head end, so that a split is left in the middle like in old-fashioned Hong Kong-made tin toy cars made of two ill-fitting halves. These people have been left ajar. Surgery is needed to make this kind of harelip into a human lip. After all no one wants to be part man, part hare, just as no person wants to have a chicken's breast or a rat's head, a dog's penis or a donkey's ears.

Nevertheless, besides doctors who transform harelips into human lips and donkey's ears into human ears, there are also doctors who replace human organs by animal ones. In 1984 the papers were full of Baby Fae, a two-year-old American girl given a baboon's heart by Dr Leonard Baily, who up to then had experimented mainly with goat and sheep hearts. The left half of the baby's own heart was missing and in the absence of a human organ of the right size that of a young baboon had been implanted. Fae survived for five weeks, long enough for an ethical commentary to be given on all the previous comments. One commentator thought

Pablo Picasso, *The Minotaur in a Good Mood*

it 'obscene sensational surgery', another implied that such things were 'not done', and the word 'inhuman' was used. When the child died the obituaries exuded a strange kind of satisfaction, as if to say: 'There you are, it was bound to go wrong, you should use only original parts, see Frankenstein's Monster.' Order had been restored, but not for long. In 1992 a thirty-five year-old man was given a baboon's liver. The baboon, aged fifteen, was killed especially for the purpose. The demonstrators were soon waving their banners outside the hospital. 'Animals are not spare parts,' *People for the Ethical Treatment of Animals* proclaimed to the world. The fear that animals are being degraded into a warehouse of spare parts is not unfounded: at that moment, in the United States alone, two thousand people were waiting for a liver and twenty-five thousand for a kidney. Although apes' organs are still not very compatible – the record is held by a man who survived for nine months with a chimpanzee's kidney – success is being achieved with organs from other animals. Heart valves from pigs function as well in a human being as artificial valves. From the outside one cannot see anything odd, and if there were ever a move to transplant the external organs of animals onto people, there would be no great surprise. It would remind us of the hieroglyphics on Egyptian temples full of gods with animal heads, or of the hybrids from Indian mythology. The Greek world of the gods was more like a zoo populated with sirens and centaurs than our well-ordered heaven with its harps and saints, even though our angels also carry a portion of bird on their backs. In their representation

76

of the gods people have from time immemorial dreamed of merging with animals. They did not immediately think of pig valves and baboon hearts. As a centaur one opted for the penis of a horse, as a griffin for the head of an eagle, as a mermaid not for the head but for the tail of a fish. It was obvious that such hybrids originated from cross-breeding. At any rate this was described in the case of the Minotaur, a monster with the body of a man and the head of a bull. The Minotaur was the son of Minos, King of Crete, himself the product of the union of Europa with her divine bull. In order to strengthen his claims to the throne of Crete, Minos had boasted that the gods would grant all his prayers. After he had prepared everything for a sacrifice he asked the sea god Poseidon that a bull should come out of the sea. One immediately swam ashore, but it was so dazzlingly white that Minos kept it for himself and sacrificed another bull. Poseidon was insulted, and in revenge ensured that Pasiphae, the wife of Minos, fell in love with the white bull. In order to satisfy her bestial lusts, she enlisted the help of Daedalus, a craftsman, who made a life-sized, hollow cow of wood, covered in real cowhide. The contraption was pushed into the meadow where the white bull was grazing under the oaks on wheels concealed in the hooves. Via the trap-doors at the back, the queen crawled into the cow, back to back, belly to belly, crotch to crotch. Daedalus withdrew discreetly and the bull attacked the casing, to the complete satisfaction of the contents. Shortly afterwards Pasiphae gave birth to the Minotaur.

Minos tried to avoid a scandal. On the advice of an oracle he hid the Minotaur in a maze with no exit, the labyrinth, which he had constructed in Knossos. Every year seven youths and seven maidens were sent into the maze to be torn to pieces by the Minotaur. The young people came from Athens, which had been conquered by Minos. But on one occasion there was a hero among them, Theseus, who had volunteered. He killed the Minotaur and thanks to Ariadne's thread was able to find his way out of the labyrinth unharmed.

The story of the Minotaur is based on the worship of bulls, which was widespread both in Crete and elsewhere long before the Greek period. A bull was a double fertility symbol: male because of its crotch, female because of its horns, which referred to the crescent shape of the moon goddess. For the transition from the old animal gods to the more modern gods in human form hybrids were very suitable. In this way people with animal heads emerged, but also animals with human heads. For centuries before the Minotaur took its first steps in the labyrinth, lions with human heads, sphinxes, had been lying in front of the gates of Egyptian towns and shrines. As the king of the animals the lion was originally given the head of the pharaoh; sphinxes with women's heads, let alone breasts, are of a later date. This transsexual operation did not benefit the sphinx's prestige. From being the proud protector of royal graves the sphinx was downgraded in the Greek period to a false harpy who terrorized the population of Thebes. Seated on a rock below the city gates, she tormented passers-by with crude riddles. Those who did not know the answer were mercilessly torn asunder. The Greeks had also given the sphinx a father and mother, but these were a very antisocial pair even by mythological standards. The mother Echidna had the lower body of a snake, from which monsters like the Chimera, the Hydra and Cerberus were born. Cerberus was the hellhound, with three heads and a snake's tail, the Hydra grew two new heads for each one that was struck off, and as regards the Chimera, the only thing on which there was general agreement was that she spouted fire; she has been described with the head of a lion, a goat and snake as well as with the head of a lion, the body of a goat and the tail of a snake. The father of the sphinx was its own brother, that is, another child of Echidna, the two-headed dog Orthus. Incest and bestiality combined: the ancient Greeks really did not know when to stop.

Maiden with Unicorn, from 'Defensorium virginitatis' by Franciscus de Resza, *c.* 1490

The sphinx has never really played a great part in Christian culture, probably because it did not feature in the *Physiologus*. This book from the second century, in which, for example, the unicorn and the phoenix occur, was the basis of all medieval writing on animals, from the first bestiary to the thirteenth-century *Flower of Nature* by Jacob van Maerlant. Undoubtedly, this is connected to the fact that each animal description was accompanied by a Christian moral. Sometimes the facts were even distorted in order to illustrate the moral better. In our eyes that seems unforgivable, but for a medieval reader it was obvious that the moral – being on a higher plane – should take precedence over earthly facts. The nature around human beings was a source of ungodliness and idolatry and only took man further away from God, except in the *Physiologus*, where on the contrary it was used as a means of pointing man towards the upward path. One of the oddest hybrid creatures in the *Physiologus* is the ant-lion.

> Of the ant-lion
> Elifax, the king of Theman, spoke: 'The ant-lion perished because it found not food.'
> The physiologist maintains that it has the countenance of a lion and the lower body of an ant. Its father is a carnivore, but its mother eats the chaff of the corn. When they together create the ant-lion, they create it as a creature with a dual nature: it cannot eat meat because of its mother's nature, nor chaff because of its father's nature. Thus it perishes through lack of food.
> Similarly the man who has two souls is uncertain wherever he goes. One must not tread two paths, nor speak ambiguously in prayer; not the Yes–No and No–Yes, but only the Yes–Yes and No–No are good.

In this description the word of the Bible is easier to recognize than the ant-lion of modern biology, an insect which in its larval form digs ant traps in the sand. Probably the author of the *Physiologus* has been misled

78

in his interpretation of the text from Job (4: II) – 'The old lion perisheth
for lack of prey' – by Aelian, who called one particular lion *Myrmex* (ant)
and, bearing in mind Matthew's words, did not wish to doubt, because
'let your yes be yes; your no, no; what is beyond this, is evil.' However, in
the thirteenth century Jacob van Maerlant doubted whether an animal
which is half-lion, half-ant is possible. What the *Physiologus* divided into
front and rear, he divided into first and then. According to him an ant-
lion begins its life as a kind of ant, well-disposed towards its fellow ants,
but later grows into an enemy, which robs or even kills ants:

> When it is grown, it attacks
> The ants and steals and sacks
> All they have gained for their daily bread,
> And sometimes even bites them dead.

There were many such adjustments. In the Middle Ages the sirens,
which in the *Physiologus* are still 'half woman as far as the navel, and for
the rest, birds' exchanged their feathers for scales. They still adorn the
coats-of-arms of Dutch towns and villages as mermaids, even those of
staunchly Christian communities from north to south. If the bird-
women who tried to seduce the Greek hero Odysseus with their song
derive from still older Sumerian bird-women, the fish-women are a
strange mixture of the Mesopotamian fish-men and the mermaids,
water fairies and sea queens from our own Western European folklore.
There was good reason to believe in women with fish tails: they were
repeatedly sighted. Columbus himself encountered three and the Dutch
nature explorer Valentijn records that fifty people have seen two, one
of which was possibly a merman, swimming in the Indies. In the
nineteenth century mermaids caught by seamen were exhibited in
London and Amsterdam, Paris and New York; in 1830 one was sold for
$40,000. The national ethnological museum in Leiden still has a pair,
but they have since been moved to the attic. They are as beautiful as they
are fake. The body is that of a monkey, the tail of course that of a fish,
expertly sewn together, probably in Japan, where there was a
flourishing trade in real specimens of unreal creatures.

How a mermaid is born, from where a human being derives such a
tail, whether a siren has to be constantly remade from human being and
a fish, are questions shrouded in mystery. The literature, which in other
cases is so keen on bestial sources, has nothing to say. One thing that is
certain is that mermaids and sirens, like almost every hybrid creature,
are not to be trusted. They turn the heads of seamen, play the whore and
consort with the devil. 'Sirens and satyrs shall dance in Babylon,'
prophesied Isaiah in the old translations, 'and onocentaurs shall dwell in
their houses.'

Female Centaurs,
classical mosaic

A centaur is a human being with the body of a horse, but what is an onocentaur, when we know that 'onos' means donkey? Bartolomeus Anglicus in his medieval encyclopedia was not entirely sure:

Onocentaurus is a strange animal which is the product of a bull and of a female ass because onos in Greek is ass in German and is a lascivious, unchaste creature like the ass, as Physiologus says that onocentaurus is an animal which from the navel upwards has a human form, and from the navel downwards the form of a bull.

Ordinary centaurs, the hippocentaurs, were in any case the sons of Centaurus, himself the son of Apollo, and the mares of Magnesia. They took their heads and arms from their father, their bodies and legs from their mother, from both sides a large horse's penis – *le meilleur des mondes possibles*. Lucretius no longer believed in them. A creature that was half-man, half-horse was impossible for him for the simple reason that the horse part would be fully grown before the human part; at a certain moment the adolescent at the front would discover that its rear was already decrepit with age. 'A combination of two bodies into a creature with a double nature, constructed of dissimilar parts, can never exist for lack of harmony between the characteristics. The slower of the two spirits could be easily overcome.' It seems more logical that the belief in centaurs is based on the sight of the first horseman. For the Greeks the horse was a fairly new animal and sitting astride them was for a long time unfamiliar. 'When the horsemen of the Thessalonians went into battle,' said the Bishop of Seville in the seventh century, explaining the centaurs, 'they merged so well with the bodies of their horses, that it seemed as though the two were actually joined together.' This view was reinforced when the Aztecs and Incas were overawed by European horsemen.

STRANGE OFFSPRING

They saw horse and rider as one creature and panicked. 'What monstrous centaurs take the field against my warriors?' exclaims the nymph America in dismay in the mystery play *El divino Narciso* (1688), written by the Mexican nun Juana Inés de la Cruz about the coming of the Spaniards. And in 1698 Father Stanislaus Arlet wrote to the general of the Jesuits of the Peruvian tribe of the Canisiers:

> The amazement which they showed when on our first appearance they saw for the first time horses and people in our kinds of colours and clothes, was very welcome to us; our appearance inspired such fear in them that their bows and arrows fell from their hands in the conviction that, as they later admitted, the man, his hat, his clothes and the horse on which he was riding formed a single animal.

Although it profited from it, the Church was not happy with the belief in centaurs. Like satyrs and sirens, they were a symbol of lust. For those who did not dare to look between the back legs there was still the bow and arrow which they held in his hands, symbolizing ejaculation. No nymph or woman was safe from his lascivious desires. But because the image of the centaur was ineradicable, it was Christianized to some extent and turned into the symbol for the eternal duality between intelligence and love on the one side, and instinct and lust on the other, or Christianity versus the heathen, the Church versus the tavern. The usual result of that conflict may be taken for granted.

In a lecture of 1901 on 'The Greek Gods and Human Monsters' the gynaecologist Professor Schatz offered another explanation for centaurs. He argued that the stories had originated from the birth of children with more than the usual number of limbs. The time was not very far off when any self-respecting book on Greek mythology would link the correct gods with the correct abnormalities. But although this prediction did not prove true, there is a striking correspondence between certain birth abnormalities and particular gods, fabulous creatures and nightmares. Human fantasy is powerful enough to invent all the mythical creatures it needs, but if reality offers something usable, imagination is willing to take inspiration from it.

It is not difficult to see the neck of a goose in a malformed human organ, or the head of a dog, the lip of a hare, a single eye of the Cyclops. The poor mother of the monster was in that case very soon exposed to the charge of bestiality. But the fear of monsters born of an animal was very great. As a preventive measure contraception was used. 'Each time', stated a man accused of bestiality to a Swedish court in 1695, 'he had withdrawn his member and allowed the seed to fall on the ground for fear that something live would be sired.' A farmer's son related in the archive documents uncovered by Liliequist that he had once heard the newly born kid of his father's goat bleating like a crying baby. Later, during his intercourse with cows and calves, he had always been careful

81

Above: Honoré
Daumier, *Centaur
Abducting a Woman,*
c. 1860

Facing: Giovanni
Battista Della Porta,
*Man-Pig, Man-Sheep,
Man-Donkey*, from 'De
Humana Physiogno-
monia', *c.* 1600

not to produce any calves. How such a monstrous calf looked – half-
animal, half-human being – could be seen in 1782 in the Swedish town of
Skirö. The owner of the mother cow showed it to anyone who wanted to
see it, until a number of stray dogs and pigs forced their way into the
room and devoured the monster.

Until recently one did not need to go to remote farmhouses in Europe
and America to see animal-humans and human-animals. Leslie Fiedler,
author of the book *Freaks*, can still hear in his head how the master of
ceremonies at a fair announced the following attraction: 'Jo-Jo, the Dog-
faced Boy, the greatest anthropological monstrosity in captivity,
brought back at great expense from the jungles. Walks like a boy. Barks
like a dog. Crawls on his belly like a snake.' Other deformed human
beings were exhibited as 'Koo Koo the Bird Girl', 'Porcupine Man', the
'Alligator Boy' and the 'Caterpillar Man'. The 'Ugliest Woman in the
World', Grace McDaniels, was known as the 'Mule Woman'. 'Her flesh
was like red, raw meat; her huge chin was twisted at such a distorted
angle, she could hardly move her jaws. Her teeth were jagged and sharp,
her nose was large and crooked. . . . Her eyes stared grotesquely in their
deep-set sockets.' 'Grace did not actually look like a mule, of course,'

admitted Edward Malone, the world's greatest collector of freak photos, 'more like a hippopotamus – in the face.'

Lionel the lion-faced Man owed his name principally to the roaring with which he sent shivers down the spines of the audience, but Jo-Jo the Dog-faced Boy, the son of *L'Homme-chien*, with silky hair covering his face, looked so like a Skye terrier that he could easily have been exhibited as the bastard child of human being and a dog. But the fair would not venture this far. They preferred to explain the animal-humans as cases of 'visual suggestion'. Lionel, for example, maintained that when his mother was pregnant with him she had been forced to witness his father being mauled by lions. In the past the notion that a pregnant woman could be adversely affected by seeing the wrong thing, just as someone else makes a logical slip or chokes on their food, was widespread. What one saw during one's pregnancy could affect one's child. For example, in 1494 a woman frightened by a bear had given birth to a child with the body of a bear, and mothers of children with a harelip must have been startled by a hare before their confinement. Ichthyosis, an hereditary affliction which produced a scaly skin, was consequently also easily explained as a result of suggestion: it was claimed that the mother of a famous seventeenth-century 'fish-child' had visited the sea too frequently during her pregnancy. To prevent giving birth to such a deformed child, one had to take care and certainly not go to fairs which exhibited monstrosities in formaldehyde. For instance, in the eighteenth century the fair at The Hague, featuring the Siamese twins Judith and Helena, was taboo. These children were so intertwined because early in her pregnancy their mother had been foolish enough to watch dogs mating.

Suggestion was also supposed to be the origin of the greatest freak of all, the Ugliest Man of All Time, the Elephant Man. In his autobiography he writes:

> The deformity which I am now exhibiting was caused by my mother being frightened by an Elephant; my mother was going along the street when a procession of Animals were passing by, there was a terrible crush of people to see them, and unfortunately she was pushed under the Elephant's feet, which frightened her very much; this occurring during a time of pregnancy was the cause of my deformity.

In reality Joseph Merrick, the Elephant Man, scarcely knew his mother, if at all. She had been alarmed not so much by an elephant as by her child, who was hired out to fairs and circuses from an early age in order to make a living from his ugliness. One look at the deformed body and spectators were reconciled with their own bodies, however unsightly, for quite some time.

All kinds of beautiful hybrids between human beings and elephants are conceivable – the Indian pantheon provides examples – but Joseph

Man with the Head of
an Elephant,
engraving from 'De
Monstrorum' by
Fortunius Licetus,
c. 1616

had the worst of all worlds: not the splendid trunk or proud bearing of the elephant, but its skin; not man's capacity to change the world, but his unfulfillable desires. Frederick Treves, the doctor who finally released him from the freak shows, was shocked at their first meeting:

> The most striking feature about him was his enormous and misshapened head. From the brow there projected a huge bony mass like a loaf, while from the back of the head hung a bag of spongy, fungus-looking skin, the surface of which was comparable to brown cauliflower. On the top of the skull were a few lank long hairs.... From the upper jaw there projected another mass of bone ... so exaggerated in the painting as to appear to be a rudimentary trunk or tusk. The nose was merely a lump of flesh, only recognizable as a nose from its position. The face was no more capable of expression than a block of gnarled wood.

Under the care of his mentor the grunting imbecile emerged as a sensitive, intelligent mind trapped in a twisted, recalcitrant body. People from the highest circles came to visit the Elephant Man, Queen Victoria sent an annual, hand-written card. But no Beauty ever appeared to bring to life the Beast's only intact external organ, his sex. The Elephant Man died in 1890, aged twenty-six, still a virgin.

Suggestion was also thought to play a part in fertilization. Commenting on an illustration of 1517 of a boy with a frog's head, Ambroise Paré quotes the testimony of the father, that 'one of his neighbours had advised him to put a live frog in his wife's hands, to cure her fever, which she must hold tight until it was dead'. That night the man went to bed with his wife, with the frog still in her hand and that is when the disaster must have happened. But Paré knew of twelve other ways of producing a monster. Monsters which were half-man, half-beast could also be produced by the 'mingling of seed' when 'Sodomites and atheists copulate unnaturally with unreasoning beasts'.

If man and animals can cross-breed so easily, animals among themselves must have even fewer problems. Consequently when new continents were discovered many unknown species of animals were at first taken to be bastards of existing species; that was less disturbing to the existing order than immediately listing new species. Among the many 'bastard animals which unite the nature of various creatures in themselves', the Greeks and Romans saw one in Africa with 'a mixture of the characteristics of the camel and the the panther': the giraffe *Camelopardalis*.

But there are also real hybrid animals and fish. Cross-breeding is possible between virtually every species of the carp family found in the Netherlands, resulting in many indeterminate hybrids and many stressed fish experts. In the countryside the hybrids of the horse family are particularly well known. After mating with a stallion a female donkey gives birth to a hinny, while a mare mounted by a donkey gives birth to a mule. The hybrid forms can be easily distinguished aurally, because the sound they produce derives exclusively from the father: a hinny neighs, a mule brays. Because they combine the advantages of a horse and a donkey, mules in particular were once very popular. But they were very difficult to acquire, since they did not reproduce among themselves. As befits a bastard of two species, mules are usually sterile. Although the hybrid females come on heat, the hybrid males cannot fertilize them because their seed is no good. There is an uneven number of chromosomes in their cells. As a product of a horse with 64 and a donkey with 62 chromosomes, a mule has 63 and hence one chromosome has to remain unpaired, which obviously results in an imbalanced development. Mules must therefore be constantly rebred from the parent species, which are not very enthusiastic. Horses and donkeys do not hit it off. In order to persuade them to mate, the breeders used all kinds of tricks, which were sometimes successful. For example, in the French region of Les Landes one used to hear the *lalandage*, an erotic song, sung by the staff of the stud when the arousal of a stallion was required.

Bear-Child, illustration from 1494

In the zoo horses and donkeys also mate with their other family members, the zebras. The result – a zebroid (horse × zebra) or zedonk (zebra × donkey) – are mostly seen in private parks, now that large zoos more than ever do their best to avoid cross-breeding between subspecies. However, in the Age of the Zoo, the nineteenth century, it was the greatest possible challenge to interbreed across species boundaries. In Victorian England yaks were enthusiastically crossed with zebus, quaggas with horses, and indigenous with foreign deer. The latter is not particularly difficult – wild red deer and sika deer cross spontaneously in the Wicklow mountains in Ireland – but the crowning achievement were the ligers and tions, which Thomas Atkins bred from lions and tigers. Liverpool Zoo was proud of the fact that 'this was the most wonderful thing ever to have happened to these animals, the most implacable foes of the jungle'. Once and for all it has been proven that 'even the wildest spirit can be subjected to man's domination'.

If the rhetoric of the 1920s and 1930s has since modified somewhat, in animal breeding bolder attempts than ever are being made to outdo the creator. What ligers and tions were to the zoo, the geep and shoats are to livestock breeders. Reports about crosses between goats and sheep have been obediently accepted for decades as a triumph of science by newspaper editors. Although the hybrids have little practical use, they are the banner under which the whole countryside is at present being bastardized. Chickens and pigs are already almost all hybrids, and the pride of the Netherlands, the pedigree Friesian cow 'Us Mem', is increasingly mated with American Holstein cattle.

When livestock breeders talk about a bastard or hybrid, they generally do not mean a mixture of species, but of breeds. There are no

Fernand Khnopff, *Art or the Caresses, c.* 1896

negative undertones; on the contrary, bastards are the cork with which modern agriculture is trying to stay afloat. If the operation is performed properly, by crossing one parent race with another, one obtains a bastard which combines the good characteristics of both races. While it is true that by crossing a variety of chicken which lays very well but is weak on its feet with a sturdy poor layer one can breed poor layers which are weak on their feet, one can equally well produce good layers which are sturdy. For the farmer such a hybrid has the disadvantage that he cannot continue breeding independently – if he does so a mishmash of characteristics will be created – but that is a boon for the breeder, who is able to continue selling the farmer chicks with a carefully balanced mix of genes. Even a farmer who creates a pure breed for himself has to acquire a cockerel from outside occasionally to avoid inbreeding.

Besides high external walls an established species of animal requires high internal walls. There is usually no question of mating with alien species, but your partners must not be too close to you. There are strong inhibitions against sex with close relatives both in human beings and in many animals: the incest taboo. Like every taboo it is sometimes transgressed, certainly by human beings, but the revulsion that this provokes has all the characteristics of a real taboo. When the TV presenter Willem Duys once announced in his programme that in his view child molesters should be castrated, he received such an ovation from the studio audience that a representative poll was taken among the general population. It found that sexual abuse of a daughter was felt to be as devastating as the child's death through an accident or illness. Because of all the emotions surrounding this phenomenon the fact is sometimes overlooked that the notion of incest refers not only to the relation between parents and children, but to all close family relationships. There is also an incest taboo between grown-ups. Although grown-ups in choosing partners still have something of a preference for their equals – rich with rich, ugly with ugly, brown with brown – incestuous marriages are largely limited to royal houses. There are sound biological reasons for this.

Lion with Woman's Face, engraving, 16th century

Incestuously bred offspring often exhibit hereditary characteristics rare in other children. These are mainly characteristics which one must have inherited from one's father and mother before they manifest themselves. The more closely related your mother and father, the greater the chance is of this happening, since they share more hereditary characteristics. Such a rare characteristic can be both advantageous and disadvantageous, but one unfavourable characteristic can cancel out all favourable characteristics. Many children of incestuous relationships will spend their lives in a sanatorium or a royal palace. If close relatives mate for generation after generation in a community, inbreeding will result and aberrations will become chronic. In dogs all kinds of breeds have been created in this way. As a rule pedigree dogs are less healthy than a mongrel chosen at random because the desired characteristics are almost always accompanied by undesirable ones: boxers are unable to bite very well, poodles have breeding difficulties, dachshunds have back problems. It is always dangerous to apply breeders' wisdom to human beings, but Rory Harrington, the man who researched the hybrid deer in the Wicklow mountains, himself a true Irish redhead, married a flaxen-haired Finn under the motto 'Hybrids do better!'

If you breed a pure race – whether of pigs or grapes – for too long, genetic degradation will occur. Positive characteristics will disappear, without being replaced by new ones. In this case 'fresh blood' has to be introduced. For rare animals which are bred in zoos, such as the Przewalski horse, international stud books are maintained in order to prevent genetic degradation. In agriculture use is also made of the fact that a hybrid of two breeds may exhibit a remarkable vitality, bastard energy. However romantic it may sound, the daily practice is very businesslike. Semen from a desired male, distributed over thousands of 'straws', is cooled in liquid nitrogen until required. If with bestiality the idea is to mate without creating descendants, with artificial insemination (AI) descendants are created without mating.

Artificial insemination is also an important aid in efforts to cross species as opposed to breeds. *Lalandages* are no longer needed to introduce horse semen into a female donkey. The difficulties involved in this way of breeding a mule have been overcome, but if, for example, one wants to cross a sheep with a goat, the problems have only just begun. The egg cell is fertilized using AI, but the body of the mother starts to produce more and more antibodies against the developing embryo, which half consists of foreign protein. After a few weeks the undeveloped monster is spontaneously aborted unless the breeder has taken preventive measures. If the mother is a sheep, he can accustom it to goat protein by injection. However, it is more elegant to mimic the tricks with which a normal embryo survives in its mother until birth. Such an embryo also half consists of protein alien to its mother: that of the father. Although the protein of a father from the same species is less alien than protein from a father of another species, measures have to be taken to combat the mother's rejection of her own child. Substances which play a part in this are also used in organ transplants. The best results with hybridization up to now have been obtained via embryo transplants. For example, at the University of California, famous for its square tomatoes, geep have been bred since 1985. Embryo cells from a seven day-old goat are introduced into a sheep embryo of the same age, after which the embryonic monster is further developed in the womb of a sheep. The geep produced in this way have the head of a goat and the body of a sheep, wool and all.

In recent years cross-breeding experiments have been pushed into the background by genetic manipulation, in which there is direct intervention in genetic materials. Pieces of it are cut out and introduced elsewhere. In the strict sense, however, much genetic manipulation is also cross-breeding, often between two species. Genetic material from one species is – via bacteria, for example – built into that of another species. Moreover, with the help of genetic manipulation one can suppress the rejection by one species of proteins from another, so that it can be an important aid in the classic cross-breeding of two species.

And now the key question: is it possible to cross a human being with an animal? Theoretically it is possible, as long as the animal is closely enough related to us. The more closely related, the better the correspondence between the proteins. In order to express the degree of relationship between two species, one can observe how violently the blood of one reacts to the other. Complete correspondence, within a pair of single-embryo twins, is put at 100; the greatest possible difference, between a human being and a flea, at zero. In the past, cross-breeding was considered possible with a relationship of 80 and above, but in view of the relationship of 75 between sheep and goats, this must be adjusted downwards. The relationship between human beings and chimpanzees is 72. The need to test the theory in practice was greatly stimulated by the rise of evolutionary theory. In 1866 the German counterpart of Charles Darwin, Ernst Haeckel, pondered on how the intermediate form between anthropoid ape and human beings might have looked. Human being and ape were so little different, in his opinion, that one link was sufficient to connect them in evolution. Haeckel christened the 'missing link' *Pithecanthropus* (ape man) in its absence. Consequently, there was great excitement when the Dutchman Eugène Dubois actually found such a transitional humanoid form on Java in 1891. A reconstruction of this *Pithecanthropus erectus*, christened Pietje by the students, can still be seen in Leiden.

A veritable gold rush erupted, which has still not subsided. Everywhere in the world people started excavating to find the link. However, all that digging struck at least one Dutchman as too indirect a method. Herman Moens saw experiment as a preferable solution. His

Félix Labisse, *The Joy of Being Loved, c.* 1943

aim was to go to Africa and inseminate female apes with semen from black human males. In 1905, as a newly qualified biology teacher, he asked the advice of Ernst Haeckel, who wrote back:

> The physiological experiments on the crossing of lower human races (negroes) and anthropoid apes, which you wish to carry out by artificial insemination, would, if the results proved *positive* of course be *very interesting* and *important*. I consider the success of these attempts possible, because since the close blood relationship between human beings and anthropoid apes has been proved in many experiments (by Friedenthal, Uhlenhuth, etc.), it is obvious that the *sexual* relationship is also very close and permits hybridization. On the basis of numerous more recent experiments it had been shown that bastards can be obtained, even from species from *different genera*, which are quite as far distant from each other in the system – perhaps even further

than negroes and gorillas or chimpanzees. However, in specific cases, only *experiment* can be decisive!

In 1908, encouraged by this letter, Moens tried to raise money for his experiments through the brochure *TRUTH. Empirical Research into the Origin of Mankind*. In this he pointed to the many correspondences between human beings and apes. They are true blood relatives:

> *Human blood serum destroys the red blood corpuscles of all experimental animals*, such as the frog, the eel, the grass snake, the adder, the pigeon, the cockerel, the heron, the horse, the pig, the cow, the rabbit, the guinea pig, the dog, the cat, the hedgehog, prosimians (Lemur), monkeys from the New World (Ateles and Pithesciurus) and monkeys from the Old World (Cynocephalus, Macacus, Rhesus), *with the exception of the blood corpuscles of anthropoid apes. Of the very closely related species, which have the same blood*: horse and donkey, horse and zebra, leopard and puma, lion and tiger, dog and wolf, hare and rabbit, lion-tailed Macaque and Brown-and-black macaque, *there are offspring* (bastards or hybrids). *Human beings and anthropoid apes also have the same blood, therefore*:

Top: *Half Man–Half Pig*, engraving from 'Monstres et prodiges' by Ambroise Paré, *c.* 1573
Bottom: Satyr, 16th-century print

> Upon conclusion of my work in the Congo I shall replace this question mark by the result of my experiments.

Moens emphasized that these experiments would comprise artificial insemination in *To Those Willing to Think (1909)*. He was aware of the stories about chimpanzees that approached native women and the reaction of a colonial doctor from the Congo: 'It could be perhaps more simply solved in this way!' Nevertheless he had not included the natural fertilization of a human being by an ape among the work to be carried out, because this could only be approved if the women consented.

> It is certain that women can be found for this purpose. Gifts and money have such power, that most blacks are prepared to allow their wife or wives to do this without much thought, and that not only the latter will be available for this research but also various women from Europe. Those persons who, purely out of scientific interest, will readily volunteer without requiring remuneration, such as a highly-educated Austrian and two German young ladies have already done for this research, are to be very highly regarded.

Although Queen Wilhelmina herself supported Moens financially, his experiments were never carried out for lack of funds. After an adventurous life, accurately reconstructed by Piet de Rooy in *In Search of Perfection*, Moens died in Casablanca in 1938. And even now, almost a century after his first plans, his 'question mark' has still not been 'replaced by the result of my experiments'. That is strange. In view of the greatly improved techniques it must be possible to cross an ape and a human being, certainly because of the new candidates who have presented themselves for this purpose. From the human side one no longer has to search for 'pygmies, dwarf races from the Congo area, or various Negro races'; every human race, as we now know, is equally close to and equally far from the apes. But as an animal partner an ape is now available which is closer to human beings than all the apes that Moens knew: the bonobo or pygmy chimpanzee.

It is not the ordinary chimpanzee, but the bonobo, first described in 1929, which is our closest relative in the animal kingdom, and that is a relief. One could call it an improved chimpanzee. Slimmer and more elegant, with a neat parting in its hair, it looks at one from under its high forehead in an almost human way. Even sexually, the gulf is smaller: sex is the bonobo's favourite activity in all positions and all combinations, with a sexual organ which is in all respects comparable with a human male's.

Hairy Girl by Ulyssis Aldrovandi, 1640

What is technically possible may be ethically unacceptable. But how could human beings, genetically manipulating, breeding fat-rumped bulls, racially discriminating, infecting anthropoid apes with AIDS, selling women into slavery, reject a scientifically controlled mating with a bonobo on ethical grounds without hypocrisy? The problem of what would happen to the child has been pointed out. That is precisely what makes it so interesting. The most common suggestion, first made by the medical sexual specialist Rohleder, who in 1918 wanted to implant negro testicles in apes, is that the bastard should be brought up under expert supervision by a pedagogue specializing in the mentally retarded. No one seems to consider that the offspring might combine the best of the apes with the best of human beings, and swinging from the chandeliers of the Royal Library, reciting poetry, improving banana-growing, and at last combining a healthy mind and a healthy body, lecture us on what we always wanted to know: what our place in this world is. At last we would find out who we are. We ourselves are the missing link.

N.A. Abildgaard, *The Primeval Cow Audumla with the Giant Ymir*, Denmark, *c.* 1777

6

Vital Juices

Everything that is full of life is liquid. So that it does not seep away into dead nature, it has a cover around it: the skin. Every organism is a vessel full of juices within which the processes that we call 'life' take place. Not much happens in dry substances. A heap of dry yeast is inanimate, and only when dissolved in water does it begin to bubble with life. The strangest organisms exist – sulphur-breathers, cephalopods, inhabitants of hot springs – but no living creature can make do with less than 50 per cent water. You too are juicy.

The most intimate thing that can take place between two organisms is therefore the exchange of juices: a drop of sperm, a gulp of blood, milk straight from the warm breast. Love is not a matter of skin on skin but of juice into juice. Nevertheless many people cherish each other's skin instead of each other's juices. Sperm makes us think of stains on the sheets, blood alarms us and saliva is spit, but the container from which those juices come often sets us on fire merely because of its elegant form, after which timely caressing is sufficient to sustain our ardour. Just as reaping follows on sowing and child-bearing on mating, so the exchange of juices follows from the cherishing of the dead container. Because everything that you see and feel about your partner – whether it be a human being or an animal – is completely dead, everywhere your partner and yourself are exposed to the air, it is horned, scaled, calloused. Stroke someone's back or hair and you are stroking precisely those parts of them that are dead: every lover is a necrophiliac. You are scarcely interested in your real partner, the juicy, flabby masses with which he or she is filled; until something goes wrong, no one is excited by a pancreas, or even an ovary, and a heart is for loving, not for embracing. We judge the content by the packaging. There is a reason for this: the packaging is where the nerve ends are located, ensuring that the exchange of juices is accompanied by pleasant feelings.

The most intimate liquid, of which no mammal is deprived in its life, is milk. Suckling is accompanied by so much warmth and tenderness that many a grown man continues to seek the safe haven of two breasts. Young fathers find it exciting to snack from the mother's breast, old fathers, as happy as babies, suck on their cigars or chew on a ball-point pen. Nipples, even his own tiny pair, continue to stimulate a man all through his life.

Milk lends itself to bestiality. Species boundaries are transgressed millions of times per day by means of this innocent liquid. By 'milk' we no longer mean the product of our own species. 'Milk' is cow's milk; human milk is called 'mother's milk', as though there was such a thing as father's milk and as though cow's milk did not come from a mother. On average each Dutch person drinks a glass-and-a-half a day from the breasts of a totally unrelated species. If our need for milk were to be satisfied by our own species, every Dutch woman would have to produce a thousand litres of milk a year, five hundred bottles a breast. Instead, the Dutch have so many cows that they determine the look of the landscape.

Elsewhere in the world people drink the milk of reindeer, sheep, camels, goats, yaks, asses and horses. This intimate udder juice is a drinkable form of Esperanto. There is no question of a high barrier between the species as in the case of sperm. Although the composition varies from species to species – seal's milk is fattier, elephant's milk sweeter than ours – nevertheless one mammal thrives more or less on the milk of another. Cats and hedgehogs eagerly slurp cow's milk (though too much is not good for them), the oddest zoo animals are given to bitches to suckle. Obviously the chances of mistaking the young for those of an alien species are so small that nature has not taken any strict preventive measures.

The compatibility comes from two sides: from the young which likes alien milk and from the mother which gives milk to an alien youngster. In anthropological textbooks one invariably sees photogaphs of Papuan women suckling piglets, and the inevitable illustration of the Thai woman with a human baby at one breast and a baby elephant at the other. But milk does not flow automatically. Just like an ejaculation the releasing of milk requires the correct nerves to be stimulated in the correct way. Young kittens give their mother a prod with their paws, which is retained in their adult behavioural repertoire as 'padding', lambs butt the udder so hard that their mother sometimes topples over. Other animals react to smell or sound, but for highly visually oriented animals like human beings the sight of an appealing youngster – a baby, a puppy, a Fiat 500 – is often sufficient to set the milk flowing. Sucking of course also stimulates and keeps the milk flowing.

In order to tap the cow's vital juices, man stimulates the largest nipples in the animal kingdom. It may escape the farmer in the course of

the years, but milking a cow is an erotically charged activity, which not for nothing is reminiscent of the 'milking of a pedigree bull'.

'Milk is the liquid obtained by unchaste caressing of a female animal, which a certain kind of person likes,' maintained Eric van der Steen in his *Alfabêtises*. Pastoral prints of milkmaids in this context are less innocent than they look and many a farmer's son must have been made to think while milking of other things that you could do with cows. On a porch in Schagen a dying cow, depicted with the distraught farmer next to it, is more highly valued than the farmer's wife:

> The Grieving Farmer:
> See the poor devil cry,
> his cow's about to die.
> For that same cow, I wager, he'd swap his very wife,
> for she makes only mischief: the cow the milk of life.

A similar sentiment is expressed in:

> If Wife-selling were allowed,
> Like one's Cows and Horses are sold and bought,
> At market there would be a crowd
> Far larger than one might have thought.

Nowadays milking by hand has been replaced by machines, but the latter could be included virtually unchanged in the arsenal of aids in a sex shop. In this respect the description in *A Thousand Faces of the Dairy Industry* leaves little to the imagination:

The machine works pneumatically, via a cleverly designed and subsequently perfected system of air and milk lines. At one end is the machine, with a

Giulio Bonasone,
Saturn and Philyra

Peter-Paul Rubens,
*Romulus and Remus being
Fed by the She-Wolf,*
c. 1618

pulsator and a vacuum pump as the most important components. At the
other end the lines are attached to an apparatus with four nipple holders.
These are double skinned and covered with rubber. They are pushed over the
udders and the pulsator, by exerting a regularly alternating pressure, mimics
the action of milking.

The cows themselves, waiting impatiently for their turn, confirm that
the machine fulfils its task in a pleasurable way. This does not mean that
personal attention has become superfluous: in the dairy industry one
worker is still available for every ten cows.

More intimate than hand or machine-milking is the direct suckling of
a human being by an animal. The traditional view has no doubt that
human beings can be suckled or even reared by animals. There are
numerous examples in history of human children growing up with

wolves, cows or other animals. Romulus and Remus, two children who were reared by a she-wolf, founded Rome, and according to Old Norse mythology, the first man on earth, the giant Ymir, drank from the udder of the first animal, the cow Audumla. But Christian creators also make use of milk. 'Hast thou not poured me out like milk, and curdled me like cheese?' is the rhetorical question addressed by Job to his Maker.

Personally such myths cost me virtually every Saturday afternoon for three years. As a cub in the scout movement I re-enacted the story of the *Jungle Books*, in which a century ago Rudyard Kipling described how a young human child, alone in the jungle and threatened by the tiger Shere Khan, was adopted by wolves as a cub. Father Wolf sees him first:

> 'Man!' he snapped. 'A man's cub. Look!'
>
> Directly in front of him, holding on by a low branch, stood a naked brown baby who could just walk – as soft and as dimpled a little atom as ever came to a wolf's cave at night. He looked up into Father Wolf's face and laughed.
>
> 'Is that a man's cub?' said Mother Wolf. 'I have never seen one. Bring it here.'
>
> A wolf accustomed to moving his own cubs can, if necessary, mouth an egg without breaking it, and though Father Wolf's jaws closed right on the child's back, not a tooth even scratched the skin, as he laid it down among the cubs.
>
> 'How little! How naked, and – how bold,' said Mother Wolf, softly. The baby was pushing his way between the cubs to get close to the warm hide. '*Ahai!* he is taking his meal with the others. And so this is a man's cub. Now, was there ever a wolf that could boast of a man's cub among her children?'
>
> 'I have heard now and again of such a thing, but never in our pack or in our time,' said Father Wolf.

Mother Wolf accepts the human child immediately: 'Do I want to keep him? Well, of course I want to keep him. Lie still, little frog. Oh, you Mowgli – because I shall call you Mowgli the frog – the time will come that you will hunt for Shere Khan as he has hunted you.' And the pack, though not without protest, also accepts the naked baby. But pretend as one may that the other species is the same, it remains alien – in this case a human being – and that is consequently the moral of the *Jungle Books*. As Mowgli grows up, the human being in the wolf finds a way out:

> Then something began to hurt Mowgli inside him, as he had never been hurt in his life before, and he caught his breath and sobbed, and the tears ran down his face.
>
> 'What is it? What is it?' he said. 'I do not wish to leave the jungle, and I do not know what this is.
>
> 'Am I dying, Bagheera?'
>
> 'No, Little Brother. That is only tears such as men use,' said Bagheera. 'Now I know thou art a man, and a man's cub no longer. The jungle is shut indeed to thee henceforward. Let them fall, Mowgli. They are only tears.'
>
> The dawn was beginning to break when Mowgli went down the hillside alone, to meet those mysterious things that are called men.

Is Mowgli more than a myth? There have been hundreds of serious reports of children who have been brought up by wolves or other animals until they behaved like animals, but seldom, in the words of Father Wolf, 'in our pack or in our time'. Moreover, great confusion has been sown by the careless use of the term 'wolf children'. The three most famous cases, Kaspar Hauser, Wild Peter of Hannover and the Wild Boy of Aveyron, were indeed representatives of *Homo ferus* (wild man), as Linnaeus called our relatives who had become wild, but they were not brought up by wolves. Although they lived outside human society for years and displayed all the resulting symptoms, they were not suckled by animals. Kaspar Hauser, for example, was a German boy who until adolescence was shut up in a dark shed, from which he was released in 1828. Rumour had it that he was a royal child who was an obstacle to other heirs. Rats that are reared in isolation in a psychology laboratory are still called Kaspar Hauser rats after him. No one assumed that the Wild Boy of Aveyron, who was discovered in 1800, aged about eleven, had been brought up by wolves. The fact that he was nevertheless examined at length by Paris scientists was due to the spirit of the age. People believed in Jean-Jacques Rousseau's 'noble savage'. The followers of Rousseau held that human beings were basically good and were corrupted only by being brought up by their evil fellow humans (themselves the product of their upbringing). Noble savages might be able to prove that thesis. A second reason for concentrating to such an extent on children who had run wild was the question of the origin of language. If they have no contact with other human beings who teach them to say things, what language will humans begin speaking? The primeval language? And if so, what language is that?

As early as the thirteenth century Kaspar Hausers were deliberately created to solve that language question. Frederick II of Hohenstaufen had children taken from their mothers' breast and entrusted to nurses who were forbidden to speak a word to them. The word 'guinea pig' was still taken literally in those days. For example, when Frederick wished to know what happens to the food we consume, he had two soldiers eat to their fill. Afterwards one soldier was allowed to sleep, the other made to walk a certain distance. In order to check on the action of the digestive system, both were finally simply cut open. No shortage of soldiers. The experiment with the children also ended in their death, although, unfortunately for Frederick, before they had spoken a word. Unlike the children entrusted to a goatherd more than 2,600 years ago for a similar experiment. After two years they said their first word, which they kept repeating: 'bekos'. Since this is the Phrygian word for bread, Pharaoh Psammètichos concluded that the Phrygians, not the Egyptians, were the oldest people on earth. However, even in antiquity it had struck some people that 'bekos' sounds not only Phrygian but also very goat-like. All in all the question of the original language was still not solved in the nineteenth century. Since experiments on human beings had in the meantime become ethically inadmissible, scientists had to content themselves with experiments conducted by nature itself. Wolf children were a popular subject of research.

The best-documented case of a true wolf child is the Indian girl Kamala. In 1920, Kamala, aged seven, and an eighteen month-old sister, were found in a termites' nest in which a she-wolf had its lair. The girls were taken into an orphanage, where the vicar's wife kept a minute record of the seven years during which Kamala was to live there and the few months in which her sister survived. On their arrival they were covered in caked dirt, smelled strongly of wolf, their nails had grown into claws and their knees, elbows and the palms of their hands were heavily calloused from walking on all fours. They could not bear being dressed or bathed, and could sniff and howl like wolves. All attempts to get them to accept any food other than milk failed until they were present one day when some dogs were being fed. The priest was no longer able to control Kamala when she saw the dogs fighting fiercely for their food. 'After a few unsuccessful attempts by the dogs to chase her off with their tails raised, she began to share their meal of meat, intestines and bones. She took one of the bones into a corner in her mouth, and held it behind her knees as though they were claws in order to gnaw it.'

Although most reports of wolf children are from warm countries, where babies have a better chance of survival out of doors, scores of children with animal foster-parents have been reported from Europe. In 1835 A. Rauber recorded a long list in his book *Homo sapiens ferus*, including the boy from Hessen, of whom 'an unknown monk' reported:

> 1344. A boy was caught in the Hessen region. As later emerged and he himself declared, he was captured by wolves at the age of three and brought up in an extraordinary way. The wolves always gave him the choicest morsel of their prey and in the winter made a pit filled with leaves and grass, on which they laid the boy, and surrounded him to protect him from the cold. They made him walk with them on his hands and knees, until he could make the greatest leaps. When found, he had to be accustomed to the standing position by the use of splints. The boy often declared that he preferred the company of wolves to that of human beings. Because of the strangeness of the case he was brought to the court of Prince Heinrich of Hessen.

In Europe the role of the wolf is usually assumed by the bear. 'When a hungry bear of the male sex finds a child which has been carelessly left somewhere,' Doctor Counar, the personal physician of the Polish king Jan III Sobieski at the end of the seventeenth century, was told, 'it immediately tears it to pieces; however, if a suckling she-bear discovers it, she will immediately take it to her lair and suckle it and rear it with her own young, so that after some time it is often captured by hunters and rescued from the bear's clutches.' •

Yamoto Bunko, *Shozan*,
c. 1840

In my time such a child was kept in a monastery, as I have reported in my
Latin treatise *De suspensione legum naturae*. This boy was approximately ten
years of age (which one could deduce only from his height and his features),
had a grotesque appearance and could neither use his intelligence, nor speak.
He walked on all fours, and looked unlike a human being, apart from the
human shape of his body. Nevertheless, because he seemed to be a human
being, he was baptised. However, he remained permanently restless, difficult
to handle and often tried to run away. He was finally taught to walk upright,
by being lifted up bodily and held against a wall, as is done with dogs being
trained to sit up.

At the time of Jan III there was also a bear child which the king 'made
into the soldiers' piper, although he – the bear-Pole – preferred moving
about on all fours to walking on two legs'. In 1661 one of the king's
predecessors – Jan II Kasimir – was given one which had been caught by
huntsmen in the forests of Lithuania, in 'the middle of a troop of bears',
'despite his resistance and screaming, the grinding of his teeth and his
lashing out with nails, which were like those of a young, untamed bear'.
The king gave him to a Polish nobleman as a servant, but from time to

time he ran away to the forest, where he tore the bark from trees with his nails in order to drink the sap. 'Once a she-bear, which had killed two people, was seen to approach him, without doing him any harm. On the contrary, she caressed him, licking his body and his face.'

An ape as foster-mother to a human being is familiar to us from the Tarzan story. In hundreds of films scores of Tarzans have been brought up by scores of chimpanzees, but whether an ape or monkey can actually rear a human being was questioned even in classical times by people, who in other cases were prepared to accept any improbable story. Aelian, who bequeathed us so much fantastic information about the world by virtue of the fact that he never set foot outside Italy in his whole life, had never been aboard a ship, knew nothing about the sea and was, moreover, proud of the fact, wrote:

> It seems that the Monkey is the most mischievous of animals; and even worse when it attempts to copy man. For example, a Monkey saw from a distance a nurse washing a baby in a tub, observed how first of all she took off its swaddling clothes and then after the bath wrapped it up tight again; it marked where she laid it to rest, and when it saw the place unguarded, sprang in through an open window from which it had a view of everything; took the baby from its cot; stripped it as it had chanced to see the nurse do; brought the tub out, and (there was some water heating on a wood fire) poured boiling water over the wretched baby and indeed caused it to die most miserably.

Centaur Mother Breastfeeding, engraving, 18th century

Whether true or not, Aelian's story, which was to be copied from one book to another, is a dire warning to people trying to do the reverse, bring up an ape. Whatever story one reads of researchers bringing up anthropoid apes from infancy, either in order to teach them a language, or out of greed, but almost always with much love, because that is the only way, one watches with dismay as the sweet infant changes into an unmanageable ape, as though the beast in man were actually emerging, as though ultimately, with all that love, you have produced a monster. For all the celebrity many wolf children enjoyed for the first few years after their discovery, their end was usually pitiful. The results of the research consequently repeatedly conflicted with the high expectations. Instead of noble savages the wolf children turned out almost invariably to be shy, sickly nobodies with limited intelligence: not unspoiled and good, but bad precisely for want of proper nurture. A human being who cannot develop among its own kind will never become a full human being: good and evil have to be drummed into us in a continuous process. In our age this truth was finally impressed on us by the moving experiments of the American psychologist Harlow. What is not permissible with human beings, he believed was permissible with apes or monkeys: he removed monkeys from their mothers immediately after birth and offered them as a substitute an iron scaffold, sometimes covered with soft hide, sometimes equipped with an artificial suckling contraption. The soft skin turned out to be much more attractive than the dummy; little monkeys which at least derived some sense of security from this, later became less disturbed than monkeys which had to begin their lives with an all-metal artificial mother. But warmth in itself is not sufficient to become a full human being. This is clearly demonstrated by the wolf children, who while they were given warmth by an animal, perhaps even milk, never had the extra human stimulus which makes a human being truly human.

Besides proving anything but noble, the savages did not speak a primeval language. The wolf children mumbled a few indistinct sounds: wolf sounds, 'pathetic growling for hours on end', gibberish with less coherence than that of any 'talking' chimpanzee. An exception was Kaspar Hauser, who spoke reasonably well, but this was because he had spent the first years of his life among human beings. Kamala knew forty-five words, which, however, she never learned to combine into proper sentences. A more recent Kaspar Hauser girl, Isabel Queresma, who had been locked up by her Portuguese mother for eight years in a chicken coop ('I couldn't take the child to work with me, and what else was I supposed to do with her?'), when released in 1980 moved her arms like wings, and was able only 'to produce peeping sounds'.

Do true wolf children exist? Does a wolf or bear suckle a human child of its own volition? One can ask the wild children themselves, but as Counar observed of his bear child in the Polish monastery: 'When asked about his life in the forest, he was as little able to say anything about it, as we are able to say what we did in the cradle.' Moreover, there are anatomical objections. However carefully Father Wolf may have carried Mowgli in his mouth, without a scratch, a real wolf can't do this with a real human child: a human has no real scruff to hang by. Moreover, a human baby does not immediately go stiff when he is grasped by his neck. A little human being would start to struggle, which would cost it its life in the wolf's jaws. For this reason it is also improbable that a human baby would be reared by an ape, since he has only two instead of four hands to hold on with. The reason why the phenomenon of the wolf child cannot be dismissed is that the animal kingdom does have examples of young being reared by a different species.

It is quite possible to put orphaned kittens in the litter of a suckling bitch to be suckled (although the American vet Bonnie Beaver says that one such kitten later lifted its leg like a dog when urinating). Of the reverse case Charles Darwin writes:

> Dureau de la Malle tells of a dog reared by a cat, which imitated the well-known feline habit of licking its paws and washing its ears and face with them; this was also observed by the famous scientist Audouin. I have received various confirmations of this; in one of them a dog had not been suckled by a

cat, but had been reared by it, together with its own young, and in consequence adopted the above-mentioned habit, in which it persisted for the remaining thirteen years of its life. Dureau de la Malle's dog also learned from the kittens how to play with a ball, by rolling it along with its front paws and pouncing on it.

Many such confusions between mammals are familiar from the popular press: many zoo animals have been fostered by a bitch. Birds are even more easily duped, because their sense of smell is too poor to be able to identify their own eggs by their scent. For example, the storks in the Dutch breeding programme at Het Liesveld are assisted by bantams in brooding. Whole aviaries of exotic birds emerge from under chickens. This is also found among wild birds, and by this method one can obtain a finch which sings in the manner of a whitethroat.

The cuckoo owes its very existence to the mistaking of eggs. It lays an egg in the nest of a different species which outwardly resembles that of the host. As soon as it hatches, the young cuckoo tips its stepbrothers and stepsisters over the edge of the nest. Instead of punishing it, its foster-parents reward it with food. They work even harder for it than they would have done with their own young, because with its larger beak it gives them an even greater stimulus to feed. An open beak triggers such an irresistible urge to feed that parent birds, loaded down with food for their young, surrender it *en route* to any carp which happens to come to the surface to breathe. However, the most remarkable case is that of the cock-pigeon Dolf, which fed three newly born dwarf rabbits rejected by their parents with the milk from its crop. The foster-parent and parents knew each other well, since they shared the same hutch in the town of Middelburg. Promptly at mealtimes the male pigeon slipped through an opening into the hutch where the young dwarf rabbits were kept.

Many species of animals are of course reared by human beings, sometimes, like the piglets in New Guinea, by breast-feeding, mostly with the bottle. This may be successful, but, for example in the case of anthropoid apes, the young are deprived of a proper upbringing. Reared by human beings outside their ape community, many apes do not learn how to deal in later life with their own young. Monkey mothers who were artificially inseminated by Harlow could not tolerate any male near them, as a result of their lack of experience with animals of their own species, and crushed the skulls of their newborn young on the ground.

Now that we are aware of this phenomenon, preventive measures are taken. The best thing, of course, is to allow the apes to grow up in a group of their own species, which they can copy. In the absence of such a group the gorillas in the Apenheul zoo in the Netherlands are given lessons in maternal care. A nurse demonstrated with a gibbon the way to hug a baby tenderly, and a friend of the director's breastfed her baby right in front of the cage of a gorilla mother-to-be, which proved a help.

While the young are being brought up by one animal species or another, imprinting may take place. If wolf children are imprinted on wolves or bear children on bears as babies, they ought, when grown up, to wish to mate with a wolf or a bear. Unfortunately few wolf children have lived long enough to provide proof; most of them died in childhood. Exceptions, such as Vincent, who lived to be forty, and Man Singh, from the North Indian district of Mathura, who survived until sixty-five, matured only physically; their minds remained infantile. For that matter, we would be very surprised if a wolf child fell for a she-wolf or an ape child for a female ape. Our vision of the object of their affections can be seen in every Tarzan film: a human female. Me Tarzan, you Jane.

Nevertheless a mild form of imprinting is certainly involved. Since shepherd boys grow up not only among people but also among cattle, and many city girls both among people and among their dogs, cows and dogs later have a head start if someone's love is not limited to one's own species. Even an alien species must have something familiar about it.

Your juicy components do not slosh around freely. Most are packed into cells and parts of cells. But the thesis that everything which is full of life is fluid is confirmed by your heaviest organ, your blood. This is full of life and flows. It occupies between 5 and 10 per cent of your body, penetrating every nook and cranny. Although calling something liquid an 'organ' requires some adjustment, blood nevertheless displays all the characteristics of an organ.

Blood feeds life. It is the mother of that other vital liquid, milk. To produce one litre of milk, four hundred litres of blood will have supplied their nutrients to the breast. Blood is hence much less nutritious than milk, being a watered-down corpuscle soup containing all kinds of things, but not too much of anything. Consequently it is only infrequently used as an intermediary between the species. Of course it is used by fleas and a handful of mosquitoes and lice, by such primitive fish as the eel and by leeches, but that is virtually all. They make their own blood out of yours. Kill a mosquito which has drunk its fill, and you have mainly killed yourself; more than half the stain on the wallpaper consists of your own blood.

The transfer of our heaviest organ to a blood-sucking insect has a hint of copulation about it. After some introductory sniffling, the insect inserts its sting and injects the victim. This undesired intimacy serves to prevent the congealing of your blood. This enables man to experience the sensation of being raped for a change, albeit by a female, since only female insects have the laying tube which is convertible into a sting, or laying eggs thirsty for blood. Killing a mosquito is consequently a curious combination of bloodshed, murderousness and reproduction, which can be very exciting.

There are also mammals which live on blood. The vampire bat creeps

Above: Vampire Biting Sleeping Victim, illustration from the 19th-century feuilleton 'Varney the Vampire'

up on sleeping cows, horses or chickens and bores a hole with its razor-sharp teeth out of which it can lick their blood. It also likes human blood, as we learn from nineteenth-century travelling scientific researchers like Henry Walter Bates. In Brazil Bates once spent the night in a long-disused room which had various openings to the outside:

> On the first evening I was fast asleep and noticed nothing unusual, on the second, however, I was woken around midnight by the noise of a numerous swarm of bats flying to and fro in my room. They had extinguished my lamp; when I had relit this, I saw that my room was crawling with bats, that the whole area was literally black with the throng, which swarmed constantly around me.... That evening various of these animals came into my hammock; I grabbed a few which were crawling around me and threw them against the wall of the room. At daybreak I found a wound on my hip which had undoubtedly been inflicted by a bat. This was too much for me; so I set about driving the animals away with the help of the Negroes; I shot a fairly large number, which were hanging on the beams, had the Negroes climb onto the roof from outside and kill several hundred bats both old and young.

Vampires are still widely attacked in South America; in one of many campaigns eight thousand caves were dynamited or poisoned, even though this also affected mainly useful species. In this way people hope to prevent the vampire spreading even more rabies among the enormous herds of cows and horses. Intimate contact between human beings and vampires is not appreciated by the former. Except, that is, by a contemporary of Bates's, Charles, the twenty-seventh Duke of Waterton, who achieved celebrity as the first nature conservationist, but mainly as an eccentric. At home in his English country house he sometimes received visitors sprawled like a dog under the table, in Rome he stood with one leg on the head of a gilt angel at the top of St. Peter's, in South America he rode a live crocodile ('if you ask me how I was able to stay on its back, I would say that I have been hunting with Lord Darlington for years') and cherished one wish:

> I should like to be sucked by a vampire.... The bite cannot hurt, because the patient is always asleep when the vampire sucks him; and as regards the loss of a few ounces of blood, that is of no significance. On many nights I have slept with my foot outside the hammock to lure this winged surgeon assuming that he was there, but I have not been successful.

A sleeping human being waiting for the vampire coming to suck his blood: outlandish as that image may seem, it strikes us as familiar, from innumerable vampire films. Except that the sleeping man is usually replaced by a blonde virgin to emphasize the erotic aspect. The vampire is not usually a bat, but a human being. Stories about vampires had existed for centuries in Europe before South America and the vampire

Hugging and Kissing,
1989

bats which are exclusive to it were discovered. If a living person dies through loss of blood, it was generally assumed, a dead person can come back to life by drinking blood. This latter was customary for the dead who could not find any rest in the grave because they were guilty of some misdeed during their lives, which had to be atoned for. Bram Stoker immortalized the Eastern European popular stories of such wandering dead in his *Dracula*. When bats which drank blood at night proved real, the creatures with their black wings fitted in perfectly with the human monsters who were mostly shrouded in a black cape. Every European child has long known the difference between ghosts with bird wings, the angels, who are good, and spirits with bat wings, the devils, who are evil.

Meanwhile more and more virgins are being penetrated in more and more films by more and more bats, making the vampire film possibly the most commonly viewed form of bestiality. The films are usually set in Transylvania or thereabouts. Unfortunately blood-sucking bats are found neither there nor here. It is too cold for them; there is too little nourishment in blood to keep a bat warm enough in cold or temperate zones. In the Netherlands a bat would have to use so much blood as fuel that it would be unable to get off the ground. In the tropics a vampire needs the blood content of one human being – five litres – to survive for a

Max Klinger, *The Siren*

year, in this country that would be one human being per month. This is a land of milk, not blood.

The most intimate contacts between two human beings begin with salivating in each other's mouth. This is called kissing. While the average American or European would not dream of using anyone else's toothbrush, he eagerly pokes his tongue into somebody else's mouth. Even if it does not reach the point of the exchange of sperm, blood or milk, exchange of saliva is widespread between partners. Just as seeing saliva or snot provokes such revulsion – the degree of civilization of a people can be calculated from the number of forests felled in order to make tissues – so the desire to have somebody else's saliva in your mouth counts as a sign of true love. Slime is the lubricant of the erotic mechanism.

This is also the case with the chimpanzees. Although they keep their mouths wide open while they kiss it looks very human when they exchange an intimate greeting, half way between the smacking kiss of a toddler and the embrace of former Eastern bloc leaders. Chimpanzees kiss people they like in the same way. Consequently a keeper who was transferred from the chimpanzees to the bonoboes at San Diego Zoo, received the shock of his life when he, as proud as a teenager with a new girlfriend, accepted a kiss from a bonobo and suddenly felt something warm and slippery entering his mouth. We are not the only species familiar with the French kiss.

Indeed for dogs, French kisses are the rule: a lick with that all-purpose household cloth is regarded as an intimate greeting. Many people dislike such a wet token of affection, but there are those who enjoy having even their faces slobbered over, to the delight of dog, human being and bacteria alike. And if you don't pick up an infection as a result, then you can combat them in the same way. In Philadelphia four hundred Americans are attending a course on mouth-to-mouth resuscitation for dogs. They hope in due course to be able to save their most loyal comrade from a heart attack, a disease of prosperity found even among dogs.

People who would never dream of mating with an animal swallow its sperm with relish. Sometimes still alive, when eating oysters, usually dead, as soft roe; sometimes unintentionally, often deliberately, with clear ulterior motives, not free of eroticism. Nice and dirty. Fishmongers all over the world wink at their customers when they buy a half a pound of soft roe and in South America it is a great treat (for the men only) when, after the calves in a herd have been castrated, the dice are rolled for the largest testicles. North American women eat 'mountain oysters' as rarely as their South American sisters. Not because they are so difficult to prepare – simply cut into slices (first taking off the skin) and then sauté gently in butter – but for fear of growing hair on their chests from the calves' testicles. They do, however, occasionally help themselves to a 'turkey fry', the turkey testicles, at smart parties.

The euphemisms – in Dutch sheep's testicles are called 'white kidneys', in imitation of the French *rognons blancs* – and the sniggering reinforce the erotic effect of the genital titbits. Although even the Romans used the euphemism *minute apicianum* when they meant a braised dish of capons' testicles, the intention of every male eater is quite clear: to increase his potency. The best thing of course is to use the testicles of the most potent animal. In Spain these are regarded as the fighting bulls from the bullring, and of these the fiercest fighting bulls from the most renowned bullrings. Consequently, in the famous *Florian* restaurant in Barcelona you are served a bull's testicles, accompanied not only by garlic and parsley, but by the name of the bull, its weight, a brief history, the pedigree, the place and time of its death and the name of the matador responsible. They taste of sweetbreads, but that is all. The essence of the virility they contained has long disappeared into the pan and into our alimentary canal before it can fortify our temperament. The French doctor Serge Voronoff understood this perfectly well, but believed he had the answer.

In the 1920s Voronoff gave older men grafts of 'monkey glands' to help them to tap fresh reserves of youth. Given a new zest for life by slices of monkey testicle sewn onto their own ageing scrota, old men did handstands before the cameras of excited press photographers, a general maintained that after the operation he felt like a young sergeant again, men who for years had used their beds only for sleeping, posed proudly with a newborn son or daughter, an insurance company refused to pay out to one of Voronoff's patients because thanks to his operation he did not look anything like the age given in his passport: there was still plenty of life in the old dog. Eternal youth seemed within reach, and Serge Voronoff moved into a château on the French Riviera, where he was rumoured to keep a particularly large anthropoid ape for himself and the treatment became so famous that it found its way into literature.

In *Nora*, by the French writer Félicien Champsaur, Anatole Frass, already half senile, has himself treated by Doctor Voronoff after falling in love with a female ape who is the rage of the *Folies Bergères* as a black dancer. In *The Adventure of the Creeping Man* Sherlock Holmes has to deal with an old professor who out of love for a young girl has had himself treated with ape serum by the obscure scientist Lowenstein. Besides the desired effect, this has an undesired effect: the professor goes around on all fours at night or swings from the treetops in his nightshirt. Obviously, concludes Holmes, he has been given serum from some gibbon or other instead of an anthropoid ape serum. 'The highest type of man may revert to the animal if he leaves the straight road of destiny', pontificates Conan Doyle's hero.

That was at the end of the 1920s. Apes' testicles were soon to be safe again. Voronoff had gone too far. Using the testicles of young horses he attempted to squeeze the last drops of super-semen from famous but ageing breeding stallions. The animals turned out to be less susceptible to suggestion than their owners and that became apparent in the view of the amount of money involved. What we all now know in our age of heart transplants became increasingly obvious: an organ from another individual is not automatically accepted by the body. The *coup de grâce* came in 1929 when the sex hormone testosterone was isolated. Monkey glands turned out to be monkey business. Popular belief in them, according to David Hamilton, the biographer of Voronoff, reflected the spirit of the age. There was a huge demand for youthful élan, once the First World War had decimated a generation of young people. In the upper classes the lack of young people was particularly disastrous, because those who were to take over the management of the English and French empires were in danger of being trampled underfoot by the far more rapidly reproducing lower orders; 'national degeneration' threatened. However, Voronoff's success was also based on the reputation of the ape or monkey as a virile rapist. The return to youth was in some sense a return to the strength and resilience of our monkey ancestor.

More recently cattle and pigs have been used for the same purpose. Because although monkey glands are no longer implanted, the demand for other species' sex hormones has remained. People have themselves injected with sex hormones, partly synthetically prepared, partly taken from our domesticated animals, so that we now know at last what it is like to have someone else's sexual juices flowing through our veins.

A. Paul Weber, *Face to Face*, c. 1962

Female sex-cells are eaten much more frequently than male ones. There are two or three in every egg sandwich, female sex-cells are eaten in their thousands and in the case of sturgeon roe – caviar – they enjoy gourmet status. Eating egg-cells is more sensible than eating sperm-cells, since the actual reproductive cell of the female is often produced with a large amount of food, the yolk. But while the eating of male sex-cells is regarded as beneficial for the sexual capacity of men, the female sex cells are not eaten to increase female pleasure. Both sperm and eggs are considered primarily to increase the man's potency.

When one eats an egg, one is eating a sexual product. But female sexual organs are also eaten. Recipes for stuffed pig's vagina are known from as far back as the Roman gourmet Apicius, and his fellow townsman Pliny maintained that the vagina of an aborted piglet (*ejectitia*) was even more delicious than that of a piglet born naturally (*porcaria*). According to Martial it was preferable if the sow were pregnant, while Horace was fairly indifferent, as long as the vagina was a good size. Penises, on the other hand, according to the culinary expert Johannes van Dam, from whom I derive my knowledge of Roman meats, were not eaten even by the Romans. He knows only one recipe for penis, from the very poor, Jewish Yemeni kitchen:

> Blanch the penis and clean it. Boil for ten minutes and cut into slices. Sweat onions, garlic and coriander in oil. Add the penis and fry. Cover the penis with mixed chopped tomato, pepper, cumin, saffron and salt. Put the lid on the pan and braise slowly for two hours until well done.

Obtaining a suitable penis can be difficult. Under Dutch law any left over after slaughter must be destroyed; police bullwhips are imported from abroad. Penis is supposed to taste better than testicles, because it seemed so unlikely to the legislators that the latter would be eaten they have simply omitted to prohibit it. Nevertheless penis was recently eaten in Netherlands by a group of inveterate foodies. The taste, according to one, was a disappointment.

The same applies to blood. One's own blood, sucked from a wound, tasting of oneself, is not too bad – nice and sweet – but the thought of the black pudding which we were forced to eat as children does not make me nostalgic for my youth. That may just be me, of course. In France there are whole culinary societies whose members, dressed in extravagant togas and strange berets, make an elaborate cult of the local *boudins* which has many similarities to the blood rituals of primitive peoples. There is a taboo on the eating or drinking of blood which is as least as old as the third oldest book of the Old Testament, Leviticus:

> And whatsoever man there be of the house of Israel, or of the strangers that sojourn among you, that eateth any manner of blood; I will even set my face against that soul that eateth blood, and will cut him off from among his people. For the life of the flesh is in the blood; and I have given it to you upon the altar to make an atonement for your soul; for it is the blood that maketh an atonement for the soul.

Like Muslims, Jews consequently allow the animals that they eat to bleed before eating them. Of course there are also peoples, such as the Tibetans, who strangle their animals precisely in order to leave plenty of blood in them, but in our part of the world blood, among Christians too, who invoke the blood of their Saviour, is treated with awe. In any case the taboo on blood was still effective in the England of 1667 when Doctor Edmund King tried to have the blood of a lamb flow through the vein of a human being, and the transfusion was at first prevented by 'some considerations of a moral nature'. The considerations must have been very like the objections that were made to vaccination in the nineteenth century: vaccinating with liquid derived from an animal would lead to 'the degradation of human beings'.

Nowadays the taboo has lost much of its potency. We inject ourselves with other people's blood and guinea pigs with our own. Cleansed of all erotic ulterior motives by the hypodermic needle and the sterilizer, juices flow from one organism into the veins of another organism unimpeded by any taboo. In such cases it is nature herself that throws up obstacles. Precisely in the case of blood one is dealing with groups and factors which make arbitrary exchange impossible. Animal blood is not admitted to our veins and even human blood has to be carefully selected and treated to prevent it meeting such a hostile reception that the motherland succumbs. Because it is liquid, blood would appear easy to transplant, but it remains an organ, chock-full of substances and particles which characterize it as ours, as mine, a piece of myself which is different from all pieces of you or them. Borderline markers indicate the boundaries like the apples of the tree of good and evil: cross me, eat me.

If the juices with which we are filled are the most intimate substance we can exchange with other beings, the most intimate but one is the exchange of the rest, the bag in which the juices are contained. One can remove an animal's coat and don it oneself. In this way you literally get into someone else's skin. You are sporting other people's feathers.

Until recently the deepest wish of every woman was to own a fur coat, and in some countries it still is. Enveloped in an animal skin you looked not only more coquettish, but strangely enough more sophisticated. The higher the society, the nearer the proportion of ladies with fur coats approaches 100 per cent. It is even more strange how quickly anti-fur campaigns have been able to change the situation. Suddenly it is, on the contrary, unsophisticated to appear in public on a Dutch pavement in a fur coat; a howling mob of youngsters will soon drum that into you. Such a rapid turnaround is only possible if there is a latent sense of aversion which can be exploited. For all its chic image, fur was always charged with a feeling of guilt, blood, death. Now people wear fake fur. But that is just as effective. Wearing an imitation leopardskin dress a woman transmits an unmistakable message, which was actually intended for male leopards but strangely enough works as powerfully on human males. As though they were themselves leopards, men on building sites ogle the fake female leopard. Many people find such a leopardskin pattern vulgar, but that only means that the symbolism is laid on too thickly. Proud, vulgar and sexy, the leopard girl walks along accompanied by a leather-clad he-man.

Stripped of its hair skin is called leather and from being feminine it has become masculine. Men feel more masculine in leather as women feel more feminine in fur, and admire other men who wear it. They derive collective excitement from motorbiking or from the various leather scenes. Both homosexuals and heterosexuals can be turned on by leather, even if they are only wearing it. Outsiders, according to Paul van Gelder in *Leather Clothes*, find this disturbing: it is a sign of sexual orientation, animalism and primitiveness. Leather and sex are inextricably connected. Hence the astonished rage of the leather boy at a pick-up from a leather bar: 'I went home with a boy dressed beautifully in leather, but once we started making love he took everything off!'

The erotic charge of fur and leather tends of necessity towards necrophilia. The animal must be dead before you can appropriate its skin. But while a beautiful girl in a leopardskin dress feels like a live leopard, possessed by the animal, the leather boy in no way identifies with the dead, shed skin of the old cow in which he is sheathed. What animal the item of clothing once was is of great importance with leopardskin and mohair socks, but makes little difference in the case of leather. The identity has vanished along with the hair.

A special case is the waistcoat of Doctor Melchior, the ship's doctor of the *Willem Barentz*. On a whaling expedition the doctor tanned the only part of a whale's skin which can be tanned and made a waistcoat of it. He had his Bible bound in the same material – penis leather. Seldom have sex, the animal, death and religion been so closely linked.

114

7

God and the Commandments

An animal is a thing. The jurists are agreed on this point. An animal is a thing and a thing has no rights, only a person has those. So you can just as easily break the legs of your dog as those of your table, unless it gives offence to a person under Dutch law. Legislators may, in the words of Professor Langemeijer, 'not give any weight to the consideration that animals suffer when they feel pain, hunger, thirst, exhaustion, but should ask themselves only whether the mass of those people living within their jurisdiction, or at least a representative group of them, are concerned about that suffering.' This is why you must not pull a dog's leg off, but may do so with a fly, that is why mistreatment of animals has found its way into the law between pornography, making children under sixteen drunk and singing offensive songs. This is why a million animals a day are put through the mincing machines of the Dutch food industry with impunity, executed without any form of trial on grounds of gross edibility.

Professor Langemeijer was writing in 1954. Since then the 'representative group' among those 'people concerned with that suffering' living within the jurisdiction of the legislators has greatly increased, both at home and abroad. If in this country the Foundation for Nice Animals is good to nice animals and if the Association of Police Officers in the Netherlands for the Protection of Animals stands firm, in America the Beaver Defenders and the Jews for Animal Rights are active, England has Chicken's Lib and where else but Switzerland would the *Konsumenten Arbeitsgruppe zur Förderung tierfreundlicher umweltgerechter Nutzung von Haustieren* (Consumer Working Party for the Promotion of the Animal and Environment-Friendly Use of Domestic Pets) flourish? If women have equal rights, along with ethnic minorities and gays and children and the mentally defective, then in the view of an increasing number of people animals too have a right to rights. They are right. Animals should

Execution of a Sow in front of the Church at Falaise, engraving from 'L'Homme et la Bête' by Arthur Mangin

not be things but persons, not objects but subjects, not a means but an end. However, rights create duties. Few campaigners are aware that an animal which has rights can also be held liable for its actions. If a court personifies the animal, the animal can find itself in the dock. In 1595 this cost the dog Provetie dear. It was charged by the Sheriff and Aldermen of Leiden with killing a child:

> Provetie (it was alleged) was guilty on Sunday last, the ninth day of May 1595 of biting the child of Jan Jacobsz van der Poel, which child was playing with its uncle and had a piece of Meat in its hand and the aforesaid Provetie snatching at it, bit the aforementioned child and thus inflicted a wound in the second Finger of the Right hand, cutting right through the skin deep into the flesh, so that blood issued from the wound and as a result of the shock the child shortly after departed this world, because of which Mr Eysser took Provetie into custody, after it emerged by the prisoner's own confession made by him without the use of torture or iron shackles.
>
> The Alderman of the city of Leiden . . . herewith condemn him to be taken to the square of Gravesteyn in this town where evildoers are customarily punished and that there he shall be hung by the executioner with a rope on the gallows until he is dead, and that subsequently his dead body shall be dragged on a cart to the Gallows field and that he shall there remain hanging from the gallows to deter all other dogs.

Old Woman Fighting against the Devil in Animal Form

It is doubtful whether the dog's carcass, hanging from the gallows, moved the other dogs of Leiden to well-behaved, prudent thoughts. Even as a means of preventing reoffending or revenge such a trial, complete with custody and judgment, seems heavyhanded in our eyes. Why go to all that trouble to put a dog on the gallows? This clearly expresses a need for order. The law had been broken and something had to be done, all the more so because the law had been laid down by God. An animal trial was a ritual in the eternal struggle between good and evil. The judges were unconcerned with whether or not an animal was a thing. The problem was that an animal was one of God's creatures and therefore good. Condemning an animal could be regarded as criticism of God's creatures, unless you assume that the good creature had been possessed by evil forces, by the devil. The devil must be driven from the world, if necessary with the animal and all. This is why there was so much attention to ritual detail: the dock, the confession, the last meal, the executioner's gloves, the tolling bells. Even though a discussion as to whether a mad dog can be declared not responsible for its actions strikes us as ridiculous, for the judges of those days it was in deadly earnest.

'In those days' includes almost the whole of the Christian era, from the earliest Middle Ages down to the nineteenth century. The trials were conducted mainly in France, but in Germany, Italy, Sweden, the Netherlands and America pigs which had bitten children, bulls which had gored farmers and she-asses which had seduced farm-hands were hanged, strangled or burnt at the stake. A billy-goat, having been found guilty, was traditionally banished to Siberia by the Russians. In 1457 six piglets which were found covered in bloodstains alongside the body of Jehan Martin, a French infant, were put on trial in 1457 as the accomplices of their mother, but because of lack of proof were released on bail. The horses or beasts of burden with which a virgin had been abducted got off less lightly. Animals could be punished not only for what they had done, but also for what they had failed to do. If someone had been raped, then according to an old German law all the animals in the house had to be slaughtered because they had obviously not done enough to help the victim. Animals could even be called to testify; in England a parrot is mentioned as a witness.

Encumbered with human duties, possessed by devils, animals were also judged on their degree of piety. In 1394 in Mortaigne a pig was hanged for sacrilege: the animal had eaten a blessed host. In the case of another pig which had eaten a piece of a child which it had killed, an aggravating circumstance was that it had done this on Friday and hence had offended against the fast laws. And if there were worldly penalties against spiritual offences, worldly offences could be punished spiritually. Swarms of insects, packs of rats and other plagues of animals which could not be put in the dock individually, were, after the necessary prayers and processions, excommunicated by a spiritual quadrumvirate. In order nevertheless to have something tangible, sometimes a number of specimens were ceremonially killed in the courtroom while the ban was being pronounced. However, acquittal was possible if the defence had successfully shown that God had created plants both for human beings and for insects as food. Sometimes the insects, by the time the Church authorities had finished splitting hairs, had long since gone into hibernation. How the protracted case brought by the church of Saint-Julien against the beetles which threatened the local wine harvest in 1545 concluded, is not known; the last page of the judgment has been eaten by insects.

If in order to judge animals it was necessary to enter into convoluted trains of thought which we today can scarcely follow, in the case of judging bestiality matters were very simple. The Bible – which, besides revelation, adventure story and pornographic collection, is also a book of laws – is unambiguous about it in the book of Leviticus:

Neither shalt thou lie with any beast to defile thyself therewith: neither shall any woman stand before a beast to lie down thereto: it is confusion ...

And if a man lie with a beast, he shall surely be put to death: and ye shall slay the beast.

And if a woman approach unto any beast, and lie down thereto, thou shalt kill the woman, and the beast: they shall surely be put to death: their blood shall be upon them!

'Their blood shall be upon them': both human being and animal must be stoned to death. One can hear the echoes of ancient curses in these words, but even the Hittites, the predecessors of the Jews in the Holy Land, were not that strict. Although the Hittites were forbidden on pain of death 'to lie' with a cow or dog, if 'a man lies with a horse or mule, there is no punishment, although this must not happen in the proximity of the king and such a man may not become a priest'. Such nuances are more concerned with a distinction between pure and impure animals than with regulating sexual activity. With its strict laws the Old Testament emphatically took issue with all the previous inhabitants of the Holy Land: 'For in all these the nations are defiled which I cast out before you: and the land is defiled . . .'. The Jews based their Talmud on the precepts of the Old Testament. In this widows were even forbidden to keep a dog, for fear that they would prefer the animal sexually to a real man. But symbolically too any mixing of animals and human beings or gods was banned. Depicting God with an animal's head or an animal's body, as the Egyptians and Greeks did, was forbidden, let alone identifying God with an animal; for the devout Jew a Lamb of God is as great an abomination as a golden calf.

The Old Testament curse on bestiality was grist to the mill of an anti-Semite like Voltaire:

> Leviticus makes this accusation against the Jewish ladies who were wandering through the desert. In their defence I must say that they were unable to wash in a country that has no water at all and which can still be reached only by camel. They were unable to put on clean clothes or shoes because by an exceptional miracle they were able to wear the same garments for forty years; they had no change of clothes. Because of their smell the local billy-goats quite possibly mistook them for nanny-goats. This likeness may well have led to amorous relations between the two species.

The Flemish jurist Joost de Damhoudere in the sixteenth century even turned Jewish laws against the Jews when in his legal handbook he counted coitus between a Christian and Jew as sodomy. A certain Jean Alard, who lived in Paris with a Jewess and had a number of children with her, was condemned for sodomy and burnt at the stake together with his girlfriend, 'since coitus with a Jewess is exactly the same as if a man were to copulate with a dog'. These views are as scandalous as they are unequivocal. There can be no doubt of what is meant by sodomy here. Elsewhere it is different. Basically sodomy is the name for the sexual debauches for which God punished the city of Sodom with destruction, but no one knows exactly what these debauches were. The term has been used for bestiality, but also a great deal for homosexuality. The New York legal code still regards anyone as guilty of sodomy who 'has carnal intercourse with any animal or any bird', 'approaches any male or female person via the anus or via or with the mouth' or 'has sexual intercourse with a dead body'. The European jurists who for centuries talked of *crimen nefandum contra naturam* or *offensa cujus nominatio crimen est* (an infamous crime which was better not named) were perhaps no broader, but they were vaguer. Psychiatrists have not made things any simpler with their dog Latin, so that 'bestiality' and 'zoophilia' are almost the only terms which are decent and yet unambiguous.

Christianity's legacy from Judaism certainly included the laws against bestiality. As far as possible these were made if anything a little stricter. Just as the Jews had made clear their opposition to their predecessors in the Holy Land, the Christians in the first centuries of existence tried to distinguish themselves from the Romans and other heathens by self-testing and temperance. That was not difficult. Adulterers, slave-seducers and holders of orgies as they were, the Romans did not even have a law against bestiality! There were ordinances against acts of homosexuality, but apart from that Roman legislators did not concern themselves juridically with the private morality of citizens. The Christians, on the other hand, abhorred every example of unchasteness, the sin which had driven man from Paradise. When aimed at reproduction, sex was just permissible, but anyone wanting to lead a really exemplary life abstained from it. Besides the constant danger of being eaten by lions, early Christianity was not a very jolly faith. Although the New Testament never gained the same legal force as the Old Testament, one commandment sounded even more loudly from it: thou shalt not commit unchastity. 'Flee fornication,' wrote the apostle Paul in his letter to the Corinthians, 'he that commiteth fornication sinneth against his own body. What? Know ye not that your body is the temple of the Holy Ghost which is in you?' Sex with another species did not serve reproduction and was therefore as strictly forbidden as in nature. Even touching an animal's genitals counted as an unnatural act. Anyone who did so from lust was committing a mortal sin; those who were merely curious were committing only a venal sin. If touching animal genitals was unavoidable, for example in husbandry, this, according to the Church's advice from as late as 1927, should be restricted to older and married persons. Such married persons, however, must be careful not to go too far, for sexual intercourse between human beings and animals counted as 'even more terrible than adultery', and 'gave the [other] spouse the right to abandon his or her marital duties'.

The Christians made one change to the Old Testament commandment: the sentence of death was as rule not carried out by stoning but at the stake. Many documents of trials have been lost, but hundreds of reports have survived from the boom in bestiality trials from the sixteenth to the eighteenth centuries. From the evidence these often concerned imbeciles, or else bestiality (and hence the death penalty)

Hugo van der Goes,
Fall, c. 1470

seemed to be a useful charge to rid oneself of a superfluous spouse or to
settle an old score. Characteristic of this is the trial of Jean de La Soille, a
26-year-old mule-driver from Villeneuve-L'Archevêque. The witnesses
were questioned on 20 November 1555:

> Aymon Groupan, cooper, had known for a long time that M. De Terron had
> employed Jean de La Soille to look after his asses and that the aforementioned

de La Soille gave most care to the she-ass mentioned in the charge, which he allowed to sleep in a stall separated from the others.

The aforementioned Josse Valcroin, a grocer of the town, declared that he had employed a young boy called La Biche, who had repeatedly said to him that the aforementioned de La Soille was an infamous Sodomite and that he misused a she-ass, to which he devoted more care than the others, in a terrible and unnatural way.

Roger Dumoulin, an innkeeper of the town, declared that he had caught the aforementioned de La Soille repeatedly in the act, for example on Saturday the thirteenth of this month, the day on which the aforementioned de La Soille was arrested.

The accused was found guilty and sentenced to be taken in an open cart with the she-ass tied to it. While the condemned man was strung up on a ladder which was put against a pole in the great square of the town, 'the aforesaid she-ass will be burned in his presence; after that has been done the aforementioned de La Soille will be hanged and strangled, after which his body shall be thrown into the fire in which the aforementioned she-ass has been consumed.'

The trial papers were often also thrown into the fire 'so that no trace of the gruesome deed should remain'. The trial of de La Soille is one of forty which have been preserved as copies in the Bibliothèque Nationale because a royal prosecutor, Simon Gueulette, had wished to include them in a weighty legal tome. In this collection is also found a trial of 1622 against the master wagon-maker Antoine de La Rue, who was destined to live to be no more than thirty-five:

Raymond Pardiat, an apothecary of the town, has maintained and declared that the aforementioned Antoine de La Rue on the Tuesday the 18th of April last came to him to ask for an ointment to alleviate a pain which he was suffering and which he, although de La Rue when asked did not wish to confess anything about the place of the affliction or the reason for it, had been easily able to see that the aforementioned de La Rue had grazed his skin through some carnal intercourse or other; and that nevertheless he had given the aforementioned de La Rue the ointment which he wished for.

Thomas Le Fèvre, nicknamed Belle Humeur, an apprentice wagon-maker in the service of the aforementioned Antoine de La Rue, has declared that he knew that the aforementioned Antoine de La Rue constantly had carnal intercourse with the white mare which he kept in his stable and which had been purchased solely for that purpose. After the customary oath declaring that she was telling the truth and nothing but the truth, Angelique Renée Millot, wife of Antoine de La Rue, declared that the aforementioned Antoine de La Rue, her husband, not only mistreated and struck her and in addition copulated daily with a mare, which she tolerated without daring to complain, but had also had asked her with great insistence and even with force to have unnatural intercourse with him in a way other than is allowed by decent marital relations, and that one night the aforementioned de La

Sexual Witchcraft:
Women Changing into
Foxes, anonymous
Japanese prints

Rue had carried out his disgusting intentions on her in her sleep by taking her by surprise, since, she had never permitted him and had even insisted on sleeping separately in her own room.

The accused denied everything, except that he had sometimes beaten his wife with a stick because she refused to stop seeing Pardiat, the apothecary with whom he maintained she was having an affair. In addition, her evidence did not worry him unduly, since she was quite simply a slut and had dreamed up the whole scheme with her lover. However, their plot succeeded. On 22 June 1622 de La Rue was sentenced. Not long after he was hanged and strangled in the market square of Montpensier. His body was burned together with that of the horse in a fire at the foot of the gallows. Their ashes have been scattered by the wind for centuries.

First hanging and strangling, then burning at the stake; it seems to be a double punishment and so it was. Of the two the more essential was burning, so that the world was cleansed for good of evil. Hanging and strangling were simply an alleviation of death by burning. It also happened that the victim was first roasted a little, then strangled and finally burned. The animal was usually killed by a blow to the head before going into the fire. In a judgment of 1684 from Ottendorf it was expressly decreed that the body of the animal abuser in question should lie under that of his accomplice, a mare, while being burnt. Only occasionally did an unnatural pair of lovers escape the flames after

sentence. The man and horse who in 1609 were thrown into a burial pit after execution in Niederrad were such an exception.

It was even more exceptional that the animal survived. This good fortune was enjoyed by the she-ass which, in 1750, according to E.P. Evans in *The Criminal Prosecution and Capital Punishment of Animals*, had been caught in the act with Jacques Ferron. It was acquitted because it had been the victim of force and had not co-operated of its own free will with the crime of its master, who was condemned to death. The she-ass owed its life to a number of local dignitaries who maintained that they had known the she-ass for four years. Since the ass, both at home and outside, had always behaved virtuously and carefully and had never caused trouble to anyone, the dignitaries of Vanvres 'were prepared to testify that both in word and deed and in her whole manner of life she is very law-abiding'. This mitigating evidence was needed not only to counter the biblical commandment that both human and animal must be punished, but also the moral and legal considerations in which, for example, de Damhoudere had packaged God's word for mankind:

> Why are animals also subject to this punishment, which have not sinned and have not been able to sin against the law, which they cannot comprehend? After all, every sin must be voluntary and the unreasoning beasts have no free will; that is why they are not considered guilty of crimes. The correct answer is consequently not that the animals are punished because they have committed a personal sin recognized by their consciences, but that the beasts

have been the means whereby human beings have committed the most terrible of all sins; therefore they must also be punished with a dreadful death; it is no more than just that the aforementioned means, that is the unreasoning animals, should be punished along with the human being: it would after all be shameful and intolerable if such an animal, devoid of reason, should continue to live in the sight of men while because of it a human being, blessed with reason, had died a wretched death.

It is no coincidence that the high point of the bestiality trials more or less coincides with that of the witch-hunts. In the case of both bestiality and witchcraft human beings and animals collaborate in the service of the devil. All kinds of animal could serve as the helpers of the witch, because Satan was very versatile, but the witch's familiar *par excellence* was the cat, which in those days reached the nadir of its popularity. As a nocturnal animal, often itself black, suddenly springing up with glinting eyes, possessing nine lives, the cat was the ideal vehicle for the devil. One should have no illusions about the nature of the relations between witches and cats: cats are there so that their arses can be kissed. Many cats died with many witches at the stake. And since heresy was associated with witchcraft, it was better not to be a heretic's cat.

When Europe began to burst at the seams, migration to America got under way. Sadly for themselves the colonists took more ancient laws than young women with them to the New World, with the inevitable results. In 1642 William Hacket, aged eighteen, was sentenced to death in colonial Massachusetts for inserting his member into a cow. His defence that such things would have been quite normal back home on the farm in England did not save him, or the cow: first the cow was burned before his eyes, then he was put to the noose. In that same year, in the words of the *Magnalia Christi Americana*, 'at New Haven, there was a most unparalleled wretch ... executed for damnable bestialities'. Although the condemned man, a certain Potter, aged about sixty, had 'been a member of the Church' and was 'zealous in reforming the sins of other people', he had for half a century given himself over to the most shameful bestialities. His wife had caught him ten years before with a bitch, but at his insistence had not said anything to anyone about it. Later he had hanged the animal, 'probably as a sort of vicarious atonement'. Now he himself had been sentenced to the gallows, 'a cow, two heifers, three sheep and two sows, with all of which he had committed his brutalities' were killed before his eyes.

The moment at which the old days, when bestiality was a capital offence, changed to the present, when judges have better things to do, can be fairly accurately pinpointed: during the French Revolution. As advocated by Montesquieu and other Enlightenment thinkers, Church and State, morality and law, God and the Commandments were separated. The time had come finally to stop avenging God all the time, in Montesquieu's opinion; after all, one could also praise Him. Morality was transferred from law to conscience. Overnight, bestiality ceased to be a capital offence, but at most cost you your friends of both sexes. This was true not only in France, but also in the countries that fell under French influence. And although the rigorous division of morality and law has been reversed in various places since the Napoleonic period, the subject of bestiality has never since been included in the civil codes of Italy, Spain, Portugal, Romania, Belgium, the Netherlands or, of course, France itself. The spirit of the age has for all that time been just liberal enough to resist such crusaders for chastity as the French doctor Lucien Nass, who as late as 1912 noted with indignation that 'the French criminal code does not include this crime. It must believe that some villainies are too disgusting to qualify for the honour of being combated.'

Countries like Germany and England also made a division between morality and law, but continued to view bestiality as in conflict with the law. Bestiality checked population growth, undermined marriage and also provoked instinctive revulsion in the mass of the population. It is characteristic of the difference between the Romance and German mentality that until long after the Second World War farmers in the German-speaking cantons of Switzerland were much less free to take liberties with their cattle than their French-speaking neighbours. Until 1969 anyone in Germany itself touching the genitalia of an animal with lewd intent risked not only a prison sentence but also the loss of his civil and political rights. The severity of the penalty, as in Austria and German-speaking Switzerland, depended on the *Beischlafähnlichkeit* (approximation to intercourse).

In England and America, where bestiality is often lumped together with homosexuality as 'sodomy', the prosecution of one has declined with that of the other, but according to the letter of the law one could be sentenced to penal servitude for between ten years and life for bestiality. All that was necessary was that 'the organ which had carnal intercourse with the male organ of reproduction, was penetrated by it in any way'. If this was not the case, then one might get off with a simple prison sentence. The spirit of such legislation survives strongest in America, where by no means all states have removed bestiality from their statute books. Nevertheless even there one is more liable to be sent to the psychiatrist than to court for bestiality today. 'Although the behaviour of adults who seek or prefer contact with animals falls outside the scope of normality,' write Donal MacNamara and Edward Sagarin in *Sex, Crime and the Law*, 'it need not exceed the tolerance of society. There is little or no point in laws against bestiality, and there is certainly no point in the long prison sentences which have been inflicted on a few unfortunates.' In that case one might just as well legislate against grave desecrators. In addition, it is becoming increasingly clear that in the last century in the fight against masturbation, homosexuality and bestiality far more harmful things such as incest and rape within the family were being ignored. Consequently attention is focused on these nowadays.

The criminal law is the simplest, but also the least effective means of combating immorality. In the case of bestiality it is most effective when used indirectly. The owner of the abused animal can lay a charge of disturbance of the peace or damage to property; on the public highway bestiality falls under offensive behaviour, and there are also, fortunately, ordinances against animal abuse. For example, no special law against bestiality was necessary in order for action to be taken in the following, fairly recent case from Saxony:

> A 38-year-old man of poor reputation forced his way into a cowshed in order to satisfy his sexual lust with a cow. First he introduced his member into the vagina of a nine month-old calf. Next he tried to do the same with a cow, which, however, kicked him to the ground. The enraged accused drove the handle of a manure fork with great force into their anus, first of the calf, then of the cow. The cow died shortly afterwards, the calf had to be slaughtered the following day. From their internal injuries it appeared that the handle had been moved forcefully back and forth a number of times. The accused was sentenced to two years and three months for damage to property.

Vets often encounter internal injuries which give rise to speculation. In the French hamlet of Trémonzey, however, it was the livestock farmer himself who thought that many of his chickens and turkeys were dying in suspicious circumstances. In May 1992 the chicken violator was caught in the act and charged with cruelty to animals. One could also talk of a crime of passion.

Apart from the physical damage it is questionable to what extent an animal need suffer in the case of a 'normal', non-sadistic coupling with a human being. Force is often required to get the animal to do what the human being wants. Barbara Noske consequently prefers to speak not of bestiality but of *interspecific rape*. The analogies with the rape of a human being by another human being – force, fear, violence, trauma – are obvious. But it is not always the human being who is responsible for the rape. Sometimes animals take the initiative and do so so impulsively, that any objective judge would conclude that a rape had been committed. Besides a stag who behaved in a sexually aggressive way to every menstruating woman who came near him, Bordemann in his *Lexicon der Liebe* mentioned a large Great Dane who forced a woman to the ground and took her literally by force. A female elephant tried to grab her female trainer in the crotch with its trunk so often that the elephant act had to be cancelled. In the case of a rape between a human being and animal it would also be very difficult to find conclusive proof because of all possible nuances.

In any event this conclusive proof was not found in the controversial donkey trials of the Dutch writer Gerard Kornelis van het Reve in

Animal Mounting Woman, Indian miniature, 17th century

1966/7. In 'Letter to my Bank', published in the magazine *Dialoog*, the writer pictured the second coming of God to earth:

> When God again takes animate form, he will return as a Donkey, capable at most of stringing together a few syllables, unrecognized and abused and beaten, but I shall understand Him and immediately go to bed with Him, though I shall put bandages around His hooves, so that I shall not receive too many grazes when He thrashes about at the moment of orgasm.

The anti-homosexual campaigner C.N. van Dis – 'they will gnaw their tongues in pain in the company of the devil, cut off from God' – asked questions in the Lower House of Parliament and a criminal action began in which the indictment did not concern sexual morality but 'scornful sacrilege offensive to religious feelings'. All kinds of experts were drummed up, but the most cogent arguments were those of the self-styled 'people's writer' himself:

> Sexual intercourse between the Divinity and a human being is normal in the history of religion. It is not even alien to Christianity: the Holy Virgin after all is made pregnant by God in the person of the Holy Ghost, who is supposed to have been not only 'the true God', but also 'fire and love'. Nowhere does it say as far as I know, and in view of the qualification 'fire and love', it is also improbable, that this intercourse was not sexual.... The divinity, Your Lordships, has from time immemorial not been particularly fastidious, but has been inclined 'to go the whole hog'.... And I should like to conclude with the following heartfelt appeal of my own: whether God is a Lamb with bloodily pierced feet or a one year-old, mousy grey donkey, which allows itself to be possessed by me at length three times in succession in its Secret Opening, what difference does it make, as long as He takes away the sins of the world, and has pity on us all?

On appeal Van het Reve was fully acquitted on 31 October 1967 by the fifth chamber of the Amsterdam court. And if he had not been, God himself would have forgiven him.

Laws against bestiality are not necessary. Even without a court in the background it is bad enough to be found committing bestiality. This is why it is a taboo. A man who is caught with a calf is a dirty old man, a woman with a dog a slut, a foreigner with a goat a laughing stock. No one who has gained notoriety as a chicken violator will get very far in life. Sexual intercourse with a pet, entrusted to your care, is regarded with almost as much disapproval as actual incest; the blackmailer who catches an American politician committing bestiality is in clover for the rest of his days. Almost anything goes these days, the pillory is usually vacant. For abusers of animals. This was discovered by the Belgian magazine *Dol*, which tried its best to destroy as many sacred cows as were left in the 1980s. Everything was printable, even the sex life of the Belgian prime minister, but problems arose when the latter was depicted having sexual intercourse with a dog; the distributor for the Netherlands refused to handle the issue. The publication's successor, *Belge*, folded after the widow of Hergé, the creator of *Tintin*, took it to court because of a cartoon strip in which Tintin has sex with Snowy. Similarly, Belgian Radio 3 was forced to promise to mend its ways in 1991 after a story had been broadcast one morning 'about two children who look on while a girl is mounted by a dog'. Telephone lines at the broadcasting company were red hot. Later that year Alan Cooper, a nature-lover from Manchester, had more to fear from the man in the street than the courts. While out swimming in a wetsuit he was alleged to have masturbated a dolphin. 'Swimming along with the dolphin was magic and the allegation completely ruined it. I have had two death threats and

unsolicited mail.' The dolphin was not after sex, but had simply hooked its penis around the knee or elbow of its human friend, so that it could pull him through the water.

Keith Haring, Man on Dolphin

Characteristic of a taboo are all kinds of vague anxieties. The fear of giving birth to a monster is no longer as great in this biologically well-informed world, but the fear of disease is if possible greater than ever. For people who wash their hands after every visit to the toilet, it is quite a triumph to stick a tender part of their body into an animal or to allow themselves to be licked by one. One fear attaches to the other. So the rumour keeps resurfacing that the AIDS virus penetrated the human realm via bestiality with infected apes. It is an almost literal allusion to the previous century, with different diseases, but the same fear. Syphilis allegedly arose through a man who was supposed to have mounted a mare with the horse disease glanders, or even more literally, through mating with an ape. But there was also a reverse belief: that one could get rid of venereal disease through bestiality. In Arab countries particularly, people hoped to be cured of gonorrhoea by copulation with an animal. In this way, according to a report by the French Académie de Médicine, the animal was itself often infected:

It is generally known in Algeria, wrote General Daumaus in 1866, that certain Arabs believe that they can be cured of their venereal disease by copulating with a she-ass. The crime of bestiality is so common in Africa under that heading that the origin of the dourine, a form of syphilis in donkeys and horses, is attributed by most vets to these unnatural contacts. And the following is an authentic case. A zouave who used a she-ass as a therapeutic aid in order to cure himself of syphilis, infected the animal. The mule stallion who later mounted her, caught the disease from her and in turn infected the mares with which he mated. The unfertilized mares were brought to horse stallions who in turn caught the disease and finally spread it so rapidly, that since then real epidemics of the disease have broken out among horses in the south of France and other parts of Europe.

On our tour of the centuries, which has taken us as far as heaven and all across the globe, we have encountered punishments for bestiality varying from the stake to fear of disease and being a target of mockery. But at all times and in all places it has been punished. People simply do not approve of others having sex with animals. That is what makes them human beings.

8

Odd Means Crazy

Alfred Haighton cannot be denied a certain picturesqueness. In the Second World War he financed the famous Dutch literary magazine *The New Guide* from the money which his father had made with the First Netherlands Company for the Insuring of Risks in Lotteries, the firm of Lotisico. He would have been a fitting subject for a satirist like Willem Elsschot, because Haighton Senior was able inexplicably to make a fortune by insuring people against misfortune in the state lottery. Alfred, the son, was a fascist, a malcontent and above all a lover of one-legged women. In order to be able to enjoy his favourite activity as often as possible, he even invested money in a factory for artificial limbs. That helped: no less than three times he was able to cajole a one-legged woman into saying 'I do'.

Is that odd or not? How many men would fall for one-legged women, how many women for one-legged men? How normal is abnormal? Is sexual intercourse with a pig abnormal in itself, or only if it has three legs? And with a kangaroo? How often does a human being actually do it with an animal?

The last question is the most difficult to answer. One-leggedness or three-leggedness can be easily established, but people do not broadcast their bestial proclivities. Homosexuality is an advantage in some circles nowadays, sadism can be pursued in clubs as long as you pay your subscription on time, and even for fathers who abuse their children, there is understanding in some quarters, but I am still waiting for the first man to tell Oprah Winfrey in vivid detail about the wonderful night he had with his goat. Because of the lack of candour estimates vary widely. 'Nowadays,' wrote the sexologist Haeberle in 1978, 'you can scarcely imagine that church, legal and psychiatric experts have taken the trouble to pay attention to the subject. We now know that such sexual acts are very uncommon. Both in men and in women they occur

so seldom that they are socially insignificant.' Maurice Chickedel, one of the American doctors who believed in a cure for homosexuality, also used to believe that things were getting out of hand with bestiality:

> When I read in the Old Testament: 'And if a woman approach unto any beast, and lie down thereto, thou shalt kill the woman and the beast,' I thought that the great Lawgiver had included an unnecessary clause. When I read Plutarch's statement regarding the sacred Egyptian goat, that the woman who were locked in with the animal were practising cohabitation with it, I regarded the words of Plutarch as an invention. But I have learned differently since then. The horrible veracity was demonstrated in many cases. The only consolation is that the practice is more common in European countries and in Asia than in the United States.

In search of firm figures in the sexual area everyone turns to the monument of data which Kinsey and his assistants created in their reports. Alfred Kinsey (a professor of veterinary studies!) asked twenty thousand Americans about their sexual experiences with animals. Not whether, but how often they had had them. That removed the worst scruples and prompted more than 5 per cent of those interviewed to confess: 8 per cent of men and $3\frac{1}{2}$ per cent of women had on some occasion had a sexual encounter with an animal. Results were even more sensational if one limited oneself to men in the countryside, when the score shot up to 50 per cent. Half the young men in the countryside had had sex with animals. That sounds plausible. Certainly, in the 1940s, in the American countryside animals were readily available for physical games, girls were not. Many farmers preferred to see their unmarried farm lads diving into a stall with their donkey than with their daughter. Some of those young neighbours, for that matter, also agreed whole heartedly with this. 'There are', writes Kinsey, 'cases known of extremely religious men who as twenty year olds or older become focused completely on animals because they find heterosexual coitus with a human female morally unacceptable.' However, for most young men, animals were simply a safety-valve until they were ready for a girl. As a rule it was limited to a few experiences over the course of several years.

Pablo Picasso, *Girl with Crow, c.* 1904

And this has been the case in many ages in many different country areas, wherever and whenever marital morality is strict and contact with animals intimate. The boys had the time, the means and the motive. They often slept in the stall with the animals or were alone with them in the fields for the whole day as shepherds. To the extent that this was necessary, the animals suggested the idea to them at mating time and otherwise there were the stories of other, older boys, if the latter did not simply show them how to do it: 'Everyone always seemed to know about it,' remembers the Swedish writer Ivar Lo-Johansson from his adolescence at the beginning of the twentieth century. 'Almost all older boys had talked about how this or that boy had mounted an animal.

Michelangelo Merisi
da Caravaggio, *John
the Baptist*, *c.* 1595

They almost never said they themselves had done it. . . . My grandfather
had told me that in earlier days they had employed only women as
shepherds. Now I myself have reached the age to understand why. The
rancid smell of the sheep's wool and their inviting behaviour aroused
you. The soft coats of the young heifers, the way they climbed on top of
each other in the woods and fields, the open way in which showed their
sex and lust, were even more seductive.'

In this way passions were excited at a young age in the countryside.

134

According to the court reports which Jonas Liliequist studied, a remarkable number of 'young boys under the age of fifteen were accused – many of them still only between nine and twelve and some even younger, the youngest only seven.' Although most of them did not want any spectators, two twelve year olds confessed in 1707 that they had taken turns to commit sodomy with a mare; one had taught the other how to do it. In 1726 a boy of ten had agreed to hold the cow on condition that his thirteen-year-old friend would afterwards do the same for him. In an address to the Swedish Parliament it was repeatedly pointed out how harmful the keeping of livestock can be if it allows young boys to see animals copulating. Later in the eighteenth century the authorities tried to draw as little attention as possible to bestiality trials in order not to make young people even wiser than they already were.

We know most about bestiality in the European countryside in the twentieth century from Ronald Grassberger, who analysed the Austrian court proceedings from 1923 to 1965. Approximately fifty people annually were sentenced for bestiality; they were almost all men from the countryside. Because many infringements of the law were reported only when 'the abused animals had suffered injury or when indignation at a strange violator who had gained access to the stall by secret or by force led to personal involvement by the livestock keeper', Grassberger assumed that the actual incidence of bestiality was between four and five times as high. From this it follows that only between 1 and 2 per cent of men in the countryside occasionally had sexual contact with an animal, thus European farmers allegedly behaved much more chastely with their livestock than their American colleagues at 50 per cent.

As befits a thorough 'kriminologische Abhandlung', Grassberger also calculated at what season animals were most abused. This turned out to be spring, but there was not a great deal of difference between the seasons, presumably because 'eighty-five per cent of the abuse took place in the stall and was therefore neither hindered nor encouraged by the weather'. Approximately a quarter of the men broke into someone else's stall; in the case of offences committed outdoors other people's livestock was not abused any more often than the offender's own. Anyone going into this in detail will also naturally have quantified what persons, how often, at what age and in what way have been involved in the abuse of animals. Vaginal copulation with cows and calves appeared to be by far the most popular. Mares and foals were mounted less often by human beings, approximately as often as goats, which in turn were five times more popular than sheep or pigs. Nevertheless the number of copulations with horses in Austria was proportionately remarkably high, especially if one considers that a horse is actually far too tall for a human being. The hussars who occasionally wished to use their horses for a different purpose traditionally used an upturned bucket. With a

Le Vainqueur

The Fun of Horse-Riding, erotic postcard, c. 1904

cow such a step up is by no means always necessary; cows regularly lie down in their stall. Calves are of course even easier to mount. In addition they have a strong sucking reflex and nothing is so like the udders of their mother as the farmer's son's penis. A colleague who confessed to me that he had had his first sexual experience in this way – 'I found it a bit creepy' – concentrated entirely on mammals after graduation. Dogs are also suited for licking genitalia, during which they are often masturbated by their human partner. This is also done with bulls as far as country people are still aroused by them in this age of artificial insemination.

Then there are of course the chicken-violators. Their pastime is in many areas still so normal that it only gets into the papers when something goes wrong. For example, in December 1990 the northern Spanish newspaper *Faro de Vigo* published a photo with the following caption:

> The remains of the 39-year-old H.R.C. were found by children playing on the banks of the Río Miño, near Orense. He had been crushed by a boulder. As can be seen in the photo, his flies were open and he was holding a chicken against his lower abdomen. Because of the violent movements during the violation of the chicken a loose boulder was toppled, costing him his life.

It was not clear from the official report whether the chicken had been killed by the boulder or by the violation; in the latter case the law protecting animals would have been broken.

Girls have much less sexual contact with livestock than their brothers. Only 1 per cent of those sentenced in Austria according to Grassberger were women and in America according to Kinsey only 1½ per cent of all girls had experience with animals (3½ per cent of adult women). This seems to confirm the impression that bestiality is what men think women do. In the countryside girls at least have less opportunity than boys, if only because almost all animals are of their own sex: cows, ewes, sows, chickens, nanny-goats. Because a few male animals are sufficient to fertilize hundreds of females, males are killed or castrated on the farm; those that are spared are banished to breeding centres. Where nevertheless there are male animals on the loose, human girls are greatly alarmed by them. Capricious as they are, bulls and rams as sexual partners for girls belong more to mythology than to reality.

In town the proportions are very different. Here cows are more difficult for men to find than women; brothels are more numerous than cowsheds. There are animals, but as a rule they are too small for a man to copulate with. Women, on the other hand, enjoy playing sexually with them. Three-quarters of the women who confessed to Kinsey that they had occasionally committed bestiality had made love with a dog. Almost all written sources confirm that preference and Grassberger even tells us that 'the few cases in which a woman has been sentenced because of immorality with animals, apart from an incitement to a male offence, concerned exclusively sexual contacts with dogs'. It is not difficult to get a male dog to copulate with his mistress. A dog simply regards her as a fellow dog. Dogs that are regularly masturbated, according to Kinsey, become so strongly fixated upon man that they no longer even look at bitches. The psychiatrist Von Maschka knew a woman of forty-five who confessed that 'as a result of her very passionate temperament had engaged in sexual activities with her pet dog, who jumped between her legs and licked her; that she took the animal between her bare legs and stroked its abdomen until its member became erect, after which she supported herself against the back of a chair, pulled the animal to her, pushed its member between the lips of her genitals and let him continue until his seed was ejaculated'. His colleague Wald had a patient, a maid, who was caught in the act while she was allowing herself to be mounted like a bitch by a dog on all fours. Of Kinsey's women only one had allowed it to reach the point of actual copulation. Most of them had stopped at touching and masturbating the animal. Moreover, those contacts had not been particularly satisfying; only half of one per cent of the women had occasionally reached orgasm through bestiality. No wonder that most women left it at one or two experiments. Six women had achieved orgasm more than 125 times with an animal, one of them almost a thousand times.

F. Hofbauer, Erotic *ex libris*

Although city women had more sexual experience with animals than their sisters in the countryside they did not match city men, 8 per cent of

Franz von Bayros, *The Blue Feather*, illustration for 'Tales of the Toilet Table', *c.* 1908

whom had occasionally had sex with an animal. Since then, however, a few things have changed. The number of pets in Western cities has more than doubled and people now have much more intimate contacts with them, through which the borderline between cuddling, sexual games and actual sex can be increasingly easily crossed, particularly now that people's views on sex are much more liberal than in the 1940s and 1950s. This seems to be of particular importance to women; men can always go to prostitutes, while on ordinary working days, even in the city, gigolos are mainly available in four-footed form.

What meadows are for country children, the zoo is for city children: the place where they first see live sex. Masturbating monkeys, stallions on heat, pseudo-copulations, very large or even very small penises are a source of instruction and entertainment. In order to record the reactions of the public, in 1979 a concealed camera was set up in the mandrils' cage at the Burgers Zoo in Arnhem. Reasonably well endowed by the Creator, one of the males aroused the sincere admiration of a women's association standing in front of the cage, until the ape got an erection. Shamefacedly the ladies stared at the monkey and particularly at each other out of the corner of their eye, till an irrepressible giggling gave way to the first remarks. Comparisons with their own husbands were made, the word 'making do', was used, in brief, they enjoyed themselves immensely. Moreover, men do not react very differently. Boys eagerly absorb every detail, old men sitting on benches try to look on like a bridge-keeper at passing ships, but choose their benches suspiciously often in a corner of the zoo where sex is rampant. The zoo is a paradise for voyeurs.

There are some who do not leave it at looking. Besides pickpockets who shout, 'The lion has escaped!' in order to make their escape and suicides who force their way into a lions cage, Heini Hediger, the 'father of zoo biology', includes among the petty criminals in the zoo 'the sexual perverts':

> The least harmful of these are the animal voyeurs, who are drawn by all forms of mating behaviour like a magnet and are among the fixed components of every zoo. Then you have the kind who in remote, dark corners of the zoo are concerned not so much with animals as with women, youngsters or children; then there are people who are obviously sexually aroused by the sight of some animal or other (a snake-necked tortoise, for example), which they subsequently visit remarkably often. The sodomites are extremely unpleasant visitors. In this area, as is well known, the most improbable combinations are possible. In otherwise inexplicable accidents one must always look in this direction, both among visitors and among unidentified and not completely reliable members of staff.

'In general we have more trouble keeping the public out of the cages than keeping the animals in,' is a remarkable pronouncement in this context, coming from a spokesman of the former zoo in Wassenaar. In Amsterdam Zoo, Artis, for example, the trouble concerned, an old man who liked to be licked by the Lüneberger sheep. The director of the zoo in Arnhem, Anton van Hooff, was once addressed by a man in the former chimpanzee house.

> He asked me whether I believed that men were descended from the apes. I said that this seemed to me a rather bold assertion and that to begin with it would be better if we established that we had much in common. Then the man, who had lived for years in Indonesia, became so embarrassing that the mouths of the people around us fell open and I took him to an adjoining room to be able to talk calmly to him. He had a request: could he spend a couple of nights with Sjimmie, a female who was on heat?
>
> I told him that he could also do it during the daytime – it seemed to me that that would be entertaining for the onlookers – but that it wasn't the job of the zoo to collaborate in his experimental approach to the question of what kind of progeny the copulation of a human being with a chimpanzee would produce. All he needed, he insisted, was to have the keys, but I didn't give them to him. Finally he went away.

Joost Veerkamp, *The Uncouth Bear*, 1991

On another occasion Van Hooff was given a monkey by private owners:

> We were glad to have the animal, although it was badly deformed, which gave rise to great concern. Obviously it missed its old owner very badly. It only wanted to eat after a period of fidgeting. It had to have contact, which was very annoying. One day the keeper had tried to get it to eat at about four or four-thirty, with only moderate success. In the evening I went round to see it myself with a tasty morsel. At a certain moment it hung in front of my head, put its hand round it and pushed it approximately in the direction of its penis. I started; suddenly I realized why it had so little appetite.

Besides zoos, city voyeurs can also resort to sex clubs and peep-shows. On payment of an admission fee you can see how a woman copulates with a wide variety of animals. If they are small enough, then they are introduced whole into her. Men's wildest fantasies become reality. In the past of course such things happened mainly in Paris, where according to Von Maschka, one woman was so morally degenerate that she 'allowed herself to be mounted by a trained bulldog before a small paying audience of libertines'. However, in his new standard work on

Devéria, *Woman Mating with Donkey*, illustration from 'Gamiani' by Alfred de Musset, 19th century

French prostitution, the historian Alain Corbin maintains that it was mainly Great Danes and Newfoundland dogs which were popular in the *Maisons de débauche*, where there were also *tableaux vivants* of the raping of nuns and SM equipment was available for giving each other electric shocks. Nowadays people seek their excitement in such cities as Bangkok, where taxi-drivers display openly on their dashboards a 'menu' of a score of sexual specialities, among which there is invariably 'girl with dog'.

Whether this indicates that people are more open about sex with animals there than here remains to be seen; the sex industry derives mainly from poverty and misery. But it is certain that there are cultures where people have fewer problems with bestiality than in ours. Although it is a sick joke to ask what the definition of a virgin is ('a goat that runs faster than an Arab'), there is a grain of truth in it, to the extent that Islam is not as violently opposed to bestiality as is Christianity. Copulation with beasts may be revolting for a follower of the Prophet, writes Vern Bullough in *Sexual Variants*, quoting a connoisseur, but it does not constitute adultery, 'since a human being can have no reason to indulge in carnal intercourse with a beast; someone does that either because he is degenerate or because he has to prevent himself committing a more serious sin.' If someone is caught, the animal has to be destroyed and the owner compensated, unless the animal belongs to an edible species, when it may be eaten. From Algeria Barbara Noske reports that boys still abuse she-asses because dowries are so high there. In the Rif mountains of Morocco the boys have an even greater reason to consort with she-asses: they believe that it gives them a larger penis. Adult men therefore turn a blind eye, but they would not do it themselves, because that would be childish.

Ford and Beach, in their hunt for strange sexual customs, found a number of other peoples where it is not such a scandal if the partner is a quadruped. On the South Sea Island of Kusai men sometimes have sex with cattle, young Masai practise with she-asses and in Fez men have magic rites which enable them 'to deflower twenty-seven cows' in one night. In South and Central America bestiality was so prevalent when the Spaniards arrived that the priests hastily included the sin in the confessional protocol. Of the Indians in North America it is particularly the Hopi who seem to love animals.

This list of facts on the frequency of bestiality can easily be expanded with other peoples, other countries, other periods, other species of animal, but this would do nothing except underline how fragmentary, heterogeneous and indirect those facts are. The amount of bestiality cannot be estimated any more precisely than the impressionistic observation that a few per cent of human beings have at one time had sexual contact with animals. However, that does not make much difference to the question of how normal or abnormal bestiality is. Statistics are not decisive in this matter. After all, something rare may be normal, something generally prevalent abnormal. If one human being out of all the five billion inhabitants of the earth sets foot on the moon, it is said that *mankind* has been to the moon and in our minds we all brush the moon dust off our soles. If eleven Dutchmen – 0.00007 per cent of the population – score one goal more than their opponents, then every Dutchman feels like a champion footballer. But if it emerges that a quarter of Dutch people have at one time been the victims of incest, then we do not feel involved; people who commit incest may live in the Netherlands, but they are not included in Dutch national feeling. For them we have a magic formula for keeping them outside our group: we call them abnormal.

So it is not only a matter of how many people occasionally have sex with an animal, it is a matter of what people who do not, think about people who do. Many of them will still agree with the judgment that Maurice Chideckel made in 1935 on a woman who had trained her dog: 'there can be no doubt that such a woman is abnormal. In every

G. Coco, cartoon from
Is it Bad, Doctor?, 1983

community there are opportunities for normal cohabitation. Any woman, virtuous or lewd, can always find a man for sexual congress however plain she may be.' Until recently this judgment was deeply anchored in laws and commandments; bestiality was castigated from the bench and the pulpit. Our age is more easy-going, but it has another stigma for the zoophile. Instead of bad he is now mad; instead of a villain he is a patient. Judges and priests have been ousted by psychiatrists. If bestiality can be easily traced in earlier centuries on the basis of court records and religious treatises, for the twentieth century you must immerse yourself in a psychiatric literature full of sexual 'perversions', 'variations', 'aberrations', 'paraphilia', 'anomalies' and 'unnatural urges'. Now so many sexual habits have been designated as perverse, that according to the Kinsey Reports two-thirds of Americans have committed them; if you include masturbation, then a full 95 per cent of American males are perverts.

In order to get the perverts out of the dock and confessional and onto their couches, the shrinks went to great lengths to explain their deviant sexual behaviour from other 'mental weaknesses' such as alcoholism, heightened libido, emotional atrophy, priapism or madness. As late as 1968 Grassberger was maintaining without a shadow of doubt that 49 per cent of those who commit abuse of animals are mentally retarded or even imbeciles', in the 19–23 age group no less than 57 per cent. Bestiality seemed to him as a rule to be explicable in terms of an anomaly in one of the following eight areas: 'intensity, tension and direction of the urge, the available and punishable opportunities for satisfaction, the process of motivation, the social adequacy of the value judgements which control it, and the function of the will'. The tone for this annexation of bestiality and other 'deviations' was set by *Psychopathologia Sexualis* by Richard von Krafft-Ebing, Professor of Psychology and Mental Illness in Vienna, which dominated sexology for half a century from 1886. Since people with deviant sexual behaviour are depicted as sick, we are presented with a procession of hunchbacked, morally stunted, gruff imbeciles and passionate consumptives who, on the eve of their death, made love to their wives. Observation 186, on a case of 'impulsive sodomy', is characteristic:

A., aged 16, gardener's assistant, father unknown, mother extremely mentally defective, hystero-epileptic. A. has a deformed, asymmetrical cranium and skull, the skeleton is also small, in his childhood he was addicted to self-abuse, always slow-witted, apathetic, lonely, very irritable, exhibiting a definitely pathological reaction in his sensitivity. He is slow-witted, certainly badly affected by self-abuse and neurasthenic. Moreover, he shows hysteropathological symptoms (limitation of the field of vision, colour blindness, poor sense of smell, taste, hearing on his right side, a disabled right testicle, collarbone, etc.). It was proved that A. partly masturbated and partly sodomized dogs and rabbits. At the age of 12, he saw some boys masturbating a dog. He imitated them and could not refrain subsequently from abusing dogs, cats, rabbits in the most dreadful way. However, he much preferred female rabbits, the only animals which had a real attraction for him. When night fell he usually went to the rabbit hutch to satisfy his dreadful urge. Rabbits were repeatedly found with torn anuses. The bestial acts were always performed in the same way. They were literally attacks, which broke out approximately every 8 weeks and always in the evening in the same way. A. felt very uncomfortable, feeling as though he was being hit on the head with a hammer. He felt he was losing his reason. He fought the compulsion to commit sodomy with rabbits, felt mounting anxieties as he did so, and intensification of the headache until it became unbearable. At the height of the condition the ringing of bells, breaking out into a cold sweat, trembling of the knees, final collapse of resistance and the impulsive execution of the perverse act. As soon as it had happened he was liberated from his fear. The nervous crisis disappeared, he is in control of himself once more, feels burning shame at what has happened and is frightened of the return of such a condition. A. assures me, that if faced with the choice in such a crisis, of using a woman or a rabbit, he could only choose the latter.

It was easily possible to point to the medical epicrisis, that this human monster is a psychic degenerate, with a compulsive illness, not a criminal.

The patient in observation 187 likewise does not give an impression of everyday domesticity:

X., farmer, 40 years of age, Greek Catholic. Father and mother were heavy drinkers. From five years of age the patient had epileptic attacks, i.e. he falls down unconscious, lies motionless for between two and three minutes, then scrambles to his feet and walks off aimlessly with eyes wide open. At the age of seventeen the onset of sexual urges. The patient had no sexual inclination either towards women or towards men, but towards animals (birds, horses, etc.). He mounted cockerels, ducks, later horses, cows. Never masturbation.

The patient is a painter of icons, very narrow-minded. For years has experienced religious madness with ecstatic feelings. He has an 'inexplicable' love for the Virgin Mary, for whom he would like to sacrifice his life. When admitted to the clinic the patient is found to be free of defects and anatomical signs of degeneracy.

Since childhood he has had an aversion to women. Whenever he attempted to have intercourse with a women he was impotent, with animals always very potent. He is very shy with women. Intercourse with them seems almost to be a sin to him.

Nevertheless Krafft-Ebing 'definitely did not' explain all abuse of animals 'on the basis of psycho-pathological conditions'. They could also arise from 'a low sense of morality', or 'a great sexual urge coupled with difficulty in obtaining natural satisfaction'. For example, a thirty-year-old man 'from the upper class', who was caught with a chicken (the chickens in his house were found to be dying one after the other), was discovered to be 'mentally completely normal'. In his defence the man pointed to his 'small genitals, which made intercourse with women impossible'.

While one part of sodomy – homosexuality – has long since ceased to be regarded as an illness by sensible people, bestiality is still fodder for psychiatrists instead of psychologists. In *Between Pets and People* Alan Beck, Director of the Centre for the Interaction of Animals and Society, quotes a psychiatric lecture by 'the famous Doctor John Money':

A female patient consented to be questioned by the class. She complained that she always had a psychosomatic upsurge of stomach gas (burping) when she wished to have sexual intercourse with her husband. She also kept fiddling with the genitalia of babies which she looked after. Almost casually she mentioned that she had had intercourse with the dog of the house. She had been in therapy for years, but had never mentioned this aspect of her difficult life because she thought that the doctors would not understand anything about it anyway.

Under the title 'Motherhood Encumbered by a Nepiophilic/Zoophilic Lovemap', Money himself gave more details. Thoroughly packaged in a psychiatric background – illegitimate child, intolerant foster-parents, more miscarriages than ordinary pregnancies, weak husband, children in therapy – he relates how the woman rubbed her genitals against those of a four-year-old nephew, which she had found 'very pleasurable'. She had herself hit on the idea of substituting dogs for boys: 'We had a dog at home, but it was a female. . . . The first dog I used, was this boy's. . . . I'd go over and take care of his younger sister.' Usually, she recalled, she kept her panties on. Even after she was married, she continued to use dogs. 'And I thought, oh my God, if anybody would catch me, you know, I'd be ruined for life. But the drive is so great to satisfy this need. . . . I would sneak dogs in the house and get them up there some way. It is ridiculous when you think about it – dirty, filthy,

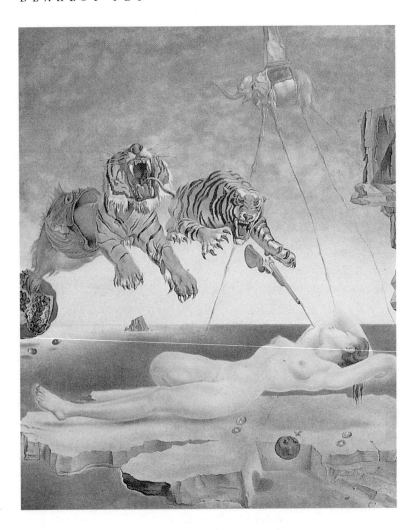

Salvador Dali, *Dream
Caused by the Flight of a
Bee around a
Pomegranate, one Second
before Waking Up,* 1944

germs – but you don't stop to think about it.' Finally, she was helped by
the pill. Obviously the hormones contained in this suppressed the need,
which can only support the notion of a pathological sexual urge.

It is fairly normal for bestiality to be linked to other sexual
'variations', much to the satisfaction of the psychiatrists. A boy who
masturbates a male dog or stallion is basically indulging in a homosexual
activity. Even though he may not experience it as such himself, many
boys have a homosexual preference for animals, if only because they at
least respond with an orgasm. Abusing chickens is by definition
heterosexual, but this automatically involves sadism. In other cases
sadism is primary and bestiality is only involved because an animal is
quite simply an easier victim than a human being. Animal abuse, as
RSPCA inspectors know, is often linked with sexual arousal. Since

animal abuse has been institutionalized in our society in the food industry, it cannot be difficult for such sadists to find satisfaction. Some of them are satisfied in an ordinary slaughterhouse:

> C.L., 42 years of age, engineer. Remembers that in his boyhood he had enjoyed watching the slaughtering of domestic animals, and particularly of pigs. It often gave him a very strong sexual feeling and an ejaculation. Later he sought out slaughterhouses to enjoy watching the spurting blood and the death throes of the animals, which always gave him a mounting feeling of sexual pleasure.

The psychiatric freak show from Vienna also mentions the 'Hendlherr' (the cockerel) whose custom it was to add excitement to intercourse with various prostitutes 'by torturing and killing chickens, pigeons and other birds'. Another gentleman, who made prostitutes buy a chicken or rabbit, 'aimed to cut off the head, tear out the eyes and the intestines. If he found a girl that was prepared to do such a thing and did it in a really cruel way, he became aroused, paid without wanting anything further from the person in question or touching her, and went on his way again.'

A third sexual peculiarity associated with bestiality, mentioned by the great French connoisseur Roland Villeneuve in his 1978 standard work, is fetishism. It is clear that dogs and particularly cats have long since surpassed the lock of hair and lace-up boot in number as fetishes. Anyone reading the terms in which dog and cat lovers sing the praises of their darlings will not have missed the similarities with high-flown love poetry. In *Le Musée de la Bestialité* Villeneuve mentions eleven other causes of bestiality besides fetishism, including frigidity of the human partner, fear of venereal disease, the lasciviousness of animals, fear of pregnancy and alcoholism. Even if he does not hit on the idea that sex with an animal might sometimes simply be pleasant, even if you are not mad, sick or stupid. Consequently it was quite a relief to read in the work of the pet animal experts Beck and Katcher about the man and woman who presented themselves at the emergency department of an animal clinic with their daughter and their Dobermann pinscher. They wanted the animal to be checked for venereal disease. Their daughter had been caught with the dog and they wanted to know whether she might have caught something. Their first resort was not to a psychiatrist, but to a vet, who could reassure them. But by this time we are already in the 1980s, when a sexologist like Haeberle can finally write that, as long as the animal is not hurt or ill treated, there is actually no need to intervene, and that it is 'not sensible' to 'psychiatrize' sexual acts between human beings and animals. But even he has reservations: 'men and women who always prefer animals to a human partner can be characterized as sexually disturbed. As in other cases of problematic sexual behaviour all one can do here is to advise them to call in the help of experts.' It is an echo of Freud's diagnosis: 'We regard exclusivity and fixation, or

Cover illustration:
Giovanni Lanfranco,
*Naked Boy on his Bed
with a Cat, c.* 1620

perversion as the principal reason for characterizing it as a symptom of illness.' It is claimed, therefore, that bestiality is a pathological deviation if it is compulsive. But in that case ordinary, heterosexual love is the same; as an ordinary heterosexual you will also simply be forced by your urges to poke your nose in places where in other cases you would scarcely have dared point. In fact, as long as none of those involved suffers pain, no form of sex should be seen as pathological, bad or mad.

Nevertheless bestiality is still a taboo, hidden away in stables and bedrooms, specialist literature and pornography, sniggers and imprecations. As long as that is the case, its prevalence is difficult to estimate. Comparison with incest presents itself. In the last few years it has emerged that the number of cases of child sex abuse by parents was much higher than one had ever thought. The reason for the turnaround was that children, having overcome the initial shame with the greatest difficulty, started talking. The more frankly they spoke, the freer the remaining silent witnesses felt to pour out their hearts. But animals cannot talk. In that respect, they are as ideal keepers of a secret as a lace-up boot or a pornographic book.

Earlier in this chapter I estimated the percentage of human beings that have sexual experiences with animals at a few per cent. If you include in bestiality only people who have sex *exclusively* with animals, then the percentage of course falls far below 1 per cent. Bestiality requires imagination and people with imagination usually have no flies on them. On the other hand, if you drop the requirement that for sexual contact something has to be inserted somewhere and that something has to be fiddled with, and it is sufficient simply to cuddle, to derive a warm feeling from each other, to kiss perhaps at times, in brief to love, then bestiality is not a deviation but the general rule, not even something shameful, but the *done thing*. After all, who does not wish to be called an animal lover?

9

A Joy For Ever

'Are you still working on that book on bestiality?' Ivo de Wijs asked me when I was still working on it. I said I was. 'Have you ever', he continued, 'thought about the expression "dog-fancier"?' A dirty mind is a joy for ever. The mind is the best sexual organ. 'If one could be condemned for one's dreams,' the expert psychiatric witness, Dr Droogleever Fortuyn, testified on behalf of Van het Reve, at the first donkey trial, 'we would all wind up behind bars.' More bestiality takes place in our heads than in any hand or vagina. In porno photos one can see a good reason for this: the girl's back still bears the scratches from the previous session, in the corner a lamp which has been knocked over also testifies to the practical problems attached to transgressing species boundaries. Putting into practice arousing thoughts can be so disillusioning that they are best left as fantasies. It is the thought that arouses; the deed can at most fan the flames in the mind. In *My Secret Garden* Nancy Friday, a wholesaler in other people's sexual fantasies, extols the imagination:

> I don't think there are many women who have actually been fucked by a bull or a donkey.... With barnyard studs, imagined or not, it's all about the visible turn-on of the prick, the incredible size of it more than anything. Imagine something *that* big – which you reacted to with such fascination, at least the first time you saw it, even if you almost immediately glanced away with embarrassment – imagine that penetrating you! How can a woman look at a prick that big and not imagine it going into her? It's like looking at a racing car and ignoring the thrill of speed.

The imagination likes having a starting point in reality, but there has to be enough left to fantasize about. This is why of all the daydreams in Nancy Friday's books those of Dawn are the richest:

King Kong with Fay Wray at the Top of the Empire State Building, drawing from the 'Press Book' of the film of 1933

151

Once when I was about fifteen, I went downstairs in the morning to get breakfast completely naked. It was summer and my parents were out, and it just felt good to walk around that big empty house naked. The dog was in the kitchen and he woke up and began to bark, then he started to nuzzle up and sniff me (he was only a young dog, not very well trained and a bit stupid). I suddenly realized the dog had this huge hard-on, and he kept trying to climb up me. I think I was fascinated and I kept stroking him. Half of me wanted to let him – let him do what? At that age I didn't really know what he'd do – and the other half was ashamed. But God, it was a strong impulse, to close my eyes and let his nose go where it would. I have always wondered what it would have been like if I hadn't got on with my breakfast. I've elaborated the picture a thousand different ways, complete with the dog's prick inside me, and my family walking in on the scene.... You name it.

Fantasy needs very little to fuel it, as was apparent in Basle Zoo, where the gorilla Achilles longed for the companionship of the new lady keeper in the adjacent bird house. In order to get her into the cage, he came up with a trick which was new to her. He pretended that his arm had got caught in the wire mesh, she came to help him, the door slammed shut, the key was left lying outside the cage and the zoo was closed; no one could help the young woman. She was not found until the following morning, drenched with sweat and dishevelled, after a whole night in the strong, persistent arms of the ape. The press was excited. Huge headlines told the story of the beautiful girl with the hairy monster. Men read the paper with more excitement than usual, women experienced a *frisson* at the news. A year-and-a-half later Achilles turned out to be a female.

Sensationalism is found not only in the sensational press. For a serious article on the trade in animals 'our correspondent Cas de Stoppelaar' in the quality newspaper NRC *Handelsblad* needed only a few facts to set his imagination racing:

A few years ago in Amstelveen an orang-utan which was no longer able to contain its sexual desires within the bounds of modesty, leapt on a little girl, breaking her back. The girl, whose father kept two of these apes in a cage in the garden as pets, was in the habit of taking them food every morning. But one fateful day in spring the call of the jungle proved too strong for the male orang.

In contrast to news-gathering, bestial acts belong largely to the realm of the imagination. In that realm art reigns supreme. As long as there have been desires, however strange or distasteful, there have been artists ready to represent them in word and image. Bestiality is no exception to this. Time and time again the unspeakable has turned out to be perfectly well depictable and describable. Down the centuries people have enjoyed scenes of bestiality depicted with great beauty, which in reality

would have inspired nothing but revulsion. Depictions of Leda and the Swan, Europa chastely lying on the back of her bull and the Holy Ghost fertilizing the Virgin Mary decorated bourgeois homes in paintings, on candelabra and as salt-and-pepper sets. In town squares and on street corners the bronze statesmen and generals, instead of mounting their wives, sat astride their bronze steeds. Our age has its own myths, from Goldilocks and the Three Bears, to creatures from outer space who carry off our women to more fertile planets. And anyone wanting to give their fantasy free rein can go to the porno shop, where books and films with very explicit pictures of *Animal Sex* are piled high between the stacks of *Rubber Sex*, *Bondage*, *Bizarre* and other 'specialities'.

After Nicolas Poussin, *Leda*

Like every product of the human mind, pornography is also art, albeit art which needs to meet only one condition: that it should titillate the senses in some way or other. One reads pornography with one hand, literature mostly with two hands. Bestiality is not bound to one such genre. The hotchpotch of pornography, literature, farce and drama which bestiality can lead to can be seen in *O de mer* by Maurice Rheims, in which Barbara, an octopus, falls in love with the Breton fisherman Jean-Marie:

Katsushika Hokusai,
*The Dream of the
Fisherman's Wife*,
illustration from
'Kinoe-no-Komatsu',
c. 1814

'Do you care for me a little?' whispered Barbara and put a tentacle around the neck of Jean-Marie (it no longer alarmed him as much), who found it quite pleasant with his shirt off, next to her damp, cool body (the nights are warm in July).

With the nets drawn up, they remained lying on the deck like that for hours. Jean-Marie looked in fascination at Barbara's body, which in the light of the full moon was seen at its best: now shining opal, now pink topaz.

The seaman introduces Barbara to his wife, but that does not prevent him being spoiled in the 'damp, soothing bed' of tentacles, until his wife presents the octopus with a set of bagpipes. Barbara immediately falls in love. The jealous seaman takes to drink and finally throws himself into the sea to see how 'that ridiculous leather bag with its belly next to Barbara plays the passionate octopus'.

One gets the impression that everything is possible with bestiality in art, but that is not the case. Even though you turn the world on its head, there are still rules, except that top is now bottom and bottom now top. *O de Mer* offends against the rule that in art bestiality is committed by the woman. Compared with reality, in which it is virtually always men who

154

actually copulate with animals, in art the roles are completely reversed. Since most artists over the centuries have been men, the reason for this role-reversal is obvious: because it corresponds with male fantasies. It seems very unselfish that the man should not assign himself a role in his own fantasies, but that is only apparent. As always a man identifies with the active party: the animal. He is the stallion, the dog, the bull, the lusty monster with its outsized organ which pumps the most insatiable women full of sperm. His fantasy is destroyed by the woman as beast. This is why *King Kong* was a box-office success and *Queen Kong* was not, this is why everyone knows the frog which one has only to kiss to turn it into a prince, and no one knows the mole in *Le roi des taupes* by Alexandre Dumas, which is actually a princess. Of course, women also have sexual fantasies, but in them – *pace* Nancy Friday – animals do not feature very prominently: only 1 per cent of the women in the Kinsey Report had passionate animal dreams. Since women dream principally about themselves, the benefit to them is not nearly as great as for a man; they do not usually share his obsession with dimensions.

The fact that the man identifies with the animal is best illustrated by all those myths and stories in which a man actually turns into an animal. Lucius Apuleius wrote the oldest Latin novel on the subject that we know in full: *The Golden Ass*. The ass in question is actually a young Roman, who had wanted to become a bird, but used the wrong magic potion:

> No little feathers appeared and no signs of wings. All that happened was that the hair grew coarser and coarser and the skin toughened into hide. Next my fingers bunched together into a hard lump so that my hands became hooves, the same change came over my feet and I felt a long tail sprouting from the base of my spine. Then my face swelled, my mouth widened, my nostrils dilated, my lips hung flabbily down, and my ears shot up long and hairy. The only consoling part of this miserable transformation was the enormous increase in the size of a certain organ of mine.

In the course of his adventures Lucius more or less reconciles himself to his fate and in the service of a master begins performing for human audiences:

> Among these visitors was a rich noblewoman. My various tricks enchanted her and at last she conceived the odd desire of getting to know me intimately. In fact she grew so passionately fond of me that, like Pasiphae in the legend, who fell in love with a bull, she bribed my trainer with a large sum of money to let her spend a night in my company. I am sorry to record that the rascal agreed with no thought for anything but his own pocket. When I had dined with Thyasus and come back to my stable, I found the noblewoman waiting for me. She had been there some time already. Heavens, what magnificent preparations she had made for her love-affair! ... Taking everything off, even

to the gauze scarf tied across her beautiful breasts, she stood close to the lamp and rubbed her body all over with oil of balsam from a pewter pot. She then did the same to mine, most generously, but concentrating mostly on my nose. After this she gave me a lingering kiss ... Then she took me by my head band and had no difficulty in making me lie down on the bed, reclining on one elbow, because that was one of the tricks I had learned, and she evidently was not expecting me to do anything that I had not done before. . . . All the same I was worried, very worried indeed, at the thought of sleeping with so lovely a woman: my great hairy legs and hard hooves pressed against her milk-and-honey skin – her dewy red lips kissed by my huge mouth with its ugly great teeth. Worst of all, how could any woman alive, though exuding lust from her very fingernails, accept the formidable challenge of my thighs? ... But her burning eyes devoured mine, as she cooed sweetly at me between kisses and finally gasped: 'Ah, ah, I have you safe now, my little dove, my little birdy.' Then I realized how foolish my fears had been. She pressed me closer and closer to her and met my challenge to the full. I tried to back away, but she resisted every attempt to spare her, twining her arms tight around my back, until I wondered whether after all I was capable of serving her as she wished. I began to appreciate the story of Pasiphae: if she was anything like this woman she had every reason to fix her affections on the bull who fathered the Minotaur on her. My new mistress did not allow me to sleep a wink that night, but as soon as the embarrassing daylight crept into the room she crept out, first pleading with my keeper to let her spend another night with me for the same fee.

As a donkey Lucius turns out to be such an erotic success that his trainer wants to have him perform as a lover in public. The lady is too respectable for this, so a criminal from prison is recruited, who after mating with the donkey will be devoured by wild beasts. Fearful that the wild animals will not be able to distinguish a condemned woman from an innocent donkey, Lucius runs away during the introductory programme, which consists of a dancing Chorus and an Arcadian-style beauty contest.

Apuleius wrote his book eighteen centuries ago and his stories are probably based on even older versions. But there is nothing new under the sun. The account in *Steps* by Jerzy Kosinkski of a visit to an unspecified carriage house has more than one parallel with the novel from antiquity:

A man dressed in city clothes came out of the carriage house and began collecting money from all of us.... A few minutes passed; the door of the carriage house was opened and four women in colourful dresses walked into the circle. The organizer followed behind them leading a large animal.... The farmers began discussing the women aloud, arguing excitedly. After a few minutes the organizer asked for quiet and explained that a vote would be taken to determine which woman would be chosen.... From the last count it became clear that the majority had elected the young girl.... The organizer led the animal into the centre of the arena, prodding its slack parts with a

E. Tapissier, *Titania and her Ass*

stick. Two peasants ran up and grabbed at the animal to keep it still. The girl then stepped forward and began playing with the creature, embracing and hugging it, fondling its genitals. She slowly began undress....

The men became frantic, urging her on to undress completely and couple with the animal. The organizer tied several ribbons on the animal's organ, each coloured bow an inch apart. The girl approached the animal, rubbing oil into her thighs and on her abdomen, and coaxing the animal to lick her body. Then, to shouts of encouragement, she lay down beneath the animal,

Johann Füssli, *Titania Caresses Bottom with the Ass's Head*, illustration for Shakespeare's 'Midsummer Night's Dream', 18th century

clasping it with her legs. Raising up her belly and thrusting it forward, she forced an insertion up to the first bow. The organizer took control again and asked the audience to pay extra for each additional inch of the animal's involvement. The price was raised for each consecutive bow removed. The peasants, still refusing to believe that the girl could survive her violation, eagerly paid again and again.

A porno version (*Spectator Sport*) of the girl-with-the-donkey takes place in Cuba before the days of Castro ('*Before the revolution down there,*

Cuba was really the place to go'). After the performance ('when the donkey came finally he must have shot half-a-gallon of juice up her alley – it came oozing back out all around her ass and dripped down the backs of her legs'), the spectator takes up with a girl who had only performed few times with a donkey and therefore is still able to give him a good, 'tight screw'. But 'give her another year or two in Havana brothels, fucking donkeys and every other damn thing that came along to fuck, and that little cunt of hers would look like the Grand Canyon.' She was not given the time. Castro came and closed down all the brothels. 'That must have been quite a blow to all those poor girls, having to go out and work. But the one I really feel sorry for is that donkey. No more screwing pretty pink pussies for him. He must've wondered what he did wrong.'

In these last two stories a third figure has slipped in to join the woman and the animal: the man, in these cases as a spectator. But the male reader still does not identify with him; the man in the story is at most an intermediary. He serves to underline the exceptional gifts of the animal (with which the reader does identify). A classic example is the story from the *One Thousand and One Nights*.

I ... came to a door, from behind which I heard could hear a storm of laughter and grunting. Putting my eye to the crack by which the light was admitted into the corridor, I saw embraced upon a couch, rolling in every lascivious contortion, the girl I had been following and an enormous ape with an almost human face. After a moment or so, the girl disengaged herself and, standing upright, took off all her clothes; then she stretched herself again upon the couch, and the ape threw itself upon her nakedness, clasping her in his arms and covering her. When he had done his act, he rose and rested for an instant; then he took her again and covered her. He rose again, rested again, only to hurl himself upon her a third time; and this continued until he had given ten assaults, while she had answered him as finely and delicately as if he had been a man. . . .

Ouchine, *Girl with Ape Lover*, illustration for the 'Arabian Nights'

Later the girl tells him:

'I am the only daughter of the wāzir. Until the age of fifteen I lived quietly in my father's palace; but one day a black slave taught me that which I had to learn and took from me that which I had to give. Perhaps you know that there is nothing like a negro for inflaming the insides of us women, especially when the assuaging of this black dung is the first the garden feels. If so, you will not be surprised to hear that my garden became so famished that it needed the negro to give it a dressing every hour.

After some time the negro died at his work, and I told my misfortune to an old woman of the palace, who had known me from infancy. She shook her head, saying: "The only thing which can replace a negro is an ape, my daughter. Apes are most marvellous in this act."

'I allowed myself to be persuaded by the old woman, and one day, seeing the master of certain performing apes pass by the palace windows with his troupe, I quickly uncovered my face before the largest of them, which happened to be looking in my direction. At once the animal broke its chain and, before its master could stop it, fled by side streets, made a great circle through the gardens, and came back to the palace. There it ran straight to my chamber and, taking me in its arms, did that which it did ten times without stopping.'

The voyeur, a butcher who had always sold the girl 'ram's eggs' kills the ape and offers to take its place, but this is a failure; lying next to her insatiable body all he can hope for is a *deus ex machina*, in the form of a miraculous potion. Baron Alcide from *Gamiani* by Alfred de Musset is also forced to acknowledge the animal as his superior when he can no longer bring his passionate Countess Gamiani to a climax and she resorts to an enormous dog: 'Medor! Medor! Take me! take ...!'

In fact the jealous man as the third figure is such an effective stylistic device for underlining the love between woman and animal that in my opinion the story could even be more subtle. This, of course, requires a cat in the leading role:

Tonight it would be different, thought Ernst. This time he must succeed. He drew Annabeth more tightly to him as the orchestra struck up the last dance. What music! What a woman! Her eyes were full of promise, and he accepted the promise eagerly.

He drove her home. He had never got this far. Once they arrived at her door, she asked without much further ado whether he wanted a cup of coffee. Well, he wouldn't say no.

While Annabeth actually went to put some coffee on, Ernst took in the interior. A real flat for a woman living alone. A flowered three-piece suite, lots of knick-knacks and as the *pièce de résistance*, a splendid cat. A Burmese, Annabeth had once told him, which would already have won many prizes if it were not a little cross-eyed. The cat lay in front of the central heating gently purring.

Along with the coffee went a cognac, and of course, one is never enough. One thing led to another and before he realized how he had managed it, Ernst was under the covers with Annabeth. She ran her fingers through his hair and cooed encouragingly. Ernst cooed back and was just about to start on the main course, when his hand got a shock. Where he had expected soft, naked woman's skin he suddenly found a great deal of hair.

Unnoticed amid all the activity the Burmese cat had pushed its way between Ernst and Annabeth and nothing indicated that he intended to leave. So let's go on caressing over the top of pussy, thought Ernst, but the animal would not have it. 'Who's a good pussums?' said Annabeth and with a well-aimed stroke put it back into purring mode. 'Yes, of course you can sleep with Mumsy.'

As well as he could, Ernst resumed his lovemaking. Stroking Annabeth and the Burmese in turn, he gradually worked the cat down to the foot end of the bed. Thoroughly aroused by now, Ernst had a towering erection. The Burmese had never seen such a sight. For a moment Ernst thought it was admiration with which the animal was looking on, but it turned out to be mostly astonishment. The Burmese came closer at its leisure and sat next to them comfortably in the teapot position. With its head cocked to one side it surveyed the phenomenon from top to bottom with its cross-eyed gaze. Once convinced that the toothless monster could not do much harm, the Burmese hesitantly extended its right paw and tapped, with its nails drawn in, playfully, against the swollen head of the penis. It bounced back amusingly. Now the left paw. The cat had to be quick, because its plaything shrank at the speed of light. It was just about to examine where it had got to, when it was seized roughly by the scruff of the neck and put outside the door.

Ernst had no sooner got back into bed than a plaintive meowing started up, accompanied by exasperating scratching.

'How could you do that?' said Annabeth reproachfully and opened the door for the Burmese, who resumed his place purring. 'Come on, sweetums.'

Ernst took his defeat like a man, tucked the meagre remnants back into his new briefs and left the flat fuming. He himself had never seen the funny side of it but it gave his psychiatrist many a good laugh.

Bestiality needs no alibi to be literature. It is a form of impossible love and that is what all literature revolves around. Romeo and Juliet or man and ape, mother and son or mother and dog, the medieval mystic Hadewijch and her Heavenly Bridegroom or Van Het Reve with his donkey – it is the never-ending song of unfulfilled desire. The literary heart of every love story is the tension between two opposite poles which attract and repel each other at the same time. In novels on the classical opposite poles of men and women a great effort is usually made to stress the differences: his firm, hairy chest contrasts with her creamy white bosom, her shy look with his piercing gaze. From there it is only a short step to transforming the man into a real bear, ape or wolf. So with the minimum of effort love becomes even more impossible, desire even more unfulfilled, tension even greater. It is the eternal theme of *La Belle et la Bête*, *Beauty and the Beast*, *The Girl and the Monster*. Beneath the repulsive exterior of the Monster, the Girl, who is herself, of course, ravishingly beautiful, soon discovers the tender lover, to whom she surrenders full of passion, although she, like the reader, knows from the outset that no good can come of it. Impossible loves, at least in literature, are required to end badly. Sooner or later the Monster can no longer suppress the beast that lurks within him and kills her, or someone else, or otherwise the outside world discovers it because their cattle are being gorily slaughtered. Only sorcery can then rescue love, and that consequently intervenes in the fairy-tale version of *La Belle et la Bête*, splendidly filmed in 1946 by Jean Cocteau. In order to rescue her father, La Belle in the film goes to live in the castle of La Bête. When the love that blossoms between them threatens to become all too impossible, La Bête changes into the handsome Jean Marais and the fairy tale that is beginning for them is over for us.

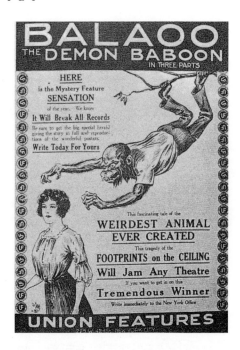

Left: *La Belle et la Bête*, illustration from a book by Madame Leprince de Beaumont, *c.* 1811
Right: *Balaoo the Demon Baboon*, the first full-length feature film on an anthropoid ape, 1913

Although the film industry has milked the theme for all it is worth, even in Cocteau's day the Girl and the Monster had already found their definitive form on the silver screen in 1933, in the form of Fay Wray and King Kong. The slim, lily-white Fay Wray from New York high society encounters her huge, dark-haired monster in the primitive setting of Death's Head Island. She is there with a film crew, he spends most of his time terrorizing the natives. The latter sacrifice Fay to Kong, but he develops a great affection for her. In order to convince us of his extraordinary strength, King Kong spars with a number of dinosaurs before being laid low by human technology and taken off to New York. Here, shackled to a cross, he is put on public display. But as soon as he sees Fay Wray he breaks his chains, and pursues his sweetheart. Crushing half of New York underfoot, he manages to find her in an apartment. The police, fire brigade and army are all in pursuit of King Kong. In an apocalyptic final scene a swarm of biplanes shoot the monster off the top of the Empire State Building. By that time, however, no one in the cinema still sees him as a monster. 'The airplanes got it,' says a policeman on the screen. 'Oh no,' says the man next to him, 'it wasn't the airplanes ... it was beauty that killed the beast.'

The success of King Kong rests in its ambiguity. He both terrifies and touches in turn, he evokes both a father figure and maternal feelings. This reflects his origin. For the brutal side of King Kong the film-maker Merian C. Cooper took his inspiration from the *Murders in the Rue Morgue* by Edgar Allan Poe, for the tender side from Jonathan Swift's *Gulliver's*

Grandville, *Giant Ape Cuddling Gulliver*, illustration for 'Gulliver's Travels' by Jonathan Swift, *c*. 1850

Travels. In the land of the giants, Gulliver is shut up in a huge doll's house, but the pet ape of the giants, itself gigantic, takes him out and cuddles him: 'He took me up in his right fore-foot, and held me as a Nurse doth a child she is going to suckle; just as I had seen the same Sort of Creature do with a Kitten in Europe.' Startled by a noise, the ape, still clutching Gulliver, flees up onto the roof tops followed by a hostile mob, just like the one that pursues King Kong onto his skyscraper. This ape, too, pays with its life for abducting a human being.

As well as to his intellectual father Poe and his intellectual 'mother' Swift, Cooper's King Kong is much indebted to the prudishness of the censors. The latter removed the most erotic scene, in which King Kong slowly peels the clothes off the body of Fay Wray and then sniffs the feminine perfumes on his finger, from most versions of the film, which relies not on open sex, but precisely on symbols and allusions. Fantasy exists to titillate, not to arouse crudely.

After *King Kong* of course there followed the film *Son of Kong*, but the only descendant who can equal the King himself is Morgan from Karel Reisz's gem, *Morgan – a Suitable Case for Treatment* (1966). Morgan is a rather confused artist, fond of flowers, children and Karl Marx, but particularly of gorillas. When he makes love with his wife – Vanessa Redgrave – in his mind he beats triumphantly on his gorilla's chest like King Kong. But his wife wants to be rid of him in order to marry a rich art dealer. 'If I'd been planted in the womb of a chimpanzee,' says Morgan, 'none of this would have happened.' At the wedding he bursts in through a window dressed in a gorilla suit. The celebration is ruined, the suit catches fire, Morgan rides into the Thames on his motorbike as a burning gorilla. In the final shot we see Morgan as a gardener in a lunatic asylum, banished from society for an offence for which he can never atone: trying to turn his fantasies into reality. This you must not do. There is already enough reality.

Literature appears to impress on one, certainly where bestiality is concerned, that one must leave things in the realm of fantasy. Even Juliette, in De Sade's book of the same name, complains that the withdrawal of the dog who had mounted her causes 'terrible pain'. And the pornographer Herb Bennett describes what happens when the swelling refuses to subside even after a quarter of an hour, so that woman and dog threaten to be coupled permanently:

> Bozo wasn't too delighted about things either. He tried to pull back and get free and it hurt like hell when he did. It felt like a barbed fishhook up inside me, tearing at my guts. . . . I guess it was the first time it had ever happened to Bozo too. . . . Every now and then he'd start thrashing around in a new try at breaking loose, and every time he did it my cunt was getting rawer and rawer inside from all that chafing. And then, as if that wasn't bad enough, after a while he started getting horny again and wanting to *fuck* some more, of all things! All of a sudden he began a whole new humping sequence and I thought I was getting my cunt reamed with a barbed wire dildo. Wow! And that miserable beast just kept on fucking me and fucking me – I thought he'd never quit. . . . I didn't have the faintest idea what to do about it. Go to the telephone? Who would I call? Imagine trying to explain a predicament like that to anyone!

The epic poem *Roan Stallion* by Robinson Jeffers is more elevated in tone, but the message comes across even more urgently. The poem's protagonist is a woman who seeks greater satisfaction than her lifeless marriage with her dull husband can give her. She falls in love with a splendid stallion. This gives her both sexual and religious and mystical experiences, but when the stallion kills her husband, the woman nevertheless chooses her own kind. However close to God she may feel when the stallion is inside her, for him, she realizes, it is merely horseplay. She kills the horse.

Even the most innocent form of disloyalty to one's own species is forbidden, as witness the charming song *Brave Margot* by Georges Brassens:

Margoton la jeune bergère
Trouvant dans l'herbe un petit chat
Qui venait de perdre sa mère
L'adopta
Elle entrouvre sa collerette
Et le couche contre son sein
C'était tout c'quelle avait pauvrette
Comm' coussin
Le chat prenant pour sa mère
Se mit à téter tout de go
Emue, Margot le laissa faire
Brav' Margot
Un croquant passant à la ronde
Trouvant le tableau peu commun
S'en alla le dire à tout l' monde
Et le lendemain

(Refrain)
Quand Margot dégrafait son corsage
Pour donner la gougoutte à son chat
Tous les gars, tous les gars du village

Gustave Doré, *Little
Red Riding Hood and the
Wolf*, illustration for
'Perrault's Fairy
Tales', *c*. 1862

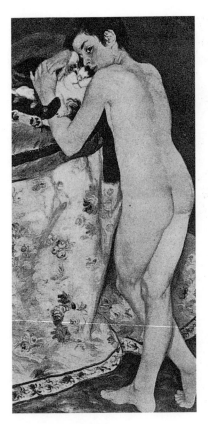

Jean Renoir, *Boy with Cat*, c. 1868

Etaient là, la la la la la la
Etaient là, la la la la la
Et Margot qu'était simple et très sage
Présumait qu' c'était pour voir son chat
Qu' tous les gars, tous les gars du village
Etaient là, la la la la la la
Etaient là, la la la la la.

Mais les autr's femme de la commune,
Privées d' leurs époux, d' leur galants,
Accumulèrent la rancune,
Patiemment.
Puis un jour ivres de colère,
Elles s'armèrent de bâtons
Et farouch's elles immolèrent
Le chaton.
La bergère après bien des larmes
Pour s' consoler prit un mari
Et ne dévoila plus ses charmes
Que pour lui.
Le temps passa sur les mémoires,
On oublia l'évènement.
Seuls des vieux racontent encore
A leur p'tits enfants:

(Refrain)

In Ernst van Altena's charming adaptation this becomes:

Margot, who was a shepherdess
Beside the broad footpath one day found
A shivering kitten on the ground.
She quickly opened up her blouse
And bared her lovely, snow-white skin
For the cold pussy to snuggle in.
In the blouse the kitten sought
A certain place on Margot's breast:
'You're thirsty, puss, I might have guessed.'

(Refrain)
When Margot unbuttoned her blouse once more
Because the kitten was hungry again,
Townsfolk and farmers flocked by the score
Oh la la la la la la la la, oh la la la la la la la.
But Margot still was very green
and thought it was the little cat
That was the reason for the scene.
Oh la la la la la la la la la, oh la la la la la la la la.
. . .
But while the men enjoyed themselves
The women almost choked with rage

And plotted how to clear the stage.
Cursing, screaming, bleating and jeering,
Swinging their sticks like mowing hay
They chased the poor meowing cat away.
Margot then, to dry her tears,
Took a husband of her own
And henceforth stripped for him alone.

(Refrain)

Of course, literature and the other arts do not concentrate exclusively on women as sexual partners for animals. The roles are so consistently reversed that in addition to many women there are also a few men who mate with animals. But it is seldom represented in such a way that it gives one as a reader or onlooker the urge to have a go oneself. Almost all examples in literature are childhood memories. As a child the writer becomes acquainted with sex through an animal, either personally, or because he sees his father or uncle on the job in the stall. In this way the animal functions as a metaphor for the disgust which the first acquaintance with all those slimy organs can inspire in a young boy. In the Dutch novel *A Golden Child* by Jean-Paul Franssens the uncle is called Jelle.

Uncle Jelle comes into the pigsty. He has his overalls on, surely that isn't right on Sunday? Didn't he have to go to church with us?

He doesn't know that I am lying up there among his apples I keep quiet because it is forbidden to go up into the apple loft.

Uncle Jelle slaps the pig's rump. It grunts with pleasure with all that shuffling around it. The piglets jostle each other to get to the fat, swollen teats, making lip-smacking and squeaking noises. Uncle Jelle keeps slapping the rump and opens the flies of his wide overall trousers. I've never seen such a big one. Actually I don't dare to look any more. But I do.

The pig grunts. Dust, gnats and cobwebs and an uncle who is standing there jerking off. When he comes he almost topples over backwards and looks up. I duck back from the crack just too late. He has spotted me. He's already coming up the steps.

'What did you see?' he asks.

'Nothing at all,' I say. 'I really didn't see anything, Uncle Jelle.' ...

'You did see. Lying is a very great sin. What you saw is also very sinful. You must never tell anyone. Anyone. Not even your mother. Do you hear that? Never. When you see something that you mustn't see, which is not intended for you, God will punish you for all eternity. It isn't right for us to see things through a crack in the loft which we should never, ever see. Do you hear me? Perhaps they do that in town.'

The writer Jan Wolkers has of course written about his own adolescent sexual experiences with animals ('then I took a firm hold of the chicken by its head and feet and impaled it on me'). Here too that is accompanied by a feeling of guilt ('the curtains of my parents' bedroom were still closed. I quickly ran behind the barn'). And if it wasn't a sin and you were not punished for it, it drove you mad, like the son of old Gilenson, in the novel *The Indolent Kings* by Hugo Raes:

> Gilenson Jr., Gerard, always took a matchbox with him when he went for a bath. In the matchbox was a fly. . . . Once in the bath he got an erection. As he lay there he adjusted the water level and the slope of his body. He is sixteen, has unsightly spots on his face, but they will disappear by themselves. He adjusted the level of the water and the angle of his soft body, so that there was only a small island left somewhere in the middle. Then he took the fly, pulled off its wings. . . . And put the insect in the water near the red island. It struggled till it was able to drag itself ashore and began crawling around like mad. . . . There followed a number of quite ecstatic moments, a second of eternity, of self-forgetfulness. Then he squashed the fly between his thumb and forefinger, but not completely flat. This took a long time, this was the finishing touch. Then he let the bath empty. He was taken to an institution outside the city, which housed mad children and young people with dangerous perversions.

From time immemorial men have had a reasonably effective antidote to hand for a sense of guilt in the sexual area: humour, from blue jokes to light-hearted poetry. As well as Hans Dorrestijn, author of the wonderful opening line: 'I had to give a French kiss to a sheep,' Lévi Weemoedt excels in the genre:

> I'd long dreamt of Tyrol, full of jollity:
> Lusty folk in a state of undress.
> Blonde women consumed by frivolity.
> Men rutting all day. No distress.

> From the bus I randily peered
> As in many nocturnal hours
> I'd devoured those films.
> The tall summits reared:
> but *where were the nudes midst the flowers?!*

> Ah, a bright Alpine meadow! Time for the show!
> I yodeled, let leather shorts glide
> Off, pants and glasses sailed way down below:
> *There the first naked girls I espied!*

> Oh, that night brought us memories galore!
> One girl cried: '*Moo-oo!*' Did she want still *more?*

10

Going to Bed with the Cat

A woman is petting her beloved. Her soft fingers fondle and caress the space between his shoulder blades from the front of his neck to the dimple in his back. Whenever he sighs softly, she whispers an endearment. When his tongue touches her neck, the caresses extend over his whole eager body, along his sides to his belly, over his buttocks, up his thighs, until he has been touched everywhere, except for that one spot between his back legs.

'Oh, Caesar,' says the woman, looking him straight in the eyes, 'how I love you.' Then she lays her head next to his. They adjust their breathing to each other. They both feel languorous and contented.

The astonishing thing about the scene just depicted is its ordinariness. It is perfectly normal to express your love to an animal bought especially for the purpose. When you see someone making love nowadays, then the odds are ten to one on that it will be with their pet. The average Dutchman is caressed less than his dog, in a quarter of households people take their dog or cat to bed with them. On the pillow, at the foot of the bed or even between the sheets the animal consoles the single person or gets in the way of the sex life of the married couple.

In no other place or time has our love been poured in such streams into alien vessels. While old people grow lonely and young people rush from one relationship into another, the love which they are denied is poured over animals in buckets. People are as flattering about animals as they are damning about human beings. In an opinion poll no less than 80 per cent of cat owners and 84 per cent of dog owners were shown to be 'completely satisfied' with their pets. Moreover, 29 per cent of the dogs and 16 per cent of the cats turned out to be over ten years old. This means that old animals are not abandoned, that human beings remain loyal to their pets until death do them part. This contrasts starkly with human loyalty to other humans: one in three marriages ends in divorce. If as

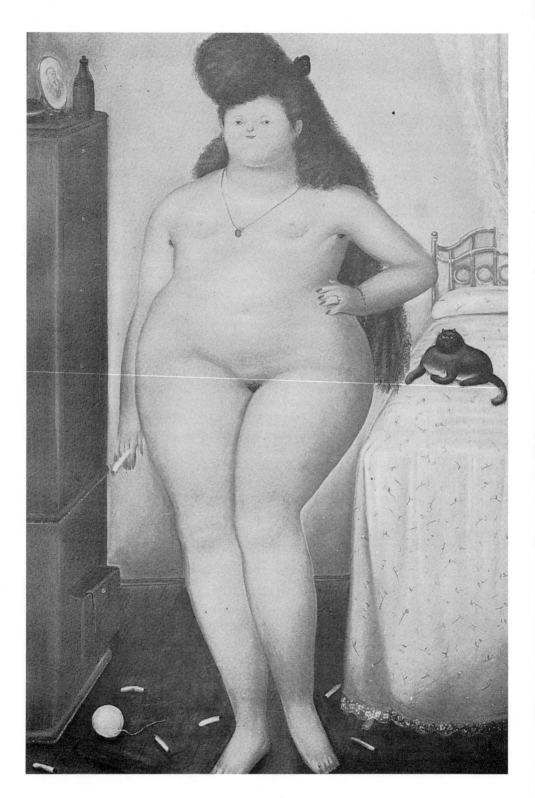

many dogs were rejected as spouses, there would not be a free tree left in our public parks. In practice it is actually after the spouse has been rejected that a tug-of-love over the dog begins. Although the dog is legally part of the goods and chattels, courts in their judgments often treat it as a member of the family. For example, like so many divorced men, Ben Miller now picks up his Bruce, aged five, every Friday evening from his ex-wife in the suburbs of New York and returns the collie on Sunday. With his visiting rights he is much better off than the man who misses his dog, which was awarded to his wife, so badly that he sleeps with postcards in his bed. He then sends these to his dog, so that it can at least sniff the smell of his ex-master and not forget him. The author Blake Green had the court state in writing that she 'was in the best position to care for the aforementioned dog and that the wife is therefore awarded custody of the dog, with reasonable visiting rights for the spouse'. 'We assure each other that Christo is much better off than if we had stayed together and battled it out. We are both determined that he suffer no adverse effects from being the product of a broken home. We don't tell him ugly tales about each other, or attempt to bribe his affections with showers of tasty treats, fancy dog apparels or extended bouts of fetch-the-stick.'

Fernando Botero, *Rosalba, c.* 1968

At the 1991 World Conference on Sexology one of the speakers told the story of a man who had complained about his lack of sex drive. Neither dirty talk nor weighty tomes helped. The disgruntled wife began cuddling her cat in bed. The moment she started playing with its tail, the man became so jealous that he jumped on top of her. Since then the complaint had vanished. 'That cat deserves a medal' was the speaker's verdict.

Often, however, it is the pet which is the source of tension in a relationship. Many women have the distinct impression that their husband cares more about the dog than about them. What is one to think of a man who refuses to get rid of his dog, even though his wife turns out to be allergic to dog hair? How can one love a woman who just before the climax gets out of bed to console the cat, which has been pushed off the end of the bed by an involuntary movement? A notorious case of a dog as a marital bone of contention is the Alsatian Blondi, the favourite of Adolf Hitler. Neither Eva Braun nor her dogs Stasi and Negus could stand her, so Blondi often had to stay in Hitler's bedroom. Eva then had to be bribed with presents, or sweetened with the prospect of a trip to Italy before Adolf dared to ask his 'Evi' whether it was all right for 'poor Blondi to spend half an hour with us'. When in March 1945 Blondi gave birth to a litter of five puppies, Hitler named the most beautiful of them Wolf, a name which he had earlier given himself. Blondi and Wolf slept in their master's bedroom, while the mistress had her sleeping quarters elsewhere in the Berlin bunker.

'I'd rather sell my husband than my Airedale', announced Mrs

Alexandra Livraghi after her Emma had been declared supreme champion at Cruft's Dog Show. Many people think likewise. You regularly hear people betraying their own species with the cliché: 'Since I've got to know people, I've come to prefer animals.' An example of this genre is the heartfelt sigh which can be found on the grave of 'Liang' (15-12-1962 – 21-9-1977) in the dog cemetery in Paris: 'Loyal soul, deceived by people, never by my dog.' Konrad Lorenz has denounced such things: 'Anyone who, disappointed and embittered by human failings, denies his love to mankind in order to transfer it to a dog or a cat, is definitely committing a grave sin, social sodomy so to speak, which is as disgusting as the sexual kind.'

In western society people certainly indulge in social sodomy on a grand scale. But what about sexual sodomy? Apart from the minority who actually make use of the sexual organs of their pets, there is a majority who stroke and cuddle, whisper and hug to the point where one becomes jealous. Although it doesn't actually reach the point of sexual intercourse, it looks for all the world like foreplay. Is loving a pet really erotic? Sir David Attenborough did not think so when asked. 'Erotic? No. Sensual? Yes. People are obsessed with sex. If they are sitting having a nice meal, they say: "Oh, how erotic! The way she gobbled that down!" But a good wine is *not* erotic, a nice steak is *not* erotic, a wonderful perfume – of a rose – really doesn't have to be erotic, they are simply nice. Otherwise you can call every perception erotic.' Sir David likes keeping both his feet on the ground and that is to his credit. But the borderlines between eroticism, sensuality, love and sex are often too blurred and too fluid to be able to settle the question of how sexually charged a relationship is in linguistic terms. You can experience a thrilling night without laying finger on each other, and you can produce a child without the slightest excitement. Which of the two alternatives is the more erotic, sensual, loving or sexual? Since the beginning of the AIDS era the idea is being propagated that sex can also be fully enjoyable without penetration of any kind, and that is precisely how hundreds of thousands of Dutch people behave with their dogs and cats.

To be able to answer the question of whether sex is involved it is more important to know the intention behind actions than the actual actions which are performed in an intimate relationship. What is the basis of the relationship between a human being and a dog, a human being and a cat, a human being and budgerigar? Are those animals friends and acquaintances or is more than friendship involved and can the relationship with your pet develop into a real relationship?

The first condition or precondition for a relationship is that you should see the other as an individual. Nature conservationists do not do this. They love a thick-beaked plover as a representative of all thick-beaked plovers and say: 'Look, *the* thick-beaked plover' or 'No, that isn't a common deer, that is *the* roe deer.' In order to love an animal, you have to see it as an individual; only then does it become a personal relationship instead of a business association. You cannot love a species, but you can love that particular animal, just as *mankind* is monstrous but each human being may be intrinsically worthwhile. Fortunately, there is a trick for seeing something as a person which renders all others superfluous: giving it a name. Naming something is appropriating it, bringing it within the fold, annexing it. A dog without a name is just a dog, name it and it is *your* dog. Hence this is not something one can take lightly and accordingly, as a rule, a lot of attention is paid to the choice of name, whether for a cat or for a child. If the decision to have a child is often taken far too quickly, the name it is to be given is debated for the full nine months. Naming is a ritual. It is the basis for the relationship which is to come.

How that relationship will develop depends to a large extent on the species of animal. One has a very different relationship with a dog than with a cat. Every cat behaves in a cat-like way towards people – it has no other behaviour in its repertoire – and a dog in a dog-like way. The difference between cat-like and dog-like can be traced back with great precision to the difference in the menu of their respective ancestors. Dogs are wolves which have been converted by human beings, and wolves like large prey such as deer or moose, provided there is ample opportunity for tearing and gnawing. Killing is what they like doing best. In order to get hold of such large prey, they have to hunt in groups. Hence their sociability, which is as great as that of the apes, but is not comparable in terms of mechanism. With apes the social structure is based on subtle interaction: bluffing, a shared history, a reproachful glance, lobbying, intriguing, politics; dogs are too stupid for this. Their wolves' community is as crude as their manner of hunting, which comes down to running, running, running and biting, biting and biting to death and eating – not necessarily in that order. For this simple tactic it is sufficient that there should be a Great Leader who likes leading, while the rest function as followers and if anything enjoy following even more. This pleasure in obeying has remained very strong in dogs and has been strengthened by selective breeding. Oddly enough, the dog sees human beings as the Great Leader. The relationship between human beings and dogs is therefore that between masters and servants, masters and slaves, monarchs and subjects. This is why in Victorian England the dog, more loyal than its owner, was held up as an example to the domestic staff and to the children of the house. Dr Samuel Johnson – 'this whale of wisdom' (Boswell) – was struck by the fact that love of dogs was seldom without a hint of an adult feeling of superiority and contempt. It is no accident that kings and princes have kept dogs from time immemorial – they were able to practise on their dogs. But many subjects also like someone below them and buy or acquire four-footed subjects. Other subjects on the

Félix Vallotton,
Languor, c. 1896

other hand prefer head-rubbing to boot-licking, and form a relationship with a cat.

Cats have not been made from another animal; they've been around as long as human beings. In contrast to wolves they're quite satisfied with small prey like mice. They need no help in catching them. Social behaviour and socialization, let alone Great Leaders, are consequently unnecessary. Precisely because they are so unfamiliar with hierarchy, one can persuade cats to eat out of the same bowl much more easily than dogs: in the absence of a top cat to which they must defer, they each start eating for themselves. This seems to contradict the behaviour of a gang of alley cats scavenging in dustbins. These act in groups and one of them is often clearly the leader. But it is not a true leader: a real leader of a real social species not only exercises power, but uses that power for the good of the whole community. With an alley cat this is out of the question.

Because cats are by nature solitary, a bond with other cats, let alone with human beings would be impossible outside mating time were it not that every cat has known a time when it was not alone: as a kitten, snug and warm with the other kittens and their mother in the litter, growling

Ludwig Knaus, *The
Cat Mother, c.* 1856

and sucking, playing cat games. From this blissful childhood the cat
derives the whole of the behavioural repertoire which it displays in
relation to human beings. The gestures, attitudes and sounds resemble
those of childhood down to the smallest details. Prodding in order to
obtain milk becomes padding, the warm nest has been exchanged for a
warm lap, allowing themselves to be licked clean becomes allowing
themselves to be stroked: what cat lovers are so fond of is infantile
behaviour. If the relationship between human beings and dogs is that of
master and servant, that of humans and cats is that of mother and child.

That someone should get a dog in order finally to be the master is
obvious, but why doesn't someone who wants to mother simply have a
real child? Can a cat replace a child? Obviously it can, the statistics
prove it: the average family has stayed the same size for the last century.

In the past it consisted of Dad, Mum and six children; nowadays there are still eight of them, except that now it is Mum, Dad, John, Sharon, two cats, the rabbit and the guinea pig. It· is not the size, but the constitution of the family which has changed, with all the advantages that offers. Those wanting love often get more satisfaction from a pet than from a child in the house. Loving is quite simply the speciality of pets, they earn their living by being lovable. They continue to play to a ripe old age and if they are really not suitable, there is no law against getting rid of them or exchanging them. In addition a pet is many times cheaper than a child and not nearly as much trouble.

All in all it is not difficult to see why people take cats into their homes. The problem is rather what on earth a cat sees in a human being. Why does the princess of creation seek the company of such a bony proletarian, with a desolate expanse of flabby, naked skin, dreadfully noisy, who consorts with dogs? As so often happens with love, the affection of cats for human beings is based on a misunderstanding. Cats love us not because we curry favour with them and we give them food, but because they were born in our houses. The moment they open their eyes they see human beings, their skins feel human hands, their brains become programmed within seven weeks onto human beings. A human, a cat realizes, is a kind of mother, because it does what mothers do: it gives food and warmth and even a clumsy kind of licking: stroking.

Thanks to such mutual misunderstandings both dogs and cats have been included as full members in the modern family. They belong as much as the children and are content with their role as children and (as far as the dog is concerned) as servant. But how sexually tinted are those roles? Master and servant, mother and child, there seems to be little sexual content in those relationships, until one realizes how important elements from the master–servant and mother–child relationship are in the sexual repertory of human beings and animals.

But one can also simply look at people with their dogs. For example, one sees a respectable lady taking her dog, a Great Dane, for a walk. We are so familiar with it that it no longer strikes us as odd that what we are actually looking at is a woman walking along with a huge prick on a lead. One has to be to be blind as a bat not to see the dangling monster, and so everyone simply closes their eyes to the offensive scene. This is strongly reminiscent of the story of the Emperor's new clothes and it seems to be why people deliberately do it, because a more embarrassing animal than the dog in this respect is scarcely conceivable. Stallions stow away their gear after use, boars put their corkscrews away neatly and bulls have a special withdrawal muscle for the purpose, but human beings walk around with the dog of all creatures, which even without an erection, despite its abundant hair, is the most naked of all animals. The respectable lady would not dare set foot on a nudist beach with her husband without his trunks on, but with that outrageous dog prick next

Christoph Schütz,
Watchdog

to her – the very word would make her blush to the roots of her hair – she strolls quite openly around her own, respectable neighbourhood. With vicarious satisfaction she stands and watches how the monster is used against lamp-posts, oaks and elms. With an average of 3.3 walks per day, one hour in the open air in all, allowing dogs to pee and poop is the most important form of open air recreation in the Netherlands. And yet again those looking on, as if by collective agreement, act as though nothing were happening. True, complaints are sometimes made about the messy waste products, but one hears nothing about the offensive behaviour that accompanies the productions, with the exception of the statement by Yvonne Kroonenberg, who writes somewhere that she doesn't have a dog because she 'doesn't know what kind of face one is supposed to pull while the dog is squatting there relieving itself'. Other people have not been deterred by this. While at one end of the leash the most uncivilized things are being done, at the other they try to put a respectable face on it, which to an unprejudiced spectator would seem to be a hopeless task. They often act as though nothing were happening, as though there wasn't a dog to be seen for miles, let alone one that might embarrass them. At the *moment suprême* these people usually hold the loop of the leash behind their backs, which only reinforces the impression of someone on the lookout while a crime is being committed. Complicity is what most dog-walkers exude. The occasional owner feels so conscience-stricken that he or she dresses the dog in trousers, as one does a human being. In America a *Society for Indecency to Naked Animals* has been set up which is pledged to conceal the genitals of stallions and cattle with clothing. However, the society has not been a great success. In their hearts dog-owners are far too proud of the organs of their alter egos and what they can do. There are some, the empathizers, who in their imagination poop along with their dogs. Lips pressed tightly together, eyebrows knitted in a slight frown, they stand there pushing like a modern father-to-be actively participating in his wife's labour. Solidarity takes strange forms.

All in all, urinating and defecating are not something incidental for dogs, but an ideal medium for the display of love between themselves and human beings. The filthier the pee and poop, the better we can show our affection. Just as dirty nappies, far from preventing us having a child, actually encourage it, so taking dogs for walks, cleaning out cat trays or scrubbing at pools of rabbit urine behind the TV are ideal ways of satisfying the urge to care and show love. In this context what is dirty can be very appealing.

The interest in everything that happens under the tail is of course not limited to processes of evacuation. The sexual life of animals is completely organized by human beings. Control of the sex life is indeed one of the conditions of being able to have a pet. Farmers exercise control for a living, animal lovers out of love. For animal lovers there are two ways of intervening in the sex life of their darlings: neutering and breeding.

The eagerness with which Dutch people have their pets neutered gives food for thought. No less than 80 per cent of tom-cats have been castrated, 68 per cent of females spayed. For dogs and bitches the percentages are 21 and 24 respectively. These figures are all the more impressive if you know that the total cost of treatment may be thirty

Jean-Marie
Poumeyrol, *Teddy
Bear*, second half of
20th century

pounds or more, and that the general purpose, of limiting the number of
dogs and cats, is not achieved. With roughly a quarter of cats and three-
quarters of dogs untreated, the population of Dutch dogs and cats is
growing just as fast it would as with 100 per cent untreated, because
there are sufficient intact animals to produce young for every vacant
habitat. It would require a much higher percentage to be castrated and
spayed before the the mortality rate equalled population growth. So
what underlies all those campaigns to have your dog or cat treated, all
the bonuses, all the nice ladies who catch stray dogs and cats to have
them neutered by the vet? What possesses people to make a love-life
impossible for the objects of their love? Of course, it reduces the chance of
a house redolent of the smell of tom-cat, or annoying tugging on the leash
in the vicinity of bitches on heat, but there are remedies for this. The

neutering of animals satisfies human needs. On the one hand, castration expunges the fear that sex inspires, and on the other, satisfies the desire for power. To castrate is to de-sex and without sex it is easier to form a friendship. Children cuddle teddy bears and dolls, which despite all the efforts of sexual reformers, are almost always sexless. Adult heterosexuals are always very positive about their friendship with homosexuals of the other sex, because one can always go into great depth about things with them 'without anything getting in the way'. Desmond Morris goes so far as to put 'sexlessness' at number eight on the list of twenty characteristics which explain the great popularity of the panda: 'The giant panda lacks any external anatomical features that are clearly sexual. Monkeys and apes often have highly obtrusive sexual structures, both in the males and in the females. These characteristics often embarrass the human eye and work against the animals' popularity. Human beings keep their sex organs carefully covered; so does the giant panda.' Of course, a neutered dog does not look as sexless as a panda, and a tom-cat looks sexless even before castration, with all that wonderful pubic hair right up to his ears, but behaviour after castration is much less offensive for those who are apt to take offence. If castration is on the one hand prudish and pacifying, on the other it is erotic and belligerent. After all, power-obsessed peoples all over the world castrate defeated enemies, and pets – whether necessarily or not – are reduced to geldings, oxen or capons. To show clearly who is the boss, even wives may be deprived of every pleasure by clitorectomy. De-sexing can be very sexual.

With breeding the same paradox is found. Although breeding by definition has everything to do with sex, breeders act as though nothing were less true. Calvinist farmers' wives, who would not dare to use the word 'prick' and conceive their own children in the dark, stand there in their black stockings tugging at a horse's penis which is pointing the wrong way. Perhaps they really can't see the erotic context any longer, just as gynaecologists rummage coolly about in all kinds of organs which are in themselves exciting. But that cannot apply to amateur breeders for whom emotions are precisely the crux of the hobby. Ladies from select suburbs in their kennels and catteries look on with straight faces while their breeding toms and dogs give free rein to the urges which they themselves have under lock and key; husbands with a talent for DIY spend Saturday afternoons constructing miniature steps to help the smallest chihuahuas clamber up onto the largest females. These dogs most probably belong to their wives, because dog-breeding is still largely women's work. 'I think that women breed dogs because they simply have an inbuilt desire to nurture', says one of them, Mrs Backx, who gets up every morning to tend her kennels. 'In the past I had to get up just as early for the children and at least dogs don't talk back.'

How gradually care and courtship merge is clear from Desmond Morris's analysis of photos of people with their pets. In 50 per cent of the

H. Armstrong Roberts,
*Who's Playing with
Whom?*, *c.* 1989

photos the human being is standing holding the animal like a babe-in-arms, in 11 per cent of cases the animal is being patted; 7 per cent of human beings have their arms around the animal, another 7 per cent held their cheeks against it and 5 per cent of human beings abandon themselves to the most intimate contact but one: kissing, on the mouth, with animals from budgerigars to whales.

Everyone knows that from the point of view of hygiene kissing animals is even riskier than kissing human beings, but by no means everyone is put off. Dogs and cats are kissed ardently, birds are fed from mouth to mouth. The attraction rests in the intimacy of the contact and the ease with which it can be achieved. Any dog or cat can be induced to kiss much more easily than any human being. Whether such a kiss has the same meaning for them as for us remains to be seen. In the absence of hands animals are quite simply more inclined to use their mouths and tongues, and would rather look with their noses than with their eyes.

A dog's kiss closely resembles a certain kind of behaviour exhibited by young wolves. When they are too large for the breast but still too young to hunt, they wait expectantly in the lair until their father comes back with the prey. Often this is obtained a long way from the lair and father has to bring it back in his stomach. In order to persuade him to regurgitate some food for them, the cubs prod their father's nose quite forcefully with their own, which to a human observer looks as though they are giving him a passionate kiss of welcome. Since a dog sees its master as a father figure, it is logical that it should beg in a similar manner with him, even though it may only be for attention, and certainly continues to do so if its master, moved by such love and devotion, rewards the behaviour.

Cats basically kiss like Eskimos; nuzzling is their way of greeting. While dogs put their noses under another dog's tail by way of greeting, cats sniff each other initially nose to nose. If they see a human being as a cat, then he or she is also given a sniff, on the nose or a calmly extended finger. A cat licks you everywhere, but seldom on your mouth. The fact is that cats lick each other mainly on the places which they cannot reach for themselves and lips are certainly not among these. For our part we do not lick in return, but stroke. This scarcely occurs in the natural cat repertoire. Consequently it is only a surrogate for the most wonderful licking that a cat has known: being licked by its mother, as a kitten in the litter. Also deriving from that time is the ultimate invitation from the realm of cats to the realm of human beings, the equivalent of two moist gleaming lips puckered in our direction: when puss puts its tail straight in the air, slightly quivering, the tip bent, demanding attention. It is the same gesture as that with which a kitten presents its divine little bottom for its mother's inspection. A stroke in response to this intimate request is definitely insufficient, if not insulting. Puss wants a lick from you. There. But human beings are so stupid. Instead of seizing this exceptional opportunity, they force a kiss on puss's nose, which puss will subsequently wash off with an aggrieved expression.

The horse probably serves better than a cat or a dog as an erotic safety-valve. In this case the need is greatest, definitely, in girls, who mature earlier than boys. While John and Fred are not even looking for the first hairs on their chest, Carol's and Anne's breasts are already swelling. Girls' dreams about blonde princesses are not really compatible with boys' dreams of windsurfing. The future of the horse lies not in forestry but in the comforting of adolescents. All over the world the Carols and Annes lovingly groom their horses and have their four-legged sweethearts shod, until they're old enough to be able to wash the socks of one of their own kind. Girls become women and acquire partners. While some lesbians may prefer motorbikes, on bridle-paths one can observe

Jean-Marie
Poumeyrol, *Giggling*,
second half of 20th
century

the same phenomenon as in churches and on buses. Adult women turn
out to be in the majority. For many women horse-riding is quite simply a
sensual experience which may not be able to replace being with a man,
but can certainly add to it.

A sexual relationship implies something reciprocal. To what extent
does an ordinary pet experience the normal intercourse between human
beings and animals as sexually arousing? According to Barbara Holland
in her *Secrets of the Cat* 'a sexual element' does creep into the relationship:

183

Cats attached to a human of the opposite sex will be sharply jealous of the spouse or lover. With Barney, in the beginning, the relationship was obviously sexual, but then, life as a cattery stud doesn't teach a cat much about other ways of feeling. From time to time he would scramble onto my back and try to hold me by the neck with his jaws, as he used to do with his Persian clients. He had strong feelings about me, and this was the only thing he knew to do about feelings. Later, after he'd had the chance to watch other cats with people, he learned the sadly limited repertoire at his disposal: the flexed paw, the purr, the stomach exposed for rubbing, the half-closed eyes.

However, an invitingly exposed belly is not that innocent: for a dog or a tom-cat rubbing the belly is an enormous stimulus during mating and anyone stroking them there could just as well have reached a little further down. For that matter, even without touching anything, the behaviour of a human being can drive a dog or wolf to ecstasy. 'Only when it comes to sex must I disappoint Igor', admitted Grada Brugman-Laeijendecker to the magazine *Panorama*. In the eyes of her wolf Igor, the 'wolf-woman' is his mate rather than that of her husband, Ben Brugman:

> Once sexually mature he had an instinctive sense of my own fertility cycle. I often didn't keep track myself of my periods, but I soon noticed them from the wolf's attempts to approach me. One day he began to prepare the bridal suite, underground, to make love to me. It's a shame I can't accept his advances. And do you know whom it's also very sad for? For the she-wolf Anuschka. She is passionately in love with Igor, but he refuses to have anything to do with her. The she-wolf then becomes terribly jealous of me. For example, she steals my brush or gives me a little nip with her teeth.

There are cases of such jealousy known in other animals. Chimpanzees, which not so long ago could still be kept as pets, often became dangerously jealous when their 'master' went to bed with their 'mistress'. Conversely it is sometimes fellow-human beings who put an end to this. For example, a 29-year-old woman wrote to me that she has had a parrot, Loortje, for nineteen years which 'is very lively', and always wants to 'play and sing'. 'The bird', she writes, 'is focused completely on me. It is also a very erotic creature. It likes to be stroked and "tickled" for hours and in its way can also caress patiently (with its beak). I even stroked it under its tail and then it "came" as they say (it is a male). I don't let things go that far anymore, because I still live with my parents, and well, they would find that very strange. At the time my mother said: "How strangely that bird's acting, what a strange noise he's making."'

In the last example a boundary has clearly been crossed – she stroked him under his tail – but I can't rid myself of the impression that even on this side of the borderline sex and eroticism play a part in the cherishing of pets. Animal lovers really love their animals: they are sodomites. How is that possible? Is there something wrong with our genes when we start

Briton Rivière, *Fellow Feeling*, c. 1877

falling for the wrong species? Aren't we heading for biological disaster? Probably not. If a disaster is happening, it is more culturally determined. That is clear if you travel southwards. By the time you get to Brussels people start thinking differently about animals and in France in our eyes they are all animal-killers. A Frenchman likes birds as much as an Englishman, but prefers them tastily prepared on the plate. A Frenchman regards nature as a well-provisioned shop window in which the Great Poulterer has displayed his wares live to ensure their freshness.

185

In France one hears not so much the birds as the bullets whistling, with the consequence that in France one finds animals on one's plate which in England one dare not even point at. And those are only differences between two neighbouring European countries. Other continents have their own distinct ideas about animals. It was, for example, a great shock to Western European animal lovers when guestworkers came to their cities. While we enliven our religious feast-days with frozen turkey, many North African immigrants do not feel that they have performed their pious duty until they have slaughtered half a dozen goats in a very un-Christian way. Their god is simply not, like ours, satisfied with the blood of His son. Newspapers reinforce the impression that you cannot leave a foreigner alone with an animal. In Canada, if given the chance, they club baby seals to death. In South East Asia they eat man's best friend. The wider our horizons become, the further the portion of the world where people like animals as much as we do shrinks. If one colours in on an atlas the countries where in cowboy films they have more sympathy with the horses than with the Indians and where they keep giving dogs tasty titbits until their legs no longer point downwards from their bodies but sideways, then the cherishing of animals seems to be an Anglo-Saxon enterprise with branches in the Low Countries, Scandinavia and Germany. Ninety per cent of all animal-coddlers speak English to their cats or dogs. Even more surprising than the limited geographical scope of animal coddling is the limited time in which this has gone on. Even in that bulwark of animal love, England, droning on about dogs and cats has been commonplace for only a short while. Two centuries ago dogs were simply there for bull-baiting. For this purpose they were aroused and let loose on a bull, which was tied to a post with a length of rope. The more vicious the dogs and the more persistent the bull, the more exciting the orgy of blood and gored bellies was for the onlookers. The bellow of the bull and the jingle of coins signalled a successful day.

In those days chickens were kept, as they are now, to lay eggs, but cocks were set against each other in an arena of which only the name survives: the cockpit. So the common people had something to bet on and could have a drink while they watched, while the lords and earls hunted nobler game. For them there was only one kind of animal, the deer.

The victory of animals began in Queen Victoria's England. Why? What was present in that place and at that time that was missing in other places and in earlier and later times? Industrial cities. Nothing fuels love of nature better than living in cities. To those far from hailstorms and hornet stings, mud and jellyfish, comfortably ensconced in the city, nature outside it seems so beautiful. Petunias, pussy-cats and romanticized depictions of country life keep the illusion alive. Characteristic of that period was the first animal protection legislation in the world, the Martin Act of 1822. This gave protection only to 'Horses, Mares,

Delmas Howe, *Zeus (on the Bull)*, c. 1981

Geldings, Mules, Donkeys, Cows, Heifers, Bull Calves, Oxen, Sheep, and other Livestock'. Pets were not on the list, they had been deleted from it during the bill's passage through the House of Commons: 'When the Honourable Member C. Smith suggested protecting donkeys, such a gale of laughter arose, that the reporter of *The Times* could scarcely hear what was being said.... Another member said that Martin would soon be wanting to have a law for dogs, which again provoked a roar of laughter and after someone cried, "And cats!" the whole House of Commons was doubled up with laughter.'

In Victorian England a change was also taking place in scientific thought. Charles Darwin confirmed the anxious suspicion that human beings are, or at least were, apes, and that in order to preserve the last grain of dignity there was only one solution. To prevent human beings, already fallen angels, descending to the level of animals, the animal was raised to the human level. Anthropomorphism was a well-tried lever and the zoological gardens which had recently sprung up everywhere offered a splendid opportunity for elevation. The apes which up till then had been stamped as hairy brutes were hurriedly given coats, caps, pipes and teacups in their cages, and the chimpanzees' tea-party was born.

Besides industrialization and the theory of evolution, the Victorian age was also marked by tender-heartedness. Almost at the same time as the sad lot of many animals, that of prisoners, city orphans, drunkards fallen on hard times – the further they had fallen the better – child labourers and old widows was discovered. It is striking that the lot of animals should have been among the first (after that of slaves) to receive organized attention. The Royal Society for the Prevention of Cruelty to Animals (RSPCA) was founded in England as early as 1824, years before children were protected. From the beginning this was a very respectable cause. Revolutionary as it might have appeared to demand rights for animals, the chairmen, secretaries, treasurers, members and honorary members were very far from revolutionary. Treasurers were recruited for their prosperity, chairmen on the basis of their social status. High subscriptions kept the man in the street away.

The American historian James Turner has offered an interesting explanation in *Reckoning with the Beast* for the attraction of animal protection for the upper classes. His starting-point is the rigid two-nation society of nineteenth-century England. This caused serious problems not only for the have-nots, but also for the haves. Materially the upper classes had little to complain about, but spiritually some of them were in a quandary. They found it difficult to reconcile the exploitation of the working class with their consciences and the Christian morality of brotherly love. Modern capitalists may have less of a problem with this, but in the Victorian period hell was still Hell, which had to be taken seriously into account. Not exploiting the working class, however, was out of the question; that would mean their own downfall. In order to ensure themselves a good night's sleep in spite of this, they introduced safety-valves. The knitting of vests for negro children became fashionable, the sick – provided they were not too infectious – were comforted, there was a hunk of bread for the hungry, and the illiterate were helped by the reading aloud of poetry and other intellectual fare. However, being kind to animals gave most satisfaction. Among animals there were no socialists, who would sooner or later bite

"I ALWAYS WASH MY PUSSY WITH SCENTED SOAP."

the hand that stroked them. Moreover, protecting animals was ideally suited to civilized people. The lower classes particularly needed to be civilized, for the good of humanity in general and for the upper classes, which felt especially threatened. And where better could one begin this progress than with children? The rough animals of the animal fables gave way to a saccharin stream of animal stories which has still not dried up. Beatrix Potter's cats, dressed in little suits, still eat their home-made pancakes instead of Mrs Tittlemouse ('Once upon a time there was a wood-mouse, and her name was Mrs. Tittlemouse. She lived in a bank under a hedge. Such a funny house!'). Our children are still introduced to the natural ecosystem as one great tea-party of sweet little rabbits and cuddly bears, with at most a rather gruff, but basically good-natured grumbler of a lion. No wonder then that later, when they are grown up, they resort to cuddling with this safe world of animals when love for their fellow human beings displays a less sunny side.

Erotic postcard, *c.* 1902

We live in a madhouse, the world upside down. Never before and in no other place has there been so much love-talk and love-making with dogs, cats and mice as here and now. In the whole history of the world there are only two periods which are to some extent reminiscent of ours: the latter days of Egypt and the decline of Rome. At the height of the decadent period people acted as coquettishly as we do now with their pets, which were treated far better than slaves. This might point to the fact that preferring pets is a sign of decadence, a short-circuit in the network of affection, a cry for help from a society which has lost its way. All the more so because the same hands which stroke dogs and cats shamelessly scoop food from the trough of the food industry, just as in the past the same eyes which enjoyed a pet bird enjoyed the mass sacrifice of animals in the Circus Maximus in Rome. Love of animals is very nice, just as all love is nice, but it must not obscure love of human beings,

Balthus, *Nude with Cat,*
second half of 20th
century

otherwise our human society will disintegrate, creaking in its joints, to
the accompaniment of heart-rending meowing and barking.

In the light of these sombre meditations it is some consolation to find
that we are not entirely alone in denying our own species. The good news
comes from San Antonio, Texas, where a colony of two thousand
baboons has been assembled for scientific purposes. The surrounding
undergrowth is teeming with cats, which have been feral for so many
generations that they want nothing more to do with human beings.
Suddenly it happened. Through a gap a half-grown cat crept into a
baboon cage. Until that point little intruders had always been eaten by
the baboons. This kitten, however, was lovingly preened by baboon
X322. The other baboons were greatly interested and also wanted to
touch the kitten. After an hour the keepers intervened. First all the
baboons had to be removed from the cage and X322 had to be
anaesthetized before they could retrieve the kitten. The animal fled into
the undergrowth, but came back regularly. A second kitten, grey this
time, also came of its own accord, and was allowed to stay for two
months. The animal was looked after by X322, carried and defended

against human beings. In short, X322 kept a cat. Moreover, this was not entirely new to science, because Charles Darwin in *The Descent of Man* also mentions 'one female baboon' which 'had so capacious a heart, that she not only adopted young monkeys of other species, but stole young dogs and cats, which she constantly carried about. . . . An adopted kitten scratched this affectionate baboon, which certainly had a fine intellect, for she was much astonished at being scratched, and immediately examined the kitten's feet, and without further ado bit off the claws.'

So we see that love takes ever new and unexpected forms. Those who are surprised by this, are surprised about themselves. And rightly so, since no one will ever be able to explain the source of that feeling that comes from deep inside, when you look a woman or a man or a cat or a rabbit in the eyes and say, 'I love you.'

Marcus Behmer, *Kalos,*
c. 1928

Bibliography

Aelian, *De natura animalium*, trans. A.F. Schofield, Harvard University Press, Cambridge, MA and Heinemann, London 1958–9.

Aldrovandi, Ulyssis, *De quadrupedibus digitalis viviparis*, Bonn 1645.

Allais, Alphonse, *A se torda*, Albin Michel, Paris n.d.

Amerongen, M. van and R.O. van Gennep, eds, *Het orgasme van Lorre – Nieuwe verhalen, gedichten en artikelen*, Van Gennep, Amsterdam 1983.

Anderson, R.S., ed., *Pet Animals and Society*, A.B.-S.A.V.A. Symposium, Baillière Tindall, London 1975.

Annan, David, *Movie Fantastic – Beyond the Dream Machine*, Bounty Books, New York 1974.

Annan, David, *Ape – the Kingdom of Kong*, Lorrimer, London 1975.

Apuleius, *The Golden Ass*, trans. Robert Graves, Penguin, Harmondsworth 1950.

Aristotle, *Historia animalium*, trans. A.L. Peck, Heinemann, London 1965.

Armstrong, Edward A., *The Life and Lore of the Bird – In Nature, Art, Myth and Literature*, Crown, New York 1975.

Arrabal, *Théâtre VI – Bestialité érotique*, Christian Bourgois, Paris 1969.

Arsan, Emmanuelle, *l'Anti-vièrge*, Le Terrain Vague, Paris 1968.

Ars erotica – Catalogo della mostra, Overart, Firenze n.d.

Ayrault, Pierre, *Des procez faicts au cadaver, aux cendres, à la mémoire, aux bestes brutes, choses inanimées, et aux contumas*, Anthoine Hernault, Angers 1591.

Banton, Michael, *The Idea of Race*, Tavistock, London 1977.

Barber, Richard and Anne Riches, *A Dictionary of Fabulous Beasts*, Macmillan, London 1971.

Barloy, Jean-Jacques, *La peur et les animaux*, Baland, Paris 1982.

Barrès, Maurice, *Du Sang, de la volupté et de la mort*, Plon, Paris 1921.

Bartholomeus Anglicus, *Dat boeck van den proprieteyten der dinghen*, Jac. Bellaert, Haarlem 1485.

Bateson, P., ed., *Mate Choice*, Cambridge University Press, Cambridge 1983

Baumann, Peter and Ortwin Fink, *Zuviel Herz für Tiere – Sind wir wirklich Tierlieb?*, Hoffmann und Campe, Hamburg 1976.

Baur, Otto, *Bestiarium humanum – Mensch-Tier-Vergleich in Kunst und Karikatur*, Heinz Moos, Munich 1974.

Bay, André, ed., *La Belle et la bête et autres contes du cabinet des fées*, Club des libraires de France, Paris 1965.

Beaver, Bonnie, *Veterinary Aspects of Feline Behavior*, C.V. Mosby, St Louis/Toronto/London 1980.

Beck, Alan and Aaron Katcher, *Between Pets and People – The Importance of Animal Companionship*,

Perigee Books, New York 1983.

Beek, Frans van der, *De koe*, Loeb, Amsterdam 1983.

Beer, Rüdiger Robert, *Einhorn – Fabelwelt und Wirklichkeit*, Georg D.W. Callwey, Munich 1972

Bennett, Herb, *The Thrill of Animal Sex*, Copley Square Press, Hollywood 1975.

Bergen, François van, *Gemengelde parnas-loof: bestaande in verscheidene soort van gedichten: zo ernstige als spot-dichten*, Amsterdam 1693.

Berkenhof, L.H.A., *Tierstrafe, Tierbannung und rechtsrituelle Tiertötung im Mittelalter*, Dissertation, Bonn, Zürich 1937.

Bessy, Maurice, *A Pictorial History of Magic and the Super-Natural*, Spring Books, London 1964.

Bevers, Holm, Peter Schathorn en Barbara Welzell, *Rembrandt: De meester & zijn werkplaats – Tekeningen & etsen*, Rijksmuseum, Amsterdam & Waanders, Zwolle 1991.

Bingham, H.C., *Sex Development in Apes*, Johns Hopkins University Press, Baltimore 1928.

Blackburn, Julia, *Charles Waterson 1782–1865 – De eerste natuurbeschermer*, G.A. van Oorschot, Amsterdam 1990.

Blount, Margareth, *Animal Land – The Creatures of Children's Fiction*, Avon Books, New York 1977.

Boardman, John and Eugenio La Rocca, *Eros in Griekenland*, Amsterdam Boek, Amsterdam 1975.

Bobis, Laurence, *Les Neuf vies du chat*, Gallimard, Paris 1991.

Boccaccio, Giovanni, *The Decameron*, trans. G.H. McWilliam, Penguin, Harmondsworth 1972.

Boerstoel, Jan, Hans Dorrestijn and Willem Wilmink, *Verre vrienden – 44 nieuwe liedjes*, J.C. Aarts, Amsterdam 1983.

Bogart, Nico, *Het paard*, Het Spectrum, Utrecht/Antwerpen 1978.

Bolen, C. van, *Dr. Kinsey en de vrouw – De Kinsey-rapporten in het licht der kritiek*, Nieuwe Wieken, Amstelveen n.d.

Bontius, J., *Historiae naturalis & medicae Indiae Orientalis*, Elzevirios, Amsterdam 1685.

Boon, Dirk, *Dierenwelzijn en recht*, Gouda Quint, Arnhem 1979.

Boon, Dirk, *Nederlands dierenrecht*, Dissertation Groningen, Gouda Quint, Arnhem 1983.

Borges, Jorge Luis, *Het boek van de denkbeeldige*

wezens, De Bezige Bij, Amsterdam 1976.

Bowell, John, *The Kindness of Strangers – The Abandonment of Children in Western Europe from Late Antiquity to the Renaissance*, Random House, New York 1988.

Boullet, Jean, *La Belle et la Bête*, Le Terrain Vague, Paris 1958.

Brassens, G., *Poésie et Chansons*, Pierre Seghers, Paris 1969.

Brongersma, E., *De historische achtergronden van wetsbepalingen – Enkele opmerkingen over de historische achtergronden van wetsbepalingen, waarin seksuele gedragingen strafbaar worden gesteld*, in *Seksinfo*, Studium Generale, Utrecht & NVSH, Amsterdam 1969.

Brown, Christopher, Jan Kelch and Pieter van Thiel, *Rembrandt: De meester & zijn werkplaats – Schilderijen*, Rijksmuseum, Amsterdam & Waanders, Zwolle 1991.

Brusendorff, Ove and Poul Henningsen, *Bilderbuch der Liebe – Aus der Geschichte der Freude und der moralischen Entrüstung vom Griechischen Altertum bis zur Französischen Revolution*, Pigalle, Stockholm n.d.

Bruijel, F.J., *Bijbel en natuur – Studies over planten en dieren uit de Heilige Schrift*, J.H. Kok, Kampen 1939.

Buddingh', C., *Gorgelrijmen*, Bruna, Utrecht 1953.

Buffon, George-Louis Leclerc, Comte de, *Histoire naturelle générale et particulière – Avec la description du Cabinet du Roy*, Imprimerie Royale, Paris 1749–1804.

Bullough, Vern L., *Sexual Variance in Society and History*, John Wiley & Sons, New York/London/Sydney/Toronto 1976.

Burroughs, E.R., *Tarzan of the Apes*, A.L. Burt, New York 1914.

Cabanés, Flavian, *Procédures singulières – Les animaux en justice*, Albin Michel, Paris 1928.

Cabanne, Pierre, *Erotik in Malerei und Graphik*, Bertelsmann, Gütersloh/Berlin/Munich/Vienna 1972.

Calvet, Jean and Marcel Cruppi, *Les animaux dans la littérature sacrée*, Fernand Lanore, Paris 1956.

Carpenter, Thomas H., *Art and Myth in Ancient Greece – A Handbook*, Thames & Hudson, London 1991.

Carr, Pattie, *Raped by her Pet*, Publisher's Consultants, South Laguna 1980.

Carrington, Richard, *Mermaids and Mastodons – A Book of Natural & Unnatural History*, Chatto & Windus, London 1957.

Carson, Gerald, *Men, Beasts and Gods – A History of Cruelty and Kindness to Animals*, Charles Scribner's Sons, New York 1972.

Cate, C.L. ten, *Wan god mast gift . . . – Bilder aus der Geschichte der Schweinezucht im Wald*, Pudoc, Wageningen 1972.

Cauldwell, D.O., *Animal Contacts*, Girard, Kansas 1948.

Chideckel, Maurice, *Female Sex Perversion – The Sexually Aberrated Woman as She Is*, Brown, New York 1963.

Chorus, A., *Het denkende dier – Enkele facetten van de betrekking tussen mens en dier in psychologische belichting*, A.W. Sijthoff, Leiden 1969.

Clark, Anne, *Beasts and Bawdy*, J.M. Dent & Sons, London 1975.

Clark, Stephen R.L., *The Nature of the Beast – Are Animals Moral?*, Oxford University Press, Oxford/New York 1982.

Clébert, Jean-Paul, *Bestiaire fabuleux*, Albin Michel, Paris 1971.

Cohen, Daniel, *A Modern Look at Monsters*, Dodd, Mead & Co., New York 1970.

Collier, John, *His Monkey Wife; or Married to a Chimp*, Peter Davies, London 1930.

Coco, G., *Is het erg dokter?* Mondria Uitgevers, Hazerswoude-dorp, Amsterdam, n.d.

Corbin, Alain, *Women for Hire – Prostitution and Sexuality in France after 1850*, Harvard University Press, Cambridge, MA 1992.

Costello, *The Magic Zoo – The Natural History of Fabulous Animals*, St Martin's Press, New York 1979.

Damhouder, Jodocus, *Rerum criminalium praxis*, Antwerp, 1562.

Dale-Green, Patricia, *Cult of the Cat*, Weathervane, New York 1963.

Darwin, Charles, *The Origin of Species by Natural Selection*, Watts, London 1951.

Darwin, Charles, *The Descent of Man and Selection in Relation to Sex*, John Murray, London 1922.

Davenport-Hines, Richard, *Sex, Death and Punishment – Attitudes to Sex and Sexuality in Britain since the Renaissance*, William Collins Sons, London 1990.

Davids, Karel, *Dieren en Nederlanders – Zeven eeuwen lief en leed*, Matrijs, Utrecht 1989.

Davidson, Gustav, *A Dictionary of Angels – Including the Fallen Angels*, The Free Press, New York 1967.

David, Murray S., *Smut*, The University of Chicago Press, Chicago & London 1983.

Dekkers, Midas, *Bestiarium*, Bert Bakker, Amsterdam 1977.

Dekkers, Midas, *Het edelgedierte – Over het vreemde verbond tussen mens en dier*, Bert Bakker, Amsterdam 1978.

Dekkers, Midas, *Bovenste Beste Beesten – Eigenzinnige dierbiografieën*, Bert Bakker, Amsterdam 1979.

Dekkers, Midas, *Het walvismeer – Op de bres met Greenpeace*, Meulenhoff Informatief, Amsterdam 1982.

Dekkers, Midas, *Houden beren echt van honing?* CPNB, Amsterdam 1985.

Dekkers, Midas, *De kanarie en andere beesten*, Contact, Amsterdam 1987.

Dekkers, Midas, *De krekel en andere beesten*, Contact, Amsterdam 1989.

Dembeck, Hermann, *Mit Ti .n Leben*, Econ-Verlag, Düsseldorf/Vienna 1961.

Dieren van stal, de – Het dier in de Griekse en Romeinse beschaving, Exhibition catalogue, Allard Pierson Museum, Amsterdam 1988.

Diodorus of Sicily, *Bibliotheca historica*, trans. C.H. Oldfather. Harvard University Press, Cambridge, MA 1962–70.

Drimmer, Frederick, *Very Special People*, Amjon, New York 1973.

Dros, Imme, *Een heel lief konijn*, Em. Querido, Amsterdam 1992.

Dröscher, Vitus B., *Leven in de dierentuin – Avonturen en ontdekkingen*, Het Wereldvenster, Baarn 1970.

Dröscher, Vitus B., *Dieren beminnen en haten elkaar – Nieuwste gedragsonderzoekingen*, Het Wereldvenster, Baarn 1974.

Dubois, Eugène, *Pithecanthropus erectus – Eine menschenähnliche Uebergangsform*, Batavia 1894.

Dubois-Dessaule, Gaston, *Étude sur la bestialité au point de vue historique, médical et juridique*, Charles Carrington, Paris 1905.

Du Chaillu, P.B., *Explorations and Adventures in Equatorial Africa*, John Murray, London 1861.

Dumas, Alexandre, *L'Homme aux contes*, Office de Publicité, Brussel 1875.

Dupuis, H.M., C. Naaktgeboren, D.J. Noordam, J. Spanjer and F.W. van der Waals, *Een kind onder het hart – Verloskunde, volksgeloof, gezin, seksualiteit en moraal vroeger en nu*, Meulenhoff Informatief & Amsterdams Historisch Museum, Amsterdam 1987.

Edey, Maitland A., *De ontbrekende schakel*, Time-Life International, Amsterdam 1973.

Engel, Marian, *Bear*, Routledge & Kegan Paul, London 1977.

Es, Ton van and Fon Zwart, *Duizend gezichten van zuivel – Recepten, wetenswaardigheden en curiosa uit de gehele wereld*, Het Nederlands Zuivelbureau, Rijswijk 1988.

Evans, E.P., *The Criminal Prosecution and Capital Punishment of Animals*, William Heinemann, London 1906.

Farson, Daniel and Angus Hall, *Vampires, Zombies, and Monster Men/Monsters and Mythic Beasts*, Aldus, London 1975.

Fekkes, Jan, ed., *De God van je tante – Ofwel het Ezelproces van Gerard Kornelis van het Reve*, De Arbeiderspers, Amsterdam 1968.

Fiedler, Leslie, *Freaks – Myths and Images of the Secret Self*, Simon & Schuster, New York 1978.

Fireman, Judy, ed., *Cat Catalog – the Ultimate Cat Book*, Workman, New York 1976.

Fogle, Bruce, ed., *Interrelations between People and Pets*, Charles C. Thomas, Springfield, Ill. 1981.

Fogle, Bruce, *The Dog's Mind*, Pelham Books, London 1990.

Fokkinga, Anno, *Koeboek*, Educaboek, Culemborg 1985.

Ford, Clellan S., *A Comparative Study of Human Reproduction*, Yale University Press, New Haven CT 1945.

Ford, Clellan S. and France A. Beach, *Vormen van seksueel gedrag*, Het Spectrum Utrecht/Antwerp 1970.

Fossey, Dian, *Gorillas in de mist*, Veen, Utrecht/ Antwerp 1984.

France, Peter, *An Encyclopedia of Bible Animals*, Croom Helm, London/Sydney 1986.

Franssens, Jean-Paul, *Een gouden kind*, De Harmonie, Amsterdam 1991.

Friday, Nancy, *My Secret Garden. Women's Sexual Fantasies*, Quartet/Virago, London 1975.

Friday, Nancy, *Men in Love*, Hutchinson, London 1980.

Friedman, John Block, *The Monstrous Races in Medieval Art and Thought*, Harvard University Press, Cambridge, MA 1981.

Frischauer, Paul, *Zeden en erotiek in de loop der eeuwen*, H.J.W. Becht, Amsterdam n.d.

Garon, Jay and Morgan Wilson, eds, *Erotica exotica*, Belmont Books, New York 1963.

Geldof, W., *De koe bij de horens gevat*, Het Spectrum, Utrecht/Antwerp 1984.

Geldof, W., *Wel verhip zei de kip*, Het Spectrum, Utrecht/Antwerp 1985.

Giese, Hans, ed., *Die sexuelle Perversion*, Akademische Verlagsgesellschaft, Frankfurt am-Main 1967.

Giese, Hans, *Zur Psychopathologie der Sexualität*, Ferdinand Enke, Stuttgart 1973.

Gmelig-Nijboer, Caroline Aleid, *Conrad Gessner's 'Historia animalium' – An Inventory of Renaissance Zoology*, Dissertation, Utrecht 1977.

Goden en hun beestenspul, Exhibition catalogue, Allard Pierson Museum, Amsterdam 1990.

Godlovitch, Stanley, Roslind Godlovitch and John Harris, *Animals, Men and Morals – an Enquiry into the Maltreatment of Non-Humans*, Grove, New York 1971.

Goldner, Orville and George E. Turner, *The Making of King Kong – Behind a Film Classic*, Ballantine, New York 1976.

Goldstein, Michael, J. and Harold Sanford Kant, *Pornography and Sexual Deviance*, University of California Press, Berkeley/Los Angeles/London 1973.

Goodall, Jane, *Through a Window – Thirty Years with the Chimpanzees of Gombe*, Weidenfeld and Nicolson, London 1990.

Gould, Charles, *Mythical Monsters*, W.H. Allen, London 1886.

Gould, James L. and Carol Grand Gould, *Sexual Selection*, Scientific American Library, New York 1989.

Gould, Stephen Jay, *The Mismeasure of Man*, W.W. Norton, New York/London 1981.

Gould, Stephen Jay, *The Flamingo's Smile – Reflections in Natural History*, W.W. Norton, New York/London 1985.

Grant, Michael and Antonia Mulas, *Eros in Pompeji – Erotische taferelen uit het geheime kabinet van het Museum van Napels*, Amsterdam Boek, Amsterdam 1985.

Grassberger, Roland, *Die Unzucht mit Tieren*, Springer, Vienna/New York 1968.

Graves, Robert, *The Greek Myths*, 2 vols, Penguin, Harmondsworth 1984.

Grimal, Pierre, *Dictionnaire de la mythologie Grecque et Romaine*, Presses Universitaires de France, Paris 1951.

Gun, Nerin E., *Eva Braun – Hitler's Mistress*, Hodder & Stoughton, London 1976.

Guthrie, R. Dale, *Body Hot Spots – The Anatomy of Human Social Organs and Behavior*, Van Nostrand Reinhold, New York/Cincinnati/Atlanta/Dallas/San Francisco 1976.

Haeberle, E.J., *Die Sexualität des Menschen – Handbuch und Atlas*, Walter de Gruyter, Berlin/New York 1983.

Hahn, Emily, *Eve and the Apes*, Weidenfeld & Nicolson, New York 1988.

Hamel, Frank, *Human Animals*, The Aquarian Press, Wellingborough 1973.

Hamilton, David, *The Monkey Gland Affair*, Chatto & Windus, London 1986.

Haneveld, G.T., *Het mirakel van het hart*, Ambo, Baarn 1991.

Hapgood, Fred, *Why Males Exist – An Enquiry into the Evolution of Sex*, William Morrow and Company, New York 1979.

Harris, Marvin, *Good to Eat – Riddles of Food and Culture*, Allen & Unwin, London/Boston/Sydney 1986.

Harrisson, Barbara, *Orang-utan*, Collins, London 1962.

Hayes, Catherine, *The Ape in our House*, Harper & Row, New York 1951.

Hearne, Vicki, *Adam's Task – Calling Animals by Name*, Heinemann, London 1987.

Hedgepeth, William, *The Hog Book*, Doubleday, Garden City, NY 1978.

Hediger, H., *Skizzen zu einer Tierpsychologie im Zoo und in Zirkus*, Europa, Stuttgart 1954.

Hediger, H., *Mensch und Tier im Zoo – Tiergarten-Biologie*, Albert Müller, Rüschlikon, Zürich/Stuttgart/Vienna 1965.

Hentig, Hans von, *Soziologie der Zoophilen Neigung*, Ferdinand Enke, Stuttgart 1962.

Hernandez, Ludovico, *Les Procès de bestialité aux XVIe et XVIIe siècles*, Bibliothèque des Curieux, Paris 1920.

Herodotus, *History*, trans. D. Grene, Penguin, Harmondsworth 1988.

Hillier, Jack, *The Art of Hokusai in Book Illustration*, Philip Wilson, London 1980.

Hirschfeld, M., *Sexual Pathology – A Study of Derangements of the Sexual Instinct*, Emerson Books, New York 1940.

Hoage, R.J., ed., *Perceptions of Animals in American Culture*, Smithsonian Institution Press, Washington/London, 1989.

Holland, Barbara, *Secrets of the Cat – Its Lore, Legend and Lives*, Ballantine, New York 1989.

Holm, Erik, *Tier und Gott – Mythik, Mantik, und Magie der südafrikanischen Urjäger*, Schwabe & Co., Basel/Stuttgart 1965.

Howell, Michael and Peter Ford, *The True History of the Elephant Man*, Allison & Busby, London 1980.

Hunold, Günther, *Abarten des Sexualverhaltens – Ungewöhnliche Erscheinungsformen des Trieblebens*, Wilhelm Heyne, Munich 1978.

Illies, Joachim, *Anthropologie des Tieres – Entwurf einer anderen Zoologie*, R. Piper & Co., Munich 1973.

Ingersoll, Ernest, *Birds in Legend, Fable and Folklore*, Longmans, Green and Co., New York 1923.

Irvine, William, *Apes, Angels and Victorians – A Joint Biography of Darwin and Huxley*, Weidenfeld & Nicolson, London 1956.

Jasper, James M. and Dorothy Nelkin, *The Animal Rights Crusade – The Growth of a Moral Protest*, The Free Press, New York 1992.

Jennison, George, *Animals for Show and Pleasure in Ancient Rome*, Manchester University Press, Manchester 1937.

Johns, Catherine, *Sex or Symbol – Erotic Images of Greece and Rome*, British Museum Publications, London 1982.

Jones, Barbara and William Ouelette, *Erotische*

prentbriefkaarten, Andreas Landshoff, Amsterdam 1977.

Kevler, Daniel, *In the Name of Eugenics – Genetics and the Uses of Human Heredity*, New York 1985.

Kinsey, Alfred C., Wardell B. Pomeroy and Clyde E. Martin, *Sexual Behavior in the Human Male*, W.B. Saunders, Philadelphia/London 1948.

Kinsey, Alfred C., Wardell B. Pomeroy, Clyde E. Martin and Paul H. Gebhard, *Sexual Behavior in the Human Female*, W.B. Saunders, Philadelphia/London 1953.

Kipling, Rudyard, *The Jungle Books*, Airmont, New York 1966.

Kirk, G.S., *Myth – Its Meaning and Function in Ancient and Other Cultures*, Cambridge University Press, Cambridge/Berkeley/Los Angeles 1970.

Kirk, G.S., *The Nature of Greek Myths*, Penguin, Harmondsworth 1974.

Klaits, Joseph and Barrie, *Animals and Man in Historical Perspective*, Harper & Row, New York/Evanston/San Francisco/London 1974.

Klingender, Francis, *Animals in Art and Thought to the End of the Middle Ages*, Evelyn Antal and John Harthan, London 1972.

Köhler, Wolfgang, *The Mentality of Apes*, Routledge & Kegan Paul, London 1925.

Kosinski, Jerzy, *Steps*, The Bodley Head, London/Sydney/Toronto 1968.

Kosinski, Jerzy, *The Painted Bird*, Bantam Books, Toronto 1981.

Kousbroek, Rudy, *De aaibaarheidsfactor*, Thomas Rap, Amsterdam 1969.

Krafft-Ebing, R. von, *Aberrations of Sexual Life*, trans. Arthur Vivian Burbury, Staples Press, London/New York 1951.

Kraus, Friedrich, *Japanisches Geschlechtsleben*, Karl Schustek, Hanau n.d.

Kraus, Werner, *Zur Anthropologie des 18. Jahrhunderts – Die Frühgeschichte der Menschheit im Blickpunt der Aufklärung*, Akademie-Verlag, Berlin 1978.

Kronhausen, Eberhard and Phyllis, *Wat is pornografie? – Eros en de vrijheid van drukpers*, Bert Bakker/Daamen, The Hague 1961.

Kronhausen, Eberhard and Phyllis, *Erotische Exlibris*, Wilhelm Heyne, Munich 1976.

Krutch, Joseph Wood, *The Great Chain of Life*, Houghton Mifflin, Boston 1956.

Langemeijer, G.E., *Het dier in de rechtsorde*, in: *Mens en dier – Bundel aangeboden aan prof. dr. F.R.L. Sassen*, 1954.

Ledda, Gavino, *Padro padrone – De opvoeding van een herderszoon*, Meulenhoff, Amsterdam 1978.

Leguat, François, *De gevaarlyke en zeldzame reyzen van den heere François Leguat met zyn byhebbend gezelschap naar twee onbewoonde Oostindische eylanden gedaan zedert den jare 1690, tot 1698 toe*, Willem Broedelet, Amsterdam 1708.

Levinson, Boris M., *Pets and Human Development*, Charles C. Thomas, Springfield, Ill 1972.

Lewontin, Richard, *Menselijke verscheidenheid – Het spel van erfelijkheid, milieu en toeval*, Natuur & Techniek, Maastricht/Brussel 1985.

Leyhausen, Pauls, *Katzen – Eine Verhaltenskunde*, Paul Parey, Berlin/Hamburg 1979.

Linden, Eugene, *Silent Partners – The Legacy of the Ape Language Experiments*, Times, New York 1986.

London, L.S. and F.S. Caprio, *Sexual Deviations*, Linacre Press, Washington 1950.

Looij, Maarten, *Van fabeldier tot wrekend beest – Negen thema's in Nederlands dicht en ondicht over dieren*, Kwadraat, Utrecht 1988.

Lopez, Barry Holstun, *Of Wolves and Men*, Charles Scribner's Sons, New York 1978.

Lucie-Smith, Edward, *Sexuality in Western Art*, Thames & Hudson, London 1991.

Mayr, E., *Animal Species and Evolution*, Belknap Press and Harvard University Press, Cambridge, MA 1963.

Maclean, Charles, *De wolfskinderen*, Het Spectrum, Utrecht/Antwerp, 1978.

MacNamara, Donal E.J. and Edward Sagarin, *Sex, Crime and the Law*, The Free Press, New York 1977.

Maerlant, Jacob van, *Naturen Bloeme*, Gijsbers & van Loon, Arnhem 1980.

Malson, Lucien, *Wolf Children and the Problem of Human Nature*, Monthly Review Press, New York/London 1972.

Manila, Gabriel Janer, *Macros – Wild Child of the Sierra Morena*, Souvenir Press, London 1982.

Marais, Eugène, *The Soul of the Ape*, Anthony

Blond, London 1969.

Mardrus, J. and Powys Mathers, transl., *The Book of the Thousand Nights and One Night*, 4 vols, Routledge, London/New York 1986.

Masters, Anthony, *The Natural History of the Vampire*, Rupert Hart-Davis, London 1972.

Masters, R.E.L., *Abnorme Triebhaftigkeit*, Lichtenberg, Munich, n.d.

Masters, R.E.L., *Sex-Driven People: an Autobiographical Approach to the Problem of the Sex-Dominated Personality*, Sherbourne Press, Los Angeles 1966.

Merki, Peter, *Die strafrechtliche Behandlung der Unzucht mit Tieren – Besonders in der Schweiz*, Dissertation, Zürich, M. Eberhard & Sohn 1948.

Michell, John and Robert J.M. Rickart, *Living Wonders – Mysteries and Curiosities of the Animal World*, Thames & Hudson, London 1982.

Mode, Heinz, *Fabeltiere und Dämonen – Die phantastische Welt der Mischwesen*, Edition Leipzig, Leipzig 1973.

Moffat, James, *Queen Kong*, Everest, London 1977.

Moller-Christensen and K.E. Jordt Jørgensen, *Dierenleven in de bijbel*, Bosch & Keuning, Baarn n.d.

Money, John, *Lovemaps – Clinical Concepts of Sexual/Erotic Health and Pathology, Paraphilia, and Gender Transposition in Childhood, Adolescence, and Maturity*, Irvington, New York 1986.

Montgomery Hyde, H., *A History of Pornography*, William Heinemann, London 1964.

Moolenburgh, H.C., *Engelen – Als beschermers en als helpers der mensheid*, Ankh-Hermes, Deventer 1983.

Morris, Desmond, *The Naked Ape*, Jonathan Cape, London 1967.

Morris, Desmond, *Dogwatching*, Jonathan Cape, London 1986.

Morris, Desmond, *Animalwatching: a Field Guide to Animal Behaviour*, Arrow, London 1993

Morris, Desmond, *Orns contract met de dieren*, A.J.G. Strengholt, Naarden 1991.

Morris, Ramona and Desmond, *Men and Snakes*, Hutchinson, London 1965.

Morris, Ramona and Desmond, *Men and Pandas*, McGraw-Hill, New York/St Louis/San Francisco 1966.

Morris, Ramona and Desmond, *Men and Apes*, McGraw-Hill, New York 1966.

Morus, *Geschiedenis der dieren – Hun invloed op beschaving en cultuur*, Het Wereldvenster, Baarn 1953.

Morus, *Het rijk van Venus – Algemene geschiedenis van de menselijke sexualiteit*, Meulenhoff, Amsterdam 1957.

Musset, Alfred de, *Gamiani*, Merlin, Hamburg 1968.

Naaktgeboren, C., *Voortplanting bij het dier – paring, bevruchting, embryonale ontwikkeling en geboorte*, Kluwer, Deventer 1967.

Naaktgeboren, C., *Mens en huisidier*, Thieme, Zutphen 1984.

Neimoller, A., *Bestiality and the Law*, Girard, Kansas 1946.

Neimoller, A., *Bestiality in Ancient and Modern Times*, Girard, Kansas 1946.

Neuhause, Ulrich, *Melk – De witte levensbron*, Pax, 's-Gravenhage n.d.

Nosek, Barbara, *Huilen met de wolven – Een interdisciplinaire benadering van de mens-dierrelatie*, Van Gennep, Amsterdam 1988.

Ovid, *Metamorphoses*, transl. by Mary M. Innes. Penguin, Harmondsworth 1955.

Pagels, Elaine, *Adam, Eve and the Serpent*, Weidenfeld & Nicolson, London 1988.

Paré, Ambroise, *Des Monstres – des prodiges – des voyages*, Club de Libraire, Paris 1964.

Parmelee, Alice, *All the Birds of the Bible – Their Stories, Identification and Meaning*, Harper & Row, New York 1959.

Patterson, Francine, *Koko's Kitten*, Scholastic, New York/Toronto/London/Auckland/Sydney 1985.

Physiologus, Der, German transl. Otto Seel, Artemis, Zürich/Munich 1960.

Pinney, Roy, *The Animals in the Bible – The Identity and Natural History of all the Animals mentioned in the bible*, Chilton, Philadelphia/New York 1964.

Pitlo, A., *De vlo in het recht – En andere curiosa uit oude rechtsliteratuur*, Gouda Quint, Arnhem 1980.

Pliny, *Natural History*, transl. by H. Rackham,

W.H.S. Jones and D.E. Eichholz, Harvard University Press, Cambridge, MA and Heinemann, London 1938–63.

Pollak, Otto, *The Criminality of Women*, A.S. Barnes & Company, New York 1961.

Polo, Marco, *The Travels*, transl. Ronald Latham, Penguin, Harmondsworth 1958.

Raes, Hugo, *De vadsige koningen*, De Bezige Bij, Amsterdam 1961.

Ramondt, Sophie, *Mythen en sagen van de Griekse wereld*, C.A.J. van Dishoeck, Bussum 1967.

Regan, Tom, *The Case for Animal Rights*, University of California Press, Berkeley 1983.

Relaties tussen mens, dier en maatschappij, Pudoc, Wageningen 1973.

Reve, Gerard Kornelis van het, *Nader tot U*, G.A. van Oorschot, Amsterdam 1966.

Reynolds, Vernon, *The Apes – The Gorilla, Chimpanzee, Orangutan, and Gibbon – Their History and their World*, Cassell, London 1968.

Rheims, Maurice, *Un Carpaccio en Dordogne*, René Julliard, Paris 1963.

Ritvo, Harriet, *The Animal Estate – The English and other Creatures in the Victorian Age*, Harvard University Press, Cambridge, MA and London 1987.

Ronay, Gabriel, *The Dracula Myth*, W.H. Allen, London/New York 1972.

Rooy, Piet de, *Op zoek naar volmaaktheid – H.M. Bernelot Moens en het mysterie van afkomst en toekomst*, De Haan, Houten 1991.

Roux, Jean-Paul, *Le Sang – Mythes, symboles et réalités*, Arthème Fayard, Paris 1988.

Rowland, Beryl, *Animals with Human Faces – A Guide to Animal Symbolism*, George Allen & Unwin, London 1974.

Sade, D.A.F de, *Histoire de Juliette, Ou les prospérités de vice*, Jean-Jacques Pauvert, Sceaux 1954

Sälzle, Karle, *Tier und Mensch, Gottheit und Dämon – Das Tier in der Geistesgeschichte der Menschheit*, BLV, 1965.

Sargent, William, *The Year of the Crab – Marine Animals in Modern Medicine*, W.W. Norton, New York/London 1987.

Schaller, George B., *The Year of the Gorilla*, University of Chicago Press, Chicago 1964.

Schilders, E. ed., *De voorhuid van Jezus – En andere roomse wonderen*, Xeno, Groningen 1985.

Schwab, Gustav, *Griekse mythen en sagen*, Het Spectrum, Utrecht/Antwerp 1956.

Schwabe, Calvin W., *Unmentionable Cuisine*, University Press of Virginia, Charlottesville 1979.

Schwartz, Jeffrey H., *The Red Ape – Orang-utans and Human Origins*, Elm Tree, London 1987.

Senn, Harry A., *Werewolf and Vampire in Romania*, Columbia University Press, New York 1982.

Serpell, James, *In the Company of Animals – A Study of Human-Animal Relationships*, Basil Blackwell, Oxford/New York 1986.

Shaffer, Peter, *Equus*, André Deutsch, London 1973.

Shattuck, Roger, *The Forbidden Experiment – The Story of the Wild Boy of Aveyron*, Secker & Warburg, London 1980.

Shephard, Odell, *The Lore of the Unicorn*, George Allen & Unwin, London 1930.

Sierksma, Kl., *De gemeentewapens van Nederland*, Het Spectrum, Utrecht/Antwerp 1960.

Simons, G.L., *The Illustrated Book of Sexual Records*, Virgin, London 1982.

Singer, Peter, *Animal Liberation*, The New York Review of Books, New York 1990.

Sliggers, Bert, *Meerminnen en meermannen – Van Duinkerken tot Sylt*, Kruseman, The Hague 1977.

Smith, Bradley, *Erotic Art of the Masters – The 18th & 20th Centuries*, Galley Press, New York n.d.

Smith, F.V., *Attachment of the Young – Imprinting and other Developments*, Oliver & Boyd Edinburgh n.d.

Smolders, Armand J.J., *De seksuele perversies – Vivisektie op een seksuele ideologie*, Boom, Meppel 1971.

Sparks, John, *Dierlijke passie & paring – Seks en erotiek in de dierenwereld*, Het Spectrum, Utrecht/Antwerp 1977.

Stanley, Susan, *Females and their Pets*, Publisher's Consultants, South Laguna 1980.

Stenuit, Robert, *The Dolphin, Cousin to Man*, J.M. Dent & Sons, London 1969.

Streepjes, Igor, *Weer een gezicht dat met de billen vloekt*, C.J. Aarts, Amsterdam 1974.

Szasz, Kathleen, *De troeteltrend – Of het petisjisme*, De Arbeiderspers, Amsterdam 1971.

Tannahill, Reay, *Vlees en bloed – De geschiedenis van het kannibalisme*, Wetenschappelijke Uitgeverij, Amsterdam 1975.

Theunissen, Bert, *Eugène Dubois en de aapmens van Java – Een bijdrage tot de geschiedenis van de paleoantropologie*, Rodopi, Amsterdam 1985.

Thomas, Keith, *Man and the Natural World – Changing Attitudes in England 1500–1800*, Allen Lane, London 1983.

Thompson, C.J.S., *The Mystery and Lore of Monsters – With Accounts of some Giants, Dwarfs and Prodigies*, University Books, New York 1968.

Timmers, J.J.M., *Symboliek en iconographie der christelijke kunst*, J.J. Romen & Zonen, Roermond/Maaseik 1947.

Toynbee, J.M.C., *Animals in Roman Life and Art*, Thames & Hudson, London 1973.

Treves, Frederick, *The Elephant Man and other Reminiscences*, Cassell, London 1923.

Tripp, Edward, *Crowell's Handbook of Classical Mythology*, Harper & Row, New York 1970.

Trumler, Eberhard, *Mit dem Hund auf du*, R. Piper & Co., Munich 1971.

Turner, James, *Reckoning with the Beast – Animals, Pain and Humanity in the Victorian Mind*, Johns Hopkins University Press, Baltimore/London 1980.

Turner, Dennis C. and Patrick Bateson, *The Domestic Cat – The Biology of its Behaviour*, Cambridge University Press, Cambridge/New York/New Rochelle/Melbourne/Sydney 1988.

Vechten, Carl van, *The Tiger in the House*, Bonanza, New York 1936.

Verroust, Jacques, M. Pastoureau and Raymond Buren, *Le Cochon – Histoire, symbolique et cuisine du porc*, Sang de la terre, Paris 1987.

Verwer, M.A.J., *De hond*, Het Spectrum, Utrecht/Antwerp 1978.

Vesper, G., *Les Procès d'animaux au moyen age*, Imprimeries réunies, Chambéry 1953.

Villeneuve, Roland, *Le Musée de la bestialité*, Henri Veyrier, Paris 1973.

Visser, M.B.H. and F.J. Grommers, eds, *Dier of ding – Objectivering van dieren*, Pudoc, Wageningen 1988.

Voltaire, *Candide – or Optimism*, transl. John Butt, Penguin, Harmondsworth 1947.

Vondel, Joost v.d., *Noah – Of ondergang der eerste wereld*, Mij voor Goede en Goedkope Lectuur, Amsterdam n.d.

Voronoff, S., *Rejuvenation by Grafting*, Allen & Unwin, London 1925.

Voronoff, S. and G. Alexandrescu, *Testicular Grafting from Ape to Man*, William & Norgate, London, 1933.

Voûte, A.M. and C. Smeenk, *Vleermuizen*, Waanders, Zwolle 1991.

Vrede, Angela de and Gerrit Jan Zwier, *Het meisje en de mol*, Meulenhoff Jeugd, Amsterdam 1989.

Vroman, Leo, *126 gedichten*, Em. Querido, Amsterdam 1964.

Waal, Frans de, *Chimpansee-politiek*, H.J.W. Becht, Amsterdam 1982.

Waal, Frans de, *Peacemaking among Primates*, Harvard University Press, Cambridge, MA 1989

Waal, M. de, *Zuivel, ei en honing – Door alle eeuwen heen*, W.J. Thieme & Cie, Zutphen n.d.

Wakefield, Pat A. and Larry Carrara, *A Moose for Jessica*, E.P Dutton, New York 1987.

Warner, Marina, *Alone of all her Sex: the Myth and the Cult of the Virgin Mary*, Knopf, New York 1983.

Webb, Peter, *The Erotic Arts*, Secker & Warburg. London 1975.

Webster, Gary, *Codfish, Oats and Civilisation*, Doubleday, Garden City, NY 1959.

Weemoedt, Lévi, *Zand erover*, Erven Thomas Rap, Baarn 1981.

Wendt, Herbert, *Ik volgde Noach – De ontdekking van de dieren*, W. de Haan, Zeist 1957.

White, David Gordon, *Myths of the Dog-Man*, The University of Chicago Press, Chicago/London 1991.

White, T.H., *The Book of Beasts – Being a Translation from a Latin Bestiary of the Twelfth Century*, Jonathan Cape, London 1954.

Wickler, W., *De aard van het beestje – Over de natuurwetten van het seksuele contact*, Ploegsma, Amsterdam 1970.

Wierenga, Tineke and Wouter van Dieren, eds., *Mensenwereld dierenwereld*, Koninklijk Verbond van Grafische Ondernemingen, Amstelveen 1986.

Willis, Roy, *Man and Beast*, Rupert Hart-Davis, London 1974.

Wilson, Glenn, *The Great Sex Divide – A Study of Male-Female Differences*, Peter Owen, London 1989.

Wilson, Glenn and David Nias, *Love's Mysteries – The Psychology of Sexual Attraction*, Open Books, London 1976.

Wit, H.C.D. de, *Ontwikkelingsgeschiedenis van de biologie*, Pudoc, Wageningen 1982–9.

Wolf, Leonard, *Monsters – Twenty Terrible and Wonderful Beasts from the Classic Dragon and Colossal Minotaur to King Kong and the Great Godzilla*, Straight Arrow, San Francisco 1974.

Wolkers, Jan, *De hond met de blauwe tong*, J.M. Meulenhoff, Amsterdam 1964.

Wulffen, Erich, *Das Weib als Sexualverbrecherin – Ein Handbuch für Juristen, Verwaltungsbeamte und Ärzte*, P. Langenscheidt, Berlin 1923.

Yerkes, Robert Mearns, *Almost Human*, Century New York 1925.

Yerkes, Robert M. and Ada W., *The Great Apes – A Study of Anthropoid Life*, Yale University Press, New Haven & Oxford University Press, Oxford n.d.

Young, J.Z., *An Introduction to the Study of Man*, Oxford University Press, Oxford/New York/ Toronto/Melbourne n.d.

Zahn, Eva, *Europa und der Stier*, Königshausen & Neumann, Würzburg 1983.

Zinsser, Hans, *Rats, Lice and History*, Little, Brown & Company, New York 1935.

Index

INDEX